teach® yourself

beginner's latin
g. d. a. sharpley

For over 60 years, more than
50 million people have learnt over
750 subjects the **teach yourself**
way, with impressive results.

be where you want to be
with **teach yourself**

The publisher has used its best endeavours to ensure that the URLs for external websites referred to in this book are correct and active at the time of going to press. However, the publisher and the author have no responsibility for the websites and can make no guarantee that a site will remain live or that the content will remain relevant, decent or appropriate.

For UK order enquiries: please contact Bookpoint Ltd, 130 Milton Park, Abingdon, Oxon,, OX14 4SB. Telephone: +44 (0) 1235 827720. Fax: +44 (0) 1235 400454. Lines are open 09.00–17.00, Monday to Saturday, with a 24-hour message answering service. Details about our titles and how to order are available at www.teachyourself.co.uk

For USA order enquiries: please contact McGraw-Hill Customer Services, PO Box 545, Blacklick, OH 43004-0545, USA. Telephone: 1-800-722-4726. Fax: 1-614-755-5645.

For Canada order enquiries: please contact McGraw-Hill Ryerson Ltd, 300 Water St, Whitby, Ontario, L1N 9B6, Canada. Telephone: 905 430 5000. Fax: 905 430 5020.

Long renowned as the authoritative source for self-guided learning – with more than 50 million copies sold worldwide – the **teach yourself** series includes over 500 titles in the fields of languages, crafts, hobbies, business, computing and education.

British Library Cataloguing in Publication Data: a catalogue record for this title is available from the British Library.

Library of Congress Catalog Card Number: on file.

First published in UK 1997 by Hodder Education, 338 Euston Road, London, NW1 3BH.

First published in US 1997 by The McGraw-Hill Companies, Inc.

This edition published 2003.

The **teach yourself** name is a registered trade mark of Hodder Headline.

Typeset by Transet Limited, Coventry, England.
Printed in Great Britain for Hodder Education, a division of Hodder Headline, an Hachette Livre UK Company, 338 Euston Road, London, NW1 3BH, by Cox & Wyman Ltd, Reading, Berkshire.

Hodder Headline's policy is to use papers that are natural, renewable and recyclable products and made from wood grown in sustainable forests. The logging and manufacturing processes are expected to conform to the environmental regulations of the country of origin.

Impression number   15 14 13 12
Year   2010 2009 2008 2007

contents

Flogging a dead course?

It may seem odd to find Latin alive and well at the beginning of the twenty-first century, and yet here it is, one of nature's survivors. And why? Because beyond this course there is a literature teeming with good things, with high life, with low life and, most of all, with life. All we have to do, of course, is read it …

Paulus and Lucia

The story is a foil for the grammar and exercises. It is set at a monastery in northern Europe around the ninth century AD. An English translation of the Latin story is available at the LATIN QVARTER (www.lingua.co.uk).

Living Latin

Assembling all the information about words and endings is a necessary but sometimes slow process. This section offers the chance to hear some excerpts of authentic Latin. You do not have to study these in detail to make progress. They are included to give you an idea of what there is to enjoy once you have mastered the language.

Recording

A recording of the story and 'Living Latin' sections of the book is available. This is not an essential aid to learning the language, but will enhance your enjoyment of the poetry, and give you an idea of what Latin sounded like.

Pronunciation guide to classical Latin

As in English (standard southern British), except:

a   'cup' (short vowel) or 'father' (long vowel)
ae   'eye'
au   'house'
c   'cat' (always hard; *never* as in 'chalice')
ch   'k' with a sharper expulsion of breath (as in 'curses!')
e   'pet' (short vowel) or 'pay' (long vowel)
ei   'reign'
eu   two sounds run together: 'e-oo'
g   'gag' (almost always hard, not as in 'George')[1]
gn   at the beginning of a word 'n', and in the middle of a word 'ngn'
i   'lip' (short vowel) or 'leap' (long vowel)
i (j) consonant: as English 'y'
ng   as in 'anger' (not 'hangar')
o   'not' (short vowel) or (long vowel) 'note' (as the Scots would say it)
oe   'oil'
ph   'p' with a sharper expulsion of breath (as in 'peasant!')
qu   'kw', as in 'quack' (as English 'qu', not French)
r   trilled with the tip of the tongue (again, think Scots...)
s   as in hiss (not his)
th   as 't' with a sharper expulsion of breath
u   'pull' (short vowel) or (long vowel) 'pool' (not with the 'y' sound in 'pew')
v   as English 'w'
y   French 'tu' (short vowel), French 'sur' (long vowel)

Yoolius Kysser, Joolius Seezer, Yoolius Chaser

The story of Lucia and Paulus, though set in a later period, is narrated according to the guidelines above. The selections in 'Living Latin' are also read in the classical manner, except post-classical ones (marked *). You will hear one or two different sounds in the post-classical sections, such as our own 'v' sound in the v; the erosion of ae to e; and the Church/Italian 'ch' sound in ci/ce (e.g. caelum: classical – kylum, ecclesiastical – chaylum).

---

1 Subsequent to publication of the first edition and the accompanying recording, I am no longer comfortable with the traditional view of a hard 'g' in all environments. It seems increasingly likely that in certain words (e.g. ego, magister, fragilis) the 'g' is softer – closer to a 'y' than 'j'. GDAS 2003

These changes should be taken as characteristic only, and not as precise, scientific reconstructions according to date, region and speaker. It's hard enough reaching any certainty about Cicero's Latin, never mind the multitude of evolving and fragmenting forms which followed.

Verse-rhythms of later Latin changed too. The rhythms of classical poetry were founded on an interplay of natural stress and quantity (i.e. the metre), but later poets came to disregard metre and used stresses alone to maintain rhythm.

Our efforts of recreation are inevitably hit and miss, no doubt betraying more than a few signs of the present day. For a further discussion of pronunciation see 'Speaking as the Romans did' (p. 25), and those who wish to explore this topic in more detail should look at *Vox Latina* (W. Sidney Allen, CUP, 1965).

Essential grammar

Nouns

A noun is a word like *mule*, *monk* or *wood*. Something you can see or at least feel. English nouns often have *the* or *a* in front of them. Latin has no equivalent words for *the* and *a* so when you translate a noun you must decide whether or not to add them. Names are also nouns, like *Paul*, *Rome*, etc., and so are abstract ideas like *peace*, *kindness*, *fear*, which are real enough but cannot be identified in the same way as concrete objects.

Verbs

A verb is a 'doing' or 'being' word; it describes the action, what happens or what is done, e.g.

> *The mule <u>watches</u> the wood.*
> *The monk <u>is</u> not <u>carrying</u> the bag.*
> *Paul <u>is</u> a student.*

English verbs often comprise more than one word (e.g. *is carrying*). Most Latin verbs are expressed by one word only. A verb like **spectat** has three possible versions in English: *watches*, *is watching* or *does (not) watch*. As with 'the' and 'a' and nouns above, a judgement has to be made from the context, from what 'sounds right'.

Index of grammar support

Grammatical words and guidance appear on these pages.

Symbols and abbreviations

▶ This indicates material that has been recorded and is available on cassette or CD.

m. masculine; f. feminine; n. neuter; pl. plural; sing. singular; nom. nominative; voc. vocative; acc. accusative; gen. genitive; dat. dative; abl. ablative; *post-classical

Acknowledgements

The publishers and author thank The Finnish Broadcasting Company, Finland, for permission to include an excerpt from Nuntii Latini (Vol.3); the Latin Qvarter (www.lingua.co.uk) for permission to adapt the story of Lucia and Paulus for the Teach Yourself series.

Thanks also to my students for their valuable feedback while the course was being developed; to P.O'R. Smiley and Amanda Lee for many helpful comments and corrections; to Keely Mitchell for her excellent drawings; to my editors at Teach Yourself; and to my wife, Sarah, and our three daughters, Rebecca, Meg and Flora.

George Sharpley

01

in silva
in the wood

In this unit you will learn about
- subjects and objects
- the cases

- and find out more about Latin in 'The classics'

Subjects and objects

Latin is an inflected language. This means that the final syllable(s) of a word can vary according to the way the word is being used in the sentence:

Mul<u>us</u> silv<u>am</u> spectat.   *The mule is watching the wood.*

Here the mule is doing the watching, the wood is being watched. The mule is the *subject* of the sentence, the wood the *object*, the difference being that the subject is the 'doer', the object is on the receiving end and is 'done to'. Latin makes this clear by having different endings for subject and object.

Mul<u>um</u> silv<u>a</u> spectat.   *The wood is watching the mule.*

Now **silva** no longer has a final 'm', and **mulus** has been changed to **mulum**. This makes **silva** the subject and **mulum** the object. English word order is more restricted because we recognize a subject by its position in a sentence, not by its ending. Latin's word order is more flexible: in general the subject appears before the object, with the verb at the end to complete a sentence or word-group, although variations, for a particular emphasis or rhythm, often occur. The verb's place at the end may seem strange at first, but you will get used to it. Reading is a process of anticipation and completion of meaning; in English this function is often performed by the object:

> *Today the milkman delivered* ... (*bottles of milk* is the anticipated object; *the post* would come as a surprise, and *twins* even more so).

Latin has us predicting the action, not the object:

> *Today the milkman* ... *two pints of milk* ... (*delivered* is what we are expecting, ahead of *stole* or *threw at the boy on the skateboard*).

▶ Paulus in silva *Paulus in the wood*

Paulus in silva ambulat. Mulus cum Paulo ambulat. Mulus non Paulum sed sarcinam portat. Fessus est Paulus et mulus est lentus. Mulus silvam non amat. Mulus silvam spectat. Silva mulum spectat. Mulus est territus.

amat	*likes, loves*
ambulat	*walks, is walking*
cum	*with, in the company of*
est	*is*
et	*and*
fessus	*tired*
in	*in, on*
lentus	*slow*
mulus, mulum, mulo	*mule*
non	*not*
Paulus, Paulum, Paulo	*Paul*
portat	*carries, is carrying*
sarcina, sarcinam	*bag*
sed	*but*
silva, silvam	*wood*
spectat	*watches, is watching*
territus	*scared*

Practice (i)

1 There are a few English words which change their form according to whether they are subject or object. These are pronouns, words we use in place of nouns. Complete the table with the missing subject or object forms:

(a)

Subject	Object
I	
she	
	him
we	

(b)

Subject	Object
silva	
	mulum
	sarcinam
Paulus	

2 Choose the correct word and translate:

(a) Mulus (sarcina/sarcinam) portat.

(b) Mulum (Paulus/Paulum) portat.

3 Choose the correct verb and translate:

(a) **Mulus silvam non (ambulat/amat).**
(b) **Paulus in silva (portat/ambulat).**
(c) **Mulus silvam (portat/spectat).**
(d) **Non Paulus sed mulus sarcinam (portat/ambulat).**

Cases

'Case' is the name given to the different kinds of word-ending:

Nominative case	*Subject*	**silva, mulus**
Accusative case	*Object, or with prepositions* (e.g. **ad**)	**silvam, mulum**
Ablative case	*'With', 'in' used (not always) with prepositions* (e.g. **cum**, **in**)	**silva, mulo**

Nouns like **mulus** (e.g. **Paulus**, etc.) all have the same case endings, and nouns like **silva** (**sarcina**, etc.) have their endings in common too.

Est and *sunt*

Est *is* and **sunt** *are* do not take objects like other verbs do. The 'object' of the verb *to be* is not on the receiving end of anything particular, but merely describes the subject. So any 'object' or rather complement of the verb 'to be' will be in the nominative case:

Paulus monach<u>us</u> est.   *Paul is a monk.*

but

Paulus monach<u>um</u> spectat.   *Paul watches the monk.*

▶ Mulus lente ambulat *The mule walks slowly*

Paulus est monachus. Benedictus etiam est monachus. Benedictus cibum desiderat. Paulus cibum emit et ad monasterium revenit. Nunc Paulus cum mulo in silva ambulat. Cibus est in sarcina. Mulus sarcinam portat. Mulus lente ambulat et silvam spectat.

ad	*to, towards*
cibum (acc. of **cibus**)	*food*
desiderat	*longs for*
emit	*buys*
etiam	*also*
lente	*slowly*
monachus	*monk*
monasterium	*monastery*
nunc	*now*
revenit	*returns*

Practice (ii)

1 Fill the gaps:

Subject Nominative case	Object Accusative case	'in', 'with', 'on' Ablative case
mulus		**mulo**
	Paulum	
	sarcinam	
silva		**silva**

2 Identify the cases of the underlined nouns, and translate:

(a) <u>Benedictus</u> <u>cibum</u> desiderat.
(b) Mulus <u>sarcinam</u> non amat.
(c) Benedictus non in <u>silva</u> est.
(d) Paulus est <u>monachus</u>.

3 Complete the words which have missing endings, and translate:

(b) In mul___ est sarcin___.

(a) Paul___ cum mul___
in silv___ ambulat.

About Latin

The classics

Latin was the language spoken in Rome and the surrounding region, Latium (mod. Lazio) as early as the sixth century BC and possibly earlier. The number of Latin speakers grew with the expansion of Rome's empire around the Mediterranean, and the vocabulary swelled and forms modified under the influence of languages in the new subject territories (especially Greek).

The classical Latin authors lived within a few decades either side of the life of Christ. In the first century BC Cicero tried to prevent the republican government falling prey to the ambitions of dictators. A compelling public speaker, his skills brought him to the attention of politicians such as Caesar and Pompey, and he was courted by them as an owner of a newspaper or television station might be today. His writing was greatly admired, and the elegance and rhetorical flair of his prose became a model for later scholars and schoolboys to imitate. He was followed by, amongst others, the historian Tacitus, whose pointed asides on the theme of moral and aristocratic

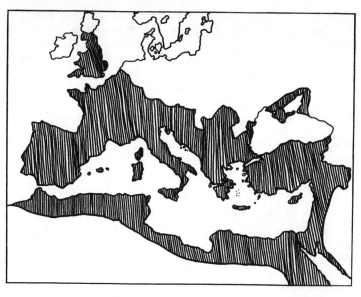

shaded area indicates where Latin was spoken at the end of the first century AD

degeneration enliven his account of Rome under the early emperors. Of the poets the best known is perhaps Virgil. His story of the founding of Rome by the Trojan fugitive Aeneas emerged within a few years of publication as a political symbol and literary masterpiece. Horace, a friend of Virgil, is remembered for his Odes, four books of lyric poetry drawing on themes of love and friendship, and yearnings, never quite fulfilled, for homely contentment and rustic ease. The erotic elegies of Propertius and Tibullus echo Catullus' earlier infatuation for Lesbia and foreshadow the work of Ovid, a decade or so later. Ovid's wit and fresh invention brought new twists to the elegiac genre, and his verse was imitated more than any other by medieval writers; partly, perhaps, because copies were available, but also because of a lightness of touch which won him universal appeal.

These classics have a timeless feel about them. They have been drummed into pupils for the best part of two thousand years (less the last few decades, perhaps). They are literature's heroes and anti-heroes. If other heroes are found, more often than not they are those heroes' heroes. Classical authors have been trotted out as arbiters of good taste throughout the centuries, medieval and Renaissance, neoclassical and new wave.

This aura of permanence is reinforced by the serene grandeur of classical civilization, by the durability of buildings and statues which survive it. Much of what actually went on, however, was anything but serene and civilized. Writers and artists are known to find inspiration under duress and in times of political insecurity. So it was with some of the best Roman literature. Throughout most of the first century BC Italy suffered from political chaos and intermittent cruelty and bloodshed. 'O Tempora O Mores!' (*What an age! What moral standards!*) cried Cicero, rounding on his peers for failing to live up to earlier times, and damning the period we have subsequently identified as one of the greatest in our history.

The classical period of Latin was a moment in the language's evolution which could not endure, for no living language can remain the same for long. The efforts of later grammarians to preserve classical Latin were a symptom of its passing. As the living, spoken language moved on, eventually evolving into French, Spanish, Italian and other Romance languages, this classical, literary Latin was preserved and 'pickled' by later generations of writers and scholars, and after the fall of the western empire, by monks in their monasteries.

Thus the rules of classical Latin, the grammar and syntax, are something of a still shot of what was essentially transitory. Nonetheless these rules are instrumental in shaping all the Latin which followed, for almost all subsequent Latinists have attempted, with different degrees of success, to remain faithful to classical norms. Where possible the Latin in this course, the grammar, syntax, idioms and pronunciation, are based on the ground rules of classical Latin, including our story set in a medieval monastery. There are some inevitable twentieth-century inventions, and a number of words are used in their medieval sense, such as **ecclesia** (*church*) and **presbyter** (*priest*).

Revision

1 Fill the gaps:

Case	silva *wood*	monachus *monk*	sarcina *bag*	cibus *food*
Nominative (subject)	silva	monachus	sarcina	cibus
Accusative (object)			sarcinam	cibum
Ablative (in, on, with)	silva	monacho		

2 Translate into Latin:
   (a) Benedict is not walking in the wood.
   (b) The bag is on the mule.
   (c) The mule does not carry Paul but the bag.
   (d) The mule does not like the wood.

3 Write a Latin sentence with:
   (a) **mulus** in the accusative;
   (b) **sarcina** in the ablative;
   (c) **Paulus** in the nominative;
   (d) **monachus** in the ablative.

4 Do you know what these words mean? If not, look back and learn them …

silva	mulus	sarcina
et	non	amat
ambulat	spectat	portat
est	cibus	sed
cum	in	nunc
etiam	monachus	

What English words have their roots (or some of them) in these Latin words?

▶ Living Latin

This section of each unit contains some authentic Latin, most but not all of which is classical. The pieces are included as both a rest and a stimulant. **You are not expected to read them too closely, in fact you are advised not to!** Many of the words and endings will be unfamiliar, so be positive and accumulate what you can. With the help of the translations see what you are able to work out, then sit back and listen to the recordings, and repeat them for pronunciation practice.

1 **Verberat nos et lacerat fortuna.**

(Seneca, Dial. i, 4, 12)

Fortune batters and torments us.

2 **Defendi rem publicam adulescens, non deseram senex.**

(Cicero, Phil. ii, 118)

I defended the republic as a young man, I shall not desert it in my old age.

3 **Ubi solitudinem faciunt, pacem appellant.**

(Tacitus, Agricola xxx)

They make a desert and call it peace.

4 **Aurora interea miseris mortalibus almam**
extulerat lucem referens opera atque labores.

(Virgil, Aeneid xi, 182–3)

Dawn now raised her nourishing light upon the suffering mortals and renewed their daily grind.

5 **O tempora, o mores! Senatus haec intellegit, consul videt.**

(Cicero, In Catilinam i, 1)

What an age! What moral standards! The senate knows what's going on, the consul has it right in front of his eyes.

02

umbrae in silva
shadows in the wood

In this unit you will learn about
- singular and plural

- and find out more about Latin in 'A question of rhetoric'

Singular and plural forms

The plural of **mulus** *mule̲s̲* is **muli** if nominative (subject), **mulos** if accusative (object) or **mulis** if ablative (*in*, *with*, etc.). The verb (**spectat, laborat,** etc.) has an '**n**' before the final '**t**' if the subject is plural:

Mul<u>us</u> in agro labor<u>at</u>.	*The mule is working in the field.*
Mul<u>i</u> in agro labor<u>ant</u>.	*The mules are working in the field.*
Monachi mulos spect<u>ant</u>.	*The monks watch the mules.*
In agro <u>est</u> mul<u>us</u>.	*A mule is (there is a mule) in the field.*
In agro <u>sunt</u> mul<u>i</u>.	*Mules are (there are mules) in the field.*

▶ Mulus equos non amat *The mule doesn't like horses*

Benedictus et Stephanus monachi sunt. Monachi in monasterio habitant. Paulus discipulus in schola est. Discipuli cum monachis in monasterio habitant. Mulus cum equis in agro habitat. Mulus saepe in agris laborat. Equi cum mulo non laborant. Equos mulus non amat.

agro	*(in) a field*
discipulus	*student*
equos (equus)	*horses*
habitat, habitant	*lives, live*
laborat, laborant	*works, work*
saepe	*often*
schola	*school*
sunt	*are*

Practice (i)

1 Choose the correct words and translate:

Mulus cum (equos/equis) in agro habitat, sed (equi/equus) cum (mulum/mulo) non laborant.

2 Choose the correct word and translate:
  (a) **Mulus sarcinam (portat/portant).**
  (b) **Monachi in monasterio (habitat/habitant).**
  (c) **Muli non equos (amat/amant).**
  (d) **Equus in agro non (laborat/laborant).**

How to look for the subject

If there is no subject, i.e. no word in the nominative case, then we add an English pronoun (*he*, *she* or *it* if the verb is singular, *they* if plural):

In monasterio labor<u>at</u>.	*<u>She</u> works in the monastery.*
In agro habit<u>ant</u>.	*<u>They</u> live in the field.*

Silvae, umbrae

The plural of **silva** (and nouns like **silva**) is **silv<u>ae</u>** (nominative), **silv<u>as</u>** (accusative) and **silv<u>is</u>** (ablative):

In silv<u>is</u> sunt umbr<u>ae</u>.	*There are shadows in the woods.*
Sarcin<u>as</u> non portat.	*(S/he/it) does not carry the bags.*

▶ Umbrae in silvis *Shadows in the woods*

Benedictus vinum desiderat. Paulus igitur vinum in oppido emit et ad monasterium cum mulo ambulat. Mulus vinum portat. Nunc sunt in silva. Mulus saepe in silvis ambulat, sed non silvas amat quod in silvis sunt umbrae. Mulus neque umbras neque sarcinas amat. Mulus amicos in agro desiderat.

amicos (amicus)	*friends*
emit	*(s/he) buys*
igitur	*and so*
in oppido	*in the town*
neque...neque	*neither...nor*
quod	*because*
umbrae (umbra)	*shadows*
vinum	*wine*

Practice (ii)

1 Choose the correct words and translate:

Mulus non (silvas/silvis) amat quod in (silvas/silvis) sunt (umbrae/umbras).

2 Choose the correct words and translate:

(a) **Sarcinae in mulo (est/sunt).**
(b) **Umbras in silva mulus non (amat/amant).**
(c) **Monachi sarcinas non (portat/portant).**
(d) **Equi in silva non (habitat/habitant).**

About Latin

A question of rhetoric

The classical period was a relatively brief period in the life of Latin. It was then immortalized by the enthusiasm of later generations, and two thousand years later the books are all we have left. But books are all it was ever meant to be. Classical Latin was composed on the page; it may have been brought to life by recital, but it was a written language. We may safely assume that the carefully weighted sentences of Cicero or the delicate rhythms of poets were not typical of everyday conversational Latin of the time.

Latin literature was the work of an educated, erudite minority. Authors all shared the same school texts, the same tutors, the same tastes, the same stock of stories and myths, the same models, Roman and Greek. Not many Romans were literate, and even fewer were literary. Authors were either themselves members of an upper-class elite or supported by someone who was. They frequently allude to myths, heroes and episodes in their history, as though to impress us with the detail of their knowledge. But their readership, the educated Roman public, were all familiar with the material. They did not judge an author by this alone, but by the use he made of it; and this material was almost all derived from Greece.

At the beginning of the second century BC, Rome controlled parts of the western Mediterranean, and her ambitious generals were contemplating further expansion eastwards, beginning with Greece. Several Romans had already visited Greece and liked what they had sampled of the refinements of Greek culture and lifestyle. Here they found an artistic inspiration and intellectual energy unmatched by anything back home, and before long Greek art and literature found a new and enthusiastic public in Italy. Talented and educated Greeks were befriended, hired, or bought in the slave markets to guide this process of cultural transfusion, a process which gathered momentum once Rome had made the step from ally to mistress of Greece.

Political control of the eastern half of the Mediterranean had belonged to the Macedonians. Greece was once part of Alexander the Great's empire, which stretched from Greece to India and south into Egypt. Alexander's travels and conquests merged the cultures of Greece with those of the near east and north Africa, creating the 'Hellenistic' culture. The city of Alexandria in Egypt became the library of the Hellenistic world, attracting writers and artists, poets and professors. This was the Greek culture which Romans inherited and experienced first-hand, but it was not the Greek culture they aspired to.

In the fifth century BC, when Rome was still struggling to assert her independence and when the Latin language was in its infancy, Greece experienced her classical age. Having fought off the menace of Persian aggression, Athens, Sparta and other city-states (Greece was not a single country at this time) all contributed to an era of virtually unparalleled excellence in the arts, in literature, architecture, philosophy and politics. The achievements of the Athenians were the most notable, and certainly now the most visible. Having organized a union of minor states, Athens turned this into an empire, and from its revenues built the Parthenon and other buildings on the Acropolis. Abroad she ruled with the heavy hand of a despot, but at home she nurtured the world's first democratic government. In this period the dramatists Aeschylus, Sophocles, Euripides and Aristophanes wrote and produced their plays; Herodotus and Thucydides wrote their histories; and Socrates and Plato confronted politicians with arguments about power and methods of persuasion in a democratic society.

Debate, discussion, argument, a willingness to talk through issues and participate in public affairs gave impetus to Athenian democracy. But by the end of the fifth century democracy was already beginning to lose its innocence. Politicians were thought to be out for all they could get, promising the world for a taste of power. Socrates himself criticized professional teachers of rhetoric, who gave lessons in how to deliver convincing arguments (and win elections) at the expense of the substance of the argument itself. Was there a value, wondered Socrates, in persuading others of a particular course of action if we did not first have a very firm grasp of the merits of that course of action? His stubborn pursuit of the truth offended a number of powerful people, and he was put to death at the close of the fifth century.

The Athenian taste for dialogue and debate was not confined to politics and philosophy but infused their plays, histories and all their literature. No one argued more convincingly than Socrates, despite his misgivings about the power of persuasion, and his conversations were recreated by his student, Plato (we have nothing written by Socrates himself), whose dialogues were an inspiration to later students of rhetoric. Rhetoric was taught as a formal subject in Greek, Roman and medieval schools – our meaning of 'rhetoric' today shows what a lost skill speaking has become.

The Greeks were known for being good speakers, and good squabblers. The difference between a debate and a quarrel is only one of degree, and while one was a symptom of freedom, the other brought that freedom to an end. A quarrel between the two most powerful city-states, Athens and Sparta, weakened the peninsula enough for Alexander's father, Philip, to overrun it in the fourth century.

The later period of Hellenism looked back on classical Greece as a golden age, and the literati deliberately recreated and imitated earlier writers. The Romans absorbed these conventions, and thus Greek ideas, rhythms, stories, their gods even, found new fertile soil in Italy, helping to shape and develop the Latin language.

Revision

1 Add the missing forms to the tables:

(a)

Case	Singular		
Nominative (subject)	**mulus**		
Accusative (object)		**discipulum**	
Ablative (by, with, from, in, on)	**mulo**		**umbra**
		Plural	
Nominative (subject)		**discipuli**	**umbrae**
Accusative (object)	**mulos**		
Ablative (by, with, from, in, on)		**discipulis**	**umbris**

(b)

Case	Singular		
Nominative (subject)	**equus**	**silva**	
Accusative (object)			**sarcinam**
Ablative (by, with, from, in, on)			
		Plural	
Nominative subject)			
Accusative (object)		**silvas**	
Ablative (by, with, from, in, on)			

2 Change the underlined word to the plural (if the subject is plural, the verb will be plural too), and translate:

(a) Paulus saepe in agro cum <u>monacho</u> laborat.
(b) <u>Sarcina</u> in mulo est.
(c) <u>Discipulus</u> in monasterio habitat.
(d) Mulus <u>umbram</u> non amat.

3 Translate into Latin:

(a) There are shadows in the woods.
(b) The monks are not carrying bags.
(c) The mule often walks in the woods.
(d) The mule does not like the horses because they do not work with mules.

4 Do you know what these words mean? If not, look back and learn them....

umbra	sunt	vinum
discipulus	equus	saepe
desiderat	quod	ad
igitur	laborat	amicus

Now look for English derivatives (they are often a clue to the meaning of the Latin word but not always identical to it).

◘ Living Latin

1 **Contra quis ferat arma deos?**

(Tibullus, Elegies i, 6, 30)

Who may take arms against the gods?

2 ***Nonne Socrates iniustae victoriam mortis promeruit?**

(Boethius, Consolation of Philosophy i, 3)

Did not Socrates reap the victory of an unjust death?

3 **Graecia capta ferum victorem cepit et artis intulit agresti Latio.**

(Horace, Epistles ii, 1, 156–7)

When Greece was captured, she in turn captivated her untamed conqueror and introduced the arts to bumpkin Lazio.

4 **Vivos ducent de marmore vultus.**

(Virgil, Aeneid vi, 848)

(The Greeks) will bring to life faces from marble.

5 ***Si quidem deus est, unde mala? Bona vero unde, si non est?**

(Boethius, Consolation of Philosophy i, 4)

If there is a god, how can there be evil? And how can there be good if there is not?

*post-classical

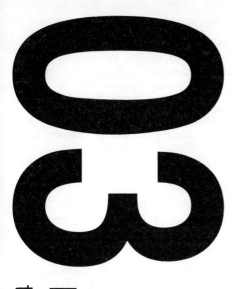

03

mulus gemit
the mule groans

In this unit you will learn about
- masculine, feminine and neuter nouns
- prepositions

- and find out more about Latin in 'Speaking as the Romans did …'

Nouns ending -*er*

Presbyter *priest*, **puer** *boy*, **liber** *book*, **magister** *master* and **ager** *field* all have endings identical to **mulus** except for the nominative singular (-**er**). Some lose the 'e' in the other cases:

			Singular		
Nom.	presbyter	puer	liber	magister	ager
Acc.	presbyterum	puerum	librum	magistrum	agrum
Abl.	presbytero	puero	libro	magistro	agro
			Plural		
Nom.	presbyteri	pueri	libri	magistri	agri
Acc.	presbyteros	pueros	libros	magistros	agros
Abl.	presbyteris	pueris	libris	magistris	agris

Masculine, feminine and neuter

Most nouns like **silva** are feminine and those like **mulus** (and **presbyter, puer,** etc.) are masculine. There are also neuter nouns. You will need to know a noun's gender when you come to matching adjectives with the nouns they qualify.

Neuter nouns ending -*um*

Vinum *wine*, **monasterium** *monastery*, **oppidum** *town*, **oleum** *oil*, **ovum** *egg* and **unguentum** *perfume* also have endings similar to **mulus**: the differences are in the nominative singular, which ends -**um** (like the accusative), and the nominative/accusative plural, both of which end -**a**:

	Singular	Plural
Nominative	vin-um	vin-a
Accusative	vin-um	vin-a
Ablative	vin-o	vin-is

These are neuter nouns, and all without exception have the same endings for both the nominative and accusative cases, so the ending alone will not tell you whether a neuter noun is subject or object. This has to be worked out from the context:

Mulus <u>vinum</u> non amat (object).	*The mule does not like wine.*
In sarcina est <u>vinum</u> (subject).	*In the bag is some wine.*

Ablative case: 'in, on, with, by, from'

English words which commonly render the ablative are: 'in, on, with, by, from'. Sometimes the ablative is used without a preposition:

Sarcina est <u>unguentis</u> onerosa.	*The bag is heavy <u>with perfumes</u>.*

Cum, *with*, is only used if it means 'in the company of'.

▶ Sarcinae onerosae *The bags are heavy*

Shared endings key

(Nouns are singular, unless stated plural. Entries in bold are included for the first time. A vowel may be long or short, e.g. nominative **silva**, ablative **silvā**.)

-um mulum, puerum, agrum : accusative
 vinum : nominative or accusative

-a silva : nominative or ablative
 vina : nominative pl. or accusative pl.

Paulus et Benedictus monachi sunt. Benedictus presbyter est, et cum ancillis in culina laborat. Paulus non presbyter sed discipulus est. In culina et in bibliotheca et in agris laborat. Benedictus, ubi cibum vinumque desiderat, Paulum ad oppidum mittit. Hodie igitur Paulus mulusque ex oppido per silvam ad monasterium reveniunt. Ager et monasterium longe absunt. Sarcinae sunt onerosae. Sarcinae vino et ovis et oleo et unguento onerosae sunt. Mulus gemit. Unguenta et cibum et vinum semper Benedictus desiderat sed semper mulus portat.

---

absunt	*(they) are away, absent*
ancillis (ancilla)	*maids*
bibliotheca	*library*
culina	*kitchen*
ex	*from, out of*
gemit	*(s/he) groans*
hodie	*today*
longe	*far, distant*
mittit	*(s/he) sends*
onerosae	*heavy*
per	*through, across, along*

-que (cibum vinumque)	*and (food and wine)*
reveniunt	*(they) come back*
semper	*always*
ubi	*when, where*

Practice (i)

1 Add the missing forms to the following tables:

Case	Singular		
Nominative (subject)	**ager**	**unguentum**	**presbyter**
Accusative (object)		**unguentum**	
Ablative (by, with, from, in, on)	**agro**		**presbytero**
		Plural	
Nominative (subject)		**unguenta**	
Accusative (object)	**agros**	**unguenta**	
Ablative (by, with, from, in, on)			**presbyteris**

2 Choose the correct words and translate:

(a) (Presbyter/presbyteri)
cum (discipulos/discipulis)
non (laborat/laborant).

(b) Sarcina (vinum/vino) et
(oleo/olea) et (unguenta/
unguentis) et (ovum/ovis)
onerosa est.

3 Change the underlined words into the plural, and alter any other words which are affected, and translate:

(a) **Monachus** in monasterio habitat.
(b) **Mulus** non **silvam** sed **agrum** amat.
(c) **Equus** neque in silvis neque in agris cum **mulo** laborat.
(d) Benedictus **vinum** et **unguentum** desiderat.

Prepositions – ablative or accusative?

These are words which form phrases with nouns. Sometimes the noun is in the accusative case, sometimes the ablative. It depends on the preposition:

+ Accusative		+ Ablative	
per	*through, by way of*	**cum**	*with*
in	*into, on to*	**in**	*in, on*
ad	*to, towards*	**a(b)** *	*from, by*
		e(x) *	*out of, away from, off*
		* the extra consonant is used before a vowel	

Prepositions like '**in**' which are used with either case are followed by the accusative if some motion is implied, or ablative if it is not:

In terram cadit.	*She falls <u>on to</u> the ground.*
In terra iacet.	*She lies <u>on</u> the ground.*
In silvam ambulat.	*She walks <u>into</u> the wood.*
In silva ambulat.	*She walks <u>in</u> the wood.*

▶ Monachus in cucullo *A hooded monk*

Paulus et mulus longe a monasterio absunt. Neque silvam neque sarcinas amat mulus. 'Io!' clamat Paulus. Mulus non ambulat.

Subito equum Paulus et mulus audiunt. Deinde equum vident. Celeriter equus per viam ad Paulum mulumque venit. In equo est monachus in cucullo. Equus est territus. Equus Paulum mulumque videt et subito e via declinat. Monachus ex equo in terram cadit et equus celeriter in silvam abit. Monachus in terra iacet.

abit	*(s/he) departs*
audiunt	*(they) hear*
cadit	*(s/he) falls*
celeriter	*quickly*

clamat	*(s/he) shouts*
cucullo (cucullus)	*hood*
declinat	*(it) swerves*
deinde	*then, next*
iacet	*(s/he) lies*
io!	*heyup!*
subito	*suddenly*
terram (terra)	*ground*
territus	*scared*
venit	*(s/he) comes*
viam (via)	*road*
vide(n)t	*see*

Practice (ii)

1 Choose the correct word and translate:

(a) Monachi per (via/viam) ambulant.

(b) Mulus in (agrum/agro) est.

(c) Equus, a (monachos/monachis) territus, e monasterio venit.

(d) Monachus ex (equum/equo) in (terra/terram) cadit.

2 Choose the correct preposition and translate:

(a) (In/Cum) silva, monachus
(in/ex) equo cadit
et (ab/in) terra iacet.

(b) Ova (in/e) sarcina
(per/in) terram cadunt.

(c) **Mulus (e/per) silvam (in/ad) monasterium ambulat.**

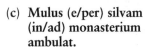

About Latin

Speaking as the Romans did ...

A recording of Cicero making a speech or Virgil reciting his poetry would be a fine thing. The best we can do twenty centuries later is tentatively reconstruct the sound of Latin, letter by letter, syllable by syllable, from various bits and pieces of evidence. Much is disputed, much open to interpretation. But we have to live with this, for no one can begin to appreciate a literature – which was written for recital – without some idea of its sound. Our reconstruction may be a somewhat incomplete jigsaw puzzle, but so too is that of Elizabethan English, and that hasn't stopped production of Shakespeare's plays. So with all the help which academic findings can give us we shall set about putting flesh on the skeleton and breathe life back into the ancient texts.

We would be hard put to identify just one correct pronunciation in any case. Latin was the first language of the empire of Rome, which lasted for over half a millennium, and stretched from the Crimea to Spain, Edinburgh to Egypt. For centuries Latin was the language of the entire known world. Looking back over the emergence of English, our international language today, whom should we choose as its most correct speaker? Alfred the Great? Abraham Lincoln? Nelson Mandela? At least with Latin we can limit our attention to the two centuries of classical Latin, but even within this briefer span changes will have occurred – a recording of Florence Nightingale suggests our own pronunciation has changed considerably in the past hundred and fifty years or so.

The clearest evidence we have is of the sound of the individual letters themselves. This evidence comes from ancient commentators who give detailed advice about certain sounds (that it was given at all can be taken as a symptom of variance if not change); other clues come from transliteration into and out of other languages (e.g. Greek *Kaisar* for 'Caesar', and *Oualerios* for 'Valerius'); also from puns and plays on words, rhymes and assonance; and from the sub-Latin, or 'Romance' languages, French, Spanish, Portuguese and Italian, of which the more isolated and conservative dialects are especially interesting – *centum*'s hard 'c', for instance, in Sardinian (*kentu*, a hundred).

Latin	English	French	Spanish	Italian
unus, una	one	un, une	un(o), una	un(o), una
septem	seven	sept	siete	sette
centum	hundred	cent	ciento	cento

Stress and intonation are less secure. Latin stress was probably similar to our own, where the accent falls on the penultimate syllable, or if that syllable is weak, the one before it: *Augústus, Cícero*. Some hold the view that the initial syllable had the weight of accent, particularly in pre-classical Latin. This idea is prompted by the weakening of first syllables when they are compounded and made second syllable: *fácere, perfícere*; *cápere, recípere*. Even after the classical period we see this stress in, for example, the Italian *pellegrino* (from Latin *peregrinus*), whose initial syllable was given enough weight for the word to arrive in English as 'pilgrim'. But we should not take this first-syllable theory too far. Almost all the examples cited involve a compound with a prefix, which would naturally be stressed on first formation. Put the accent on the second syllable of a compound, and it will soon lose the prefix and revert to the simple form. Even *pellegrino* was once a compounded form, being 'a person from across the field': *per-ager-inus*.

An 'm' in the middle of a word was very similar to ours, but at the end of a word appears to lose much of its consonantal value. For instance, say *septem (seven)* without closing your lips on the final 'm'. It is interesting to note that many other European languages, such as Bulgarian, Dutch and German, have a nasalized ending (-m/-n) for their word for 'seven' but the Romance languages derived directly from Latin all lose it (see the table above). This 'm' is also missing from some Latin inscriptions: e.g. *scriptum est (it was written)*: written as *scriptust*. In classical Latin poetry a final 'm' is treated like a vowel if it appears before another vowel, and is elided. In medieval Latin the final 'm' appears to be a more complete sound, no doubt reinforced by students of classical Latin learning the accusative case: a schoolmaster had to be impressed that you knew *silvam* from *silva* and so you spelt and hummed it for all it was worth with none of the halfway nasalizing of the classical sound. Literacy is a conservative influence on the inflexions of any language: it is no coincidence that the English language lost many of its own inflexions after the Norman Conquest took away its function as a written language.

Thus we can guess with some confidence that the final 'm' of *septem* was sounded, if openly, by educated speakers who were taught both to spell words and enunciate them until their tongues were sore; but that this sound tended to be reduced in ordinary speech, with its stress on the syllable-before-last, to the point of eventual extinction in the Romance languages.

Differences between literary and spoken Latin – or 'vulgar' Latin (*vulgus: crowd, public*) – were not confined to sound. The syntax of speech was inevitably looser and more straightforward than that of the page. There were also differences in vocabulary: *equus* was the literary man's word for horse (*equestrian, equine, equitation* are among the learned and 'posh' words coined after the Middle Ages), while a cart-driver made do with a *caballus* (*cheval, caballo, cavalry* and possibly *cabbie*). We shall never know how far Cicero carried his literary style into ordinary speech, but he certainly retained something of his elaborate style in letters to his friends. One thinks of Queen Victoria's famous grumble at Gladstone, the Prime Minister, telling him not to address her as if she were a public meeting.

Spoken idioms will, conversely, have in some measure been employed by writers, not so much to create a simple, plain style but to embellish a dramatic effect or intimate moment. Our unlettered cart-driver, however, would have struggled with all the allusions to Greek mythology and legends, and even in the one or two more accessible pieces, he might have found satirists firing sharpened verses at him for the din he made in going about his daily business.

In the fourth and fifth centuries AD, the early Christians gave fresh impetus to literary Latin and for a while welded it to the vulgar form. The gospels had originally been written in Greek but it was Latin translations, in particular St Jerome's bible (the

Vulgate), which wooed the western world to the new religion. The language of the pulpit had to be simple and straightforward since it was aimed primarily at those with little or no schooling in literacy and rhetoric. In tandem with Christianity's populist tendency was the intellectualizing of theologians caught up in debates such as the nature of the Trinity, the 'three-in-one-ness' of the Father, Son and Holy Spirit, a controversy which fuelled the fires of early heresies, and which gave renewed life to the language of philosophy and rhetoric.

Revision

1 Add the missing forms to the tables:

Case	Singular		
Nominative (subject)			**puer**
Accusative (object)	**silvam**		
Ablative (by, with, from, in, on)		**mulo**	**puero**
	Plural		
Nominative (subject)			
Accusative (object)	**silvas**		
Ablative (by, with, from, in, on)			**pueris**

Case	Singular		
Nominative (subject)	**vinum**	**liber**	**ancilla**
Accusative (object)		**librum**	
Ablative (by, with, from, in, on)	**vino**		**ancilla**
	Plural		
Nominative (subject)	**vina**		**ancillae**
Accusative (object)	**vina**	**libros**	
Ablative (by, with, from, in, on)		**libris**	

2 Change the underlined words into the singular, alter any other words which may be affected, and translate:

   (**a**) <u>Discipuli</u> in culinam ambulant.
   (**b**) <u>Presbyteri</u> cibum vinumque saepe desiderant.
   (**c**) Mulus per <u>silvas</u> semper venit.
   (**d**) Magister <u>libros</u>, discipuli vinum desiderant.

3 Translate into Latin:

   (**a**) The horses work in neither the wood nor the field.
   (**b**) The monk carries the perfumes in the bag.
   (**c**) The priest walks with the students through the wood towards the monastery.
   (**d**) Students are not priests.

4 Do you know what these words mean? If not...

ager	magister	ovum
terra	via	per
e(x)	oppidum	ubi
iacet	a(b)	habitat
culina	venit	mittit
audiunt	vident	hodie
semper	clamat	subito

How many English words can you think of which are related to these?

▶ Living Latin

1 Illa quidem iurata negat, sed credere durum est.

                                  (Tibullus, Elegies i, 6, 7)

She denies it under oath, but it's hard to believe her.

2 *Beati mites quoniam ipsi possidebunt terram.

                                  (St Matthew v, 4)

Blessed are the meek for they will inherit the earth.

3 *Gloria in excelsis Deo et in terra pax hominibus bonae voluntatis.

                                  (Gloria)

Glory be to God on high and on earth peace to men of good will.

4 Dum nos fata sinunt oculos satiemus amore.

                                (Propertius ii, 15, 23)

While the fates allow us let us fill our eyes with love.

5 **Oro, si quis adhuc precibus locus, exue mentem.**

(Virgil, Aeneid iv, 319)

I beg you, if there's still time for entreaties, change your mind.

6 ***Non veni vocare iustos, sed peccatores in paenitentiam.**

(St Luke v, 32)

I have not come to welcome the righteous, but the sinners to repentance.

7 **Exitiabilis superstitio rursum erumpebat, non modo per Iudaeam, originem eius mali, sed per urbem etiam quo cuncta undique atrocia aut pudenda confluunt celebranturque.**

(Tacitus, Annals xv, 44)

The deadly superstition broke out again, not only in Judaea, the source of this trouble, but also in the capital where from every corner all things sleaze-ridden and shameful ooze together and come into vogue.

*post-classical

04

figura feminae
the figure of a woman

In this unit you will learn about
- the genitive
- questions

- and find out more about Latin in '"Anyone" for a cancan?'

The genitive ('of') case

The nominative case is for subjects, the accusative for objects (and also follows some prepositions), and the ablative is the *in*, *on*, *with*, *by* or *from* case. Now for the genitive:

	Nominative	Accusative	Genitive	Ablative
Sing.	silva	silvam	**silvae**	silva
	mulus	mulum	**muli**	mulo
	vinum	vinum	**vini**	vino
Plural	silvae	silvas	**silvarum**	silvis
	muli	mulos	**mulorum**	mulis
	vina	vina	**vinorum**	vinis

The genitive can almost always be translated with the preposition '*of...*'. This may be the possessive '*of*':

| <u>Benedicti</u> vinum | *the wine <u>of Benedict</u> (<u>Benedict's</u> wine)* |
| <u>feminae</u> cucullus | *the hood <u>of the woman</u> (<u>the woman's</u> hood)* |

The '*of*' case may also describe a quantity:

| amphora <u>vini</u> | *an amphora <u>of wine</u>* |
| sarcina <u>ovorum</u> | *a bag <u>of eggs</u>* |

The 'of' case can be 'subjective' or 'objective':

| timor <u>Danorum</u> | *fear <u>of the Danes</u> (either another's fear of them or the Danes' own fear)* |
| amor <u>Dei</u> | *love <u>of God</u> (either another's love of God or God's own love)* |

▶ Femina in terra iacet *The woman lies on the ground*

Shared endings key

-i muli: nominative plural   **-ae** silvae: nominative plural
  muli, vini : 'of ...' genitive case   silvae: 'of ...' genitive case

---

Monachus in terra iacet. Equus, ab umbris territus, e via in silvam effugit. Vento enim folia et rami crepitant et equus, umbrarum ramorumque timidus, nunc per silvas ad monasterium festinat.

Immotus in terra iacet monachus. Paulus ad monachum currit. Figura tamen non monachi sed feminae est. Paulus feminam spectat. Cucullus feminae est scissus. Paulus feminam tunica protegit.

crepitant	*(they) rustle*
currit	*(s/he) runs*
effugit	*(s/he) flees*
enim	*for, you see*
feminam, feminae (femina)	*woman*
festinat	*(s/he) hurries*
figura	*shape*
folia (folium)	*leaves*
immotus	*still, motionless*
protegit	*(s/he) covers*
rami (ramus)	*branches*
scissus	*torn*
tamen	*however*
timidus	*fearful*
tunica	*tunic, dress*
vento (ventus)	*wind*

Practice (i)

1 Add the missing forms:

Case	Singular		
Nominative (subject)	**terra**	**ramus**	**folium**
Accusative (object)			
Genitive (of)			
Ablative (by, with, from, in, on)	**terra**		
	Plural		
Nominative (subject)	**terrae**		**folia**
Accusative (object)		**ramos**	
Genitive (of)			
Ablative (by, with, from, in, on)	**terris**		

2 Add the missing endings and translate:

(a) Feminae in culina monasteri__ laborant.

(b) Ova in tunicam femin__ cadunt.

(c) Discipuli vinum Benedict__ bibunt.

3 Identify the cases of the underlined nouns, and translate:

(a) <u>Discipuli</u> vinum <u>ancillarum</u> desiderant.
(b) <u>Stephanus</u> est magister <u>scholae</u>.

(c) **Paulus est <u>Stephani discipulus</u>.**
(d) **Mulus est <u>silvarum</u> timidus.**

4 Put these nouns into the genitive singular, and genitive plural:

(a) **ramus** *branch* (b) **ager** *field* (c) **ovum** *egg*
(d) **umbra** *shadow* (e) **ancilla** *maid*

Questions

A question may be introduced by a question word such as **ubi?** *where?*, **quis?** *who?* and **quid?** *what?* Without such an interrogative word to introduce the question, the suffix **-ne** is added to the first word:

Tu-<u>ne</u> vales?	*Are you well?*
Ubi femina habitat?	*Where does the woman live?*
Cur in terra femina iacet?	*Why is the woman lying on the ground?*

The 'is' in the third example above is part of the verbal phrase 'is lying', represented in Latin by **iacet** (and not **est**: see 'Verbs' on p. vii).

Some questions expect the answer 'yes' or 'no'. **Nonne** expects the answer 'yes', **num** the answer 'no':

<u>Nonne</u> **Benedictus in culina est?**	*Surely Benedict is in the kitchen?*
<u>Num</u> **Paulus est episcopus?**	*Surely Paul is not a bishop?*

▶ Ubi sum? *Where am I?*

Paulus neque videre neque audire equum feminae potest. Equus e silvis ad monasterium festinat. Femina diu iacet immota. Paulus est anxius et mulus trepidus. 'Te miseram!' gemit Paulus. Femina oculos aperit et Paulum spectat. 'Nonne es mortua?' rogat Paulus.

'Mortua? Non ita. Ubi sum? In silvis?'

'Ita vero,' inquit Paulus.

'Ubi est equus?'

'Lente, lente! Vales-ne? Vis-ne aquam bibere?'

'Non ita, tibi gratias. Equus-ne adest?'

'Non ita. Ramos umbrasque timet. Et tu, vales-ne?'

'Valeo. O malum est!' clamat femina.

'Lente! Quis es?'

adest	*(s/he, it) is present, here*
anxius	*concerned*
aperit	*opens*
aquam (aqua)	*water*
audire	*to hear*
bibere	*to drink*
diu	*for a long time*
es	*you are*
inquit	*(s/he) says, said*
ita vero	*yes*
malum est	*it is bad! curses!*
mortua	*dead*
non ita	*no, not so*
oculos (oculus)	*eyes*
potest	*(s/he) is able, can*
rogat	*(s/he) asks*
sum	*I am*
te miseram	*you poor thing*
tibi gratias	*thank you*
timet	*(s/he, it) fears*
trepidus	*nervous*
valeo (-es)	*I am (you are) well*
videre	*to see*
vis	*you want, wish*

Practice (ii)

1 Answer the questions with the correct form of the verb *to be*:

(a) Quis es? _____ Paulus.
(b) Qui estis? _____ Stephani discipuli.
(c) Quis est? _____ episcopus.
(d) Ubi sum? _____ in silva.

sum	*I am*	**sumus**	*we are*
es	*you are*	**estis**	*you are* (pl.)
est	*s/he, it/there is*	**sunt**	*they/there are*

2 Make up questions which lead to these answers:

(a) Mulus est in silva.
(b) Paulus in bibliotheca laborat quod est discipulus.
(c) Non ita, femina non mortua est.
(d) Stephanus est magister.

About Latin

'Anyone' for a cancan?

In the medieval period a 'clerical' worker was more often than not a clergyman. The Church first became active in government and administration during the latter days of the Roman empire, and became even more so after it collapsed. Libraries and schools might have died out altogether if the early monasteries had not survived to house them. Monks would sing, read and write Latin, much of which was religious and some secular. Hymns, liturgy, lives of saints, histories, charters, letters and poems all contribute to a rich variety of writing produced over more than a millennium. Sub-classical imitations were carefully crafted, and there was looser stuff too influenced by the respective native languages.

The spoken Latin of the empire had long since disintegrated into the Romance languages, intermingling with local speech habits and evolving with the peoples who spoke it. In France students of Latin have tended to pronounce Latin as they do French (e.g. 'qu' as 'k', not 'kw'). This has an interesting bearing on the origin of the word 'cancan', which is said by some to be derived from the Latin word *quamquam*. *Quamquam* usually means 'although', but the connection between 'although' and a dance is not easy to fathom. More likely is a less well-known meaning of *quamquam* – 'anyone' in the feminine, 'any girl', i.e. no fixed partner. Another theory ascribes the cancan to a 'scandalous' dance, again the origin being the Latin word *quamquam*, the scandal being a row during the Reformation: a few priests in France had adopted the pronunciation favoured in northern (and Protestant) Europe, 'kwamkwam', only to incur the severe displeasure of the French authorities. Even the pronunciation of a dying language could have life-threatening implications.

In England, as elsewhere, Latin was pronounced according to local speech habits. In the years following the Norman Conquest of 1066, English was strongly influenced by French. 'Julius Caesar', which was 'Yoolius Ky-sser' in classical times, was pronounced 'Joolius Seizer' by the many schoolmasters of French origin, and 'Kikero' became 'Sissero', 'Wergilius' 'Vurdgil'.

Latin is not a parent language of English, but the number of loan-words, of which many arrived via French, make it a most generous uncle. New words have one of three sources: they are either new formations, or taken from another language, or a mixture of the two. The spelling of certain words may be changed, or stabilized, at a later date (e.g. Old English *discipul* and *munuc* which were to become *disciple* and *monk*). It may be that a parent language coined the word, or itself borrowed from another source (e.g. *elephant*: Egyptian to Greek to Latin to French to English). Origins are not always clear, and there is sometimes more than one source behind a word's widespread use.

Some loan-words taken before the Norman Conquest (1066)	Some post-1066 arrivals via French
castle (castellum-i)	desire (désirer/desiderare)
disciple (discipulus-i)	oil (huile/oleum)
monk (monachus-i)	silence (silence/silentium)

In the eighth century Charlemagne had wanted to improve the schools within his empire, and employed an English scholar, Alcuin, to raise the standard of Latin taught in them. Similar initiatives followed over the next few centuries, culminating at the end of the middle ages in the Renaissance, when writers, artists and scholars were guided and inspired almost exclusively by classical models.

It was less easy to impose uniformity on the spoken language. The spoken Latin of the empire had already evolved into the vernacular languages of the Romance countries, and the Latin-as-a-second-language spoken in the medieval period became rather homeless and fragmentary. Different countries and regions could barely understand each other's use of the language, and the sound of ecclesiastical Latin was far from uniform. Even in the churches Latin was not going to last long, at least not in the countries where the Reformation was gathering momentum and allegiance to Rome would be cast aside. Latin's fading role as an international language and the continued rise of the vernacular languages was in one sense the eventual triumph of vulgar Latin over its literary counterpart. But once retired from active life, Latin becomes provider, and feeds the vernacular languages with vast numbers of new words and expressions.

Revision

1 Write sentences as answers to these questions:

    (a) **Ubi est femina?**
    (b) **Cur equus feminae e silva festinat?**
    (c) **Ubi magister scholae laborat?**
    (d) **Quid mulus portat?**

2 Translate into Latin:

    (a) Are we in a wood?
    (b) The woman's horse is able to hear the wind.
    (c) The mule carries the monk's bags.
    (d) Surely the students do not long for Benedict's wine?

3 Add the missing forms:

	Singular		
Nominative		**tunica**	
Accusative			
Genitive			
Ablative	**vento**	**tunica**	
	Plural		
Nominative	**venti**		
Accusative		**tunicas**	**ova**
Genitive			
Ablative			**ovis**

4 How well do you know these words?

cur	**ventus**	**tunica**
currit	**tamen**	**enim**
nonne	**num**	**quis**
quid	**femina**	**schola**
timet	**folium**	**ramus**
ita vero	**non ita**	**adest**

What English words can you think of, which are in part at least descended from these Latin words? The English word *via* is derived from the ablative of **via**. Can you see how?

▶ Living Latin

1 ***Nemo servus potest duobus dominis servire.**

(St Luke xvi, 13)

No one can be a slave to two masters.

2 ***Quis maior est, qui recumbit an qui ministrat?**

(St Luke xxii, 27)

Whom do we value more, the one who sits for dinner or the one who serves?

3 ***Alcuinum, de Britannia Saxonici generis hominem, virum undecumque doctissimum, praeceptorem habuit.**

(Einhard, Vita Karoli xxv)

He (Charlemagne) employed Alcuin as teacher, a fellow from Britain, of Saxon blood, in every respect a most learned man.

4 ***Heu, cuculus nobis fuerat cantare suetus,**
   quae te nunc rapuit hora nefanda tuis?
Heu, cuculus, cuculus, qua te regione reliqui,
   infelix nobis illa dies fuerat.

(Alcuin, Versus de Cuculo)

Mourn the little cuckoo who liked to sing to us.
   What unspeakable moment snatched you from your friends?
Little cuckoo, little cuckoo, where did I leave you?
   What a wretched day that was for us.

5 ***Hic Harold Rex interfectus est et fuga verterunt Angli.**

(Bayeux Tapestry)

Here King Harold was slain and the English turned and fled.

6 ***Sidus clarum**
puellarum,
flos et decus omnium
rosa veris,
quae videris
clarior quam lilium.

(12th century anon.)

Bright star of maidens, everything's flower and ornament, you are like a spring rose, more lovely than a lily.

*post-classical

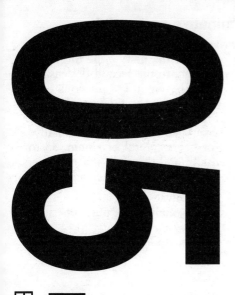

05

Egbertae filia

Egberta's daughter

In this unit you will learn about

- the vocative case
- adjectives: -us, -a, -um

- and find out more about Latin in 'Reformation and Renaissance – life after death'

Declensions: the nominative and genitive

All nouns belong to one of five groups, or 'declensions'. Nouns like **silva**, **umbra** or **Lucia** belong to the first, while those like **mulus**, **magister** or **vinum** all belong to the second declension. **Amor** and **timor**, which appeared briefly in the previous unit, belong to the third – but more about them later. All these declensions and cases mean that some endings do double and treble duty: the ending -a, for example, might be the nominative or ablative singular of **silva**, or neuter plural of **vinum**. So to help establish a noun's declension (and therefore the endings), dictionaries show a noun's nominative and genitive endings:

First declension: **silva, silvae**
Second declension: **mulus, muli** (also: **puer, pueri;**
                      ager, agri *a field*
                      vinum, vini (neuter)

▶ Lucia

'Quis es? Ubi habitas?' rogat Paulus.
'In castello,' inquit femina.
'Tu-ne es Egberta, castelli domina?'
'Non Egberta, sed Egbertae filia, Lucia sum. Et tu, quis es?'
'Sum Paulus, et in monasterio habito.'
'Es presbyter?'
'Non presbyter, sed discipulus sum.'
'Episcopi-ne discipulus es?'
'Non episcopi sed Stephani.'
'Quis est Stephanus? In monasterio habitat?'
'Stephanus est monachus et scholae magister.'
'Me miseram! Ubi est ille caballus?'
'Lente! Fortasse est in agris cum monasterii equis. Age, mecum ad monasterium veni. In mulum ascendas.'

age	*come on!*
ascendas	*you may climb*
caballus-i [m]	*horse*
castellum-i [n]	*castle*
domina-ae [f]	*lady, mistress*
Egberta-ae	*Egberta*
episcopus-i [m]	*bishop*
filia-ae [f]	*daughter*
fortasse	*perhaps*
habito (-as) (-at)	*I (you) (s/he) live*
ille	*that*

Lucia-ae	*Lucia*
me miseram	*just my luck*
mecum	*with me*
veni	*come!*

Practice (i)

1 Fill the gaps:

Nominative	Genitive
sarcina	**sarcinae**
umbra	
ovum	
puer	
	magistri
episcopus	
	Egbertae
liber	

2 Make a list of all the nouns you have met (showing the nominative and genitive endings) similar to:

(a) **silva, silvae** (e.g. sarcina-ae, Lucia-ae, etc.)
(b) **mulus, muli** (e.g. episcopus-i, Paulus-i, etc.)
(c) **vinum, vini** (e.g. ovum-i, castellum-i, etc.)

The vocative case

Second declension nouns (those like **mulus-i**) have a special ending for when they are being spoken to. This is called the 'vocative case': **mule** for **mulus**, (**Brute** for **Brutus** in **Et tu Brute!**). Most other vocative forms are the same as the nominative, e.g. '**o Lucia**'.

Adjectives: *sanctus, sancta, sanctum*

Adjectives give nouns more detail or colour: *a saintly bishop, a tired maid*. A Latin adjective is said to 'agree' with the noun it describes in gender (masculine, feminine or neuter), number (singular or plural) and case (nominative, accusative, etc.):

Sanctus episcopus et ancilla fessa in agro sedent.	*The saintly bishop and tired maid sit in the field.*
Multae feminae per silvam obscuram ambulant.	*Many women are walking through the dark wood.*
Liber magnus in monasterio est.	*The large book is in the monastery.*

The <u>masculine</u> endings of adjectives like **sanct-us** are identical to those of **mul-us,** the <u>feminine</u> to those of **silv-a,** and <u>neuter</u> to those of **vin-um.** In the final example above **magnus** agrees with **lib<u>er</u>** even though their endings are not identical: both words are nominative masculine singular.

The position of an adjective may be before or after the noun it describes. You will come across adjectives placed several words before or after the nouns they qualify, especially in poetry. The endings help you match the two together. Some adjectives appear after a verb (as in English):

Mulus est lentus. *The mule is slow.*

▶ E silvis veniunt *They come out of the woods*

Obscuram per silvam ad monasterium veniunt. Paulus mulum ducit. Lucia in mulo sedet. Mulus est lentus. Silva est umbrosa. Lucia Paulum rogat: 'Episcopus-ne sanctus in monasterio manet?'

'Episcopus? Nescio. Sanctus episcopus? Vel saevus?'

'Nonne est sanctus?'

'Episcopus est saevus, quod semper Stephanum nos discipulos in bibliotheca claudere iubet.'

'Discipuli-ne estis boni studiosique?'

'Certe, semper.'

'Num vos discipuli semper boni estis? Fortasse mali, ignavi, somnulenti estis.'

'Mali? Ignavi? Nos? Iocosa es.'

'Cur in silva ambulas? Cur studiosus in bibliotheca non laboras?'

'Episcopus certe est malus, gulosus, saevus, vinolentus ....'

'Ssst. Maledicis. Episcopus est Egbertae avunculus.'

'Vero? Episcopus est cognatus Egbertae? Quid ergo? Hic, o Domina, est mulus. Mulus est cognatus equorum qui in monasterii agris habitant, eho mule?' Paulus ridet. Sed neque Lucia neque mulus ridet. Nunc enim mulus et Luciam et onerosas cibo multo vinoque sarcinas portat. 'Ignoscas, o Lucia!' inquit Paulus. Per silvas silentio procedunt. Mox magnos monasterii muros vident et e silvis in agros veniunt.

ambulas	*you walk*
avunculus-i [m]	*uncle*
bonus-a-um	*good*
certe	*certainly, yes*
claudere	*to lock*
cognatus-i [m]	*kinsman*
ducit	*(s/he) leads*
eho	*eh*
et... et	*both... and*
gulosus-a-um	*greedy*
hic	*here*
ignavus-a-um	*lazy*
ignoscas	*forgive (me), sorry*
iocosus-a-um	*full of jokes, humorous*
iubet	*(s/he) orders, tells*
laboras	*you work*
magnus-a-um	*great, large*
maledicis	*you slander*
malus-a-um	*troublesome, bad*
manet	*(s/he) stays*
mox	*soon, presently*
multus-a-um	*much, many*
murus-i [m]	*wall*
nescio	*I don't know*
nos	*us*
num	*surely... not*
obscurus-a-um	*dark*
procedunt	*(they) go forward*
qui	*who*
quid ergo?	*so what?*
ridet	*(s/he) laughs*
saevus-a-um	*cruel, mean*
sedet	*(s/he) sits*
silentium-i [n]	*silence*
somnulentus-a-um	*sleepy*
studiosus-a-um	*hard-working*
umbrosus-a-um	*full of shadows*
vel	*or*
veniunt	*(they) come*
vero	*indeed*
vinolentus-a-um	*fond of wine*
vos	*you*

Practice (ii)

1 Fill each gap with the appropriate form of **furiosus** *angry* and **sanctus** *saintly*: (**fugat** = *chases*)

   (a) Bestiae _____
       Christianos _____ fugant.

(b) Christianus _____
     bestias _____ fugat.

(c) Christianum _____
     bestiae _____ fugant.

2 Change the underlined words to the plural form (other endings should be changed if affected) and translate the new version:

(a) <u>Bestia</u> furiosa sanctum monachum spectat.
(b) <u>Liber</u> magnus in bibliotheca est.
(c) <u>Discipulus</u> ignavus <u>mulum</u> furiosum in <u>agro</u> videt.
(d) <u>Monachus</u> somnulentus in bibliotheca non laborat.

About Latin

Reformation and Renaissance – life after death

The Renaissance was a 'rebirth', a renewal of interest in classical literature and art. Many Greek and Latin books which had previously been ignored or unknown were brought to light and translated. There were imitations as well as translations, and original works were written in the authors' own languages which echoed classical precedents in form or content. Schoolmen and scholars redoubled their efforts to introduce classical standards of grammar and syntax, and medieval Latin as a living language was all but laid to rest, helped on its way by the Reformers' distrust of anything Roman. Latin, in its classical form, had achieved immortality: dead languages do not change, and the linguistic rules which govern their use will always remain the same.

The translation of classical texts into English demanded a wider range of vocabulary than it was able to supply. There were not the words to express the many new ideas of religion, astronomy, science and philosophy which were stimulated by the interest in these ancient texts, and often the simplest solution was to import a word direct from the Latin or Greek. Many of these words in time lost their foreign status, and became part of our language (some with slight modifications, e.g. *splendidus* was first *splendidious* and then settled as *splendid*). The anglicized pronunciation of these loan-words will in turn have influenced our pronunciation of original Latin.

Latin was very closely caught up in the religious conflicts in the sixteenth century. It was, after all, the language of the Church, where it had survived as a spoken language for over a thousand years. Latin was a symbol of all things Roman, and since scholars were being strangled, burned and beheaded for denying or affirming Rome, it's no small mercy that Latin survived at all. In England, classical scholars took sides in the dispute over the correct language for the liturgy – Sir John Cheke spoke out against Latin and assisted Cranmer with his Book of Common Prayer. Some wanted to follow the lead of the Dutch scholar, Erasmus, and recreate a more authentic classical sound. Others wanted most of all to rid Latin of its association with the Church. Thus the sound of Latin, now deprived of its status as an independent, if ritualized, language, lived for a brief while in a limbo of learned good intentions before slipping into the stream of English and a pronunciation along the lines of our own speech habits.

A further complication is the famous 'vowel shift' which occurred in English at this time. Vowel quantities of Latin-derived words had been changing since pre-Conquest times. *Pater*, for instance, has a short 'a' in Latin which was lengthened on arrival in English, possibly by association with the long 'a' in 'father'. The vowel shift then brought about a further change, leaving us with the 'pay-ter' we hear in period dramas. Through change of quantity or vowel shift or both, we now have in English (and, until as late as the nineteenth century, in Latin): b*o*ne-us from *bonus* (classical pronunciation: 'b*o*nnus'); m*i*se-er from *miser* ('m*i*ssair'), f*i*ll-ial from *filius* ('feelius'), *wine* from *vinum* ('w*ee*num').

If Latin in this country was somewhat anglicized, it is even more pertinent to say English was Latinized. Coining new words became something of a fad, beyond the requirement of scientists and translators. Some loan-words which had settled into English, many having arrived via French, were reformed to make them resemble the original Latin ones more closely. We now have many cases of pairs of words, which have subsequently developed different meanings:

Latin	Pre-1500	Post-1500
securus	sure	secure
computare	count	compute
desiderare	desire	desiderate

Not all these later additions survived (e.g. *desiderate*). Some words were respelt and replaced the earlier forms altogether – a headache for all those who struggle with spelling:

Latin	Pre-1500	Post-1500
dubium	doute	doubt
septem	set (French)	sept (French)
subtilis	sutil	subtle

Some Latin-derived words can appear dry and pompous. Comedians from Molière to Mrs Bucket have had plenty of mileage from unnecessarily tortuous circumlocutions. In the sixteenth century one poor fellow closed a letter to someone he hoped to impress with 'I relinquish to fatigate your intelligence....'. However, quirk and affectation aside, Latin has proved to be a rich source of new words. Some loan-words have settled in so well that you would not notice their origin, and their crispness and nuance help to give English its unequalled richness and variety.

Revision

1 Fill the gaps:

Latin	English	Derivative(s)
ovum-i	egg	oval
lucidus-a-um	bright	
murus-i		
bestia-ae		
folium-i		
dubium-i	doubt	
loquax	talkative	
vir-i	man	
iratus-a-um	angry	

2 Change the underlined words into the plural and alter any other words which are affected, and translate:

(a) <u>Monachus</u>-ne ignavus in agris laborat?
(b) Num <u>discipulus</u> cognatus Luciae est?
(c) Paulus magistri <u>librum</u> in bibliotheca spectat.
(d) Num Benedictus <u>ancillae</u> avunculus est!

3 Write out **sanctus-a-um**, singular and plural, in all the cases you have met so far.

4 Check you know these words:

castellum-i	episcopus-i	manet
sedet	iubet	ridet
mox	certe	vero
bonus-a-um	malus-a-um	multus-a-um
magnus-a-um	gulosus-a-um	saevus-a-um
sanctus-a-um	furiosus-a-um	lentus-a-um
fessus-a-um	bibliotheca-ae	

What English words are derived from these?

5 During the Renaissance many new adjectives were coined from Latin roots. Identify the English meanings of the Latin nouns below, and the English adjective derived from the Latin word:

e.g. **noctes**	*nights*	**nocturnal**
noctes	*son*	
canis	*church*	
culina	*house*	
decem	*sun*	
domus	*brother*	
ecclesia	*nights*	
filius	*mother*	
frater	*dog*	
mater	*cattle*	
sol	*ten*	
boves	*kitchen*	

6 Translate into Latin:

(a) Surely the bishop is not greedy?
(b) The tired students often sit in the field.
(c) Is the lady furious, Stephen?
(d) Do mules work in the dark wood?

▶ Living Latin

1 *Ne nos inducas in tentationem, sed libera a malo.

(Pater Noster)

Do not lead us into temptation but free us from evil.

2 *Beati pauperes, quia vestrum est regnum Dei.

(St Luke vi, 20)

Blessed are the poor, for yours is the kingdom of God.

3 Sequitur clades, forte an dolo principis incertum (nam utrumque auctores prodidere), sed omnibus quae huic urbi per violentiam ignium acciderunt gravior atque atrocior.

(Tacitus, Annals xv, 38)

A disaster followed – whether accidental or by Nero's hand no one knows (both versions have their supporters) – but this city had never experienced a more serious or damaging fire.

4 **Eorum multitudo ingens haud proinde in crimine incendii quam odio humani generis convicti sunt.**

(Tacitus, Annals xv, 44)

A large number of Christians were condemned, not so much on any charge of arson but because of their aversion to the human race.

5 **Quamquam adversus sontis et novissima exempla meritos miseratio oriebatur, tamquam non utilitate publica sed in saevitiam unius absumerentur.**

(Tacitus, Annals xv, 44)

Despite their guilt and the deserved severity of their punishment, people began to feel pity because their destruction was not so much in the interests of the public but rather for the sadistic amusement of one man.

6 **Pervaserat rumor ipso tempore flagrantis urbis inisse eum domesticam scaenam et cecinisse Troianum excidium.**

(Tacitus, Annals xv, 39)

A rumour circulated that at the very time of the fire in Rome Nero had gone on to his stage in the palace and sung of the Fall of Troy.

*post-classical

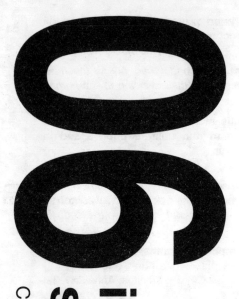

06

in amphitheatro saevitia

cruelty in the amphitheatre

In this unit you will learn about
- verbs: potest, vult, debet
- infinitives
- adjectives: -er, -era, -erum

- and find out more about Latin in 'Latin wanted – dead or alive'

Adjectives: *miser, misera, miserum* *wretched*

The endings of these adjectives are almost identical to those of **sanct-us-a-um** but for the nominative masculine singular (cf. **presbyter** and **mulus**). So **mulus miser, mulum miserum, femina misera, feminam miseram**, etc.

Verbs: *potest, vult, debet*

	is/are able	want(s)	ought, owe(s)
s/he	**potest**	**vult**	**debet**
they	**possunt**	**volunt**	**debent**

These verbs are usually followed by an infinitive (an infinitive of an English verb is formed with 'to....' , e.g. *to see, to believe, to say*.

Abbatissa cantare non potest. *The abbess is unable to sing.*
Pecuniam dare debent. *They ought to give some money.*

Latin infinitives *-re*

amat	*s/he loves*	**amare**	*to love*
videt	*s/he sees*	**videre**	*to see*
scribit	*s/he writes*	**scribere**	*to write*
audit	*s/he hears*	**audire**	*to hear*
facit	*s/he makes*	**facere**	*to make, do*

The five verbs above each represent a different group (or conjugation). With the exception of irregular verbs like **esse** and **posse**, all Latin verbs belong to one of these five conjugations.

▶ In bibliotheca *In the library*

Shared endings key	
-o	mulo, vino: ablative **mulo, vino: dative ('to... / for...')**
-ae	silvae: genitive, nominative plural **silvae: dative ('to... / for...')**
-is	mulis, silvis, vinis: ablative plural **mulis, silvis, vinis: dative plural ('to.../ for...')**

Est meridies. Discipuli Stephanusque sunt in bibliotheca. Scholae magister discipulis historiam Christianorum bestiarumque narrat.

'Christiani multi in amphitheatro occisi sunt. Romani pro suffragiis populi ludos faciebant et magnam opulentiam ostentare volebant. Miseros Christianos! Pagani semper videre multam saevitiam volunt. Ludos in amphitheatro spectabant etiam docti, qui eos non saevos sed ineptos existimabant. Nulla enim victimis erat misericordia. Nunc nobis libri non ludi sunt grati, eho Paule? Age, Paulus-ne nobis recitare potest? Paule? Ubi est Paulus?'

'Quando Christiani, o Domine, in amphitheatro paganos mutilaverunt?' rogavit Augustinus ex discipulis unus.

'Ubi est Paulus?' inquit Stephanus qui eum non audit.

'Hodie Paulus in culina laborat,' inquit Augustinus.

'Quid? Cur Paulus in culina laborare vult? Adesse in schola debet. Paulus enim non coquus sed discipulus est.'

adesse	*to be here*
amphitheatrum-i [n]	*amphitheatre*
bestia-ae [f]	*beast*
Christianus-i [m]	*Christian*
coquus-i [m]	*cook*
debet	*(s/he) ought*
doctus-i [m]	*learned man*
dominus-i [m]	*lord, sir*
eos	*them*
erat	*(s/he, it, there) was*
eum	*him*
existimabant	*(they) thought*
faciebant	*(they) prepared*
gratus-a-um	*pleasing*
historia-ae [f]	*story*
ineptus-a-um	*foolish*
laborare	*to work*
ludus-i [m]	*game, show*
meridies	*midday*
miseros Christianos!	*wretched Christians*
mutilaverunt	*(they) did mutilate*
narrat	*(s/he) tells, relates*
nobis	*to us, for us*
nulla misericordia(-ae)	*no pity*
occisi sunt	*were killed*
opulentia-ae [f]	*wealth*
ostentare	*to show*
paganus-i [m]	*pagan*
populus-i [m]	*people*

pro [+abl.]	*in return for*
quando	*when*
qui	*who*
recitare	*to recite, read aloud*
rogavit	*(s/he) asked*
Romanus-i [m]	*a Roman*
saevitia-ae [f]	*cruelty*
spectabant	*(they) used to watch*
suffragium-i [n]	*vote*
unus	*one*
victima-ae [f]	*victim*
volebant	*(they) wanted*
vult, volunt	*(s/he) wants, (they) ...*

Practice (i)

Choose the correct words and translate:

(a) Monachi abbatissam videre non (debet/possunt).
(b) Abbatissa in culina laborare (debet/volunt) sed in ecclesia
monachos spectare (vult/possunt).

Accusative of exclamation: *Miseros Christianos!*
Me miserum!

The phrases are both in the accusative without on the face of it
being objects. This expression is called the 'accusative of
exclamation'. The use of the accusative suggests they are
implied objects of a hidden verb.

Dative case: 'to, for'

This is the last of the cases to be studied. If the genitive is the 'of'
case, the ablative the 'by, with, in, on' or 'from' case, then the

dative may be known as the 'to' or 'for' case. 'To' a place, or 'towards' somewhere, is expressed by **ad** followed by the accusative (e.g. **ad monasterium** *to(wards) the monastery*). Otherwise 'to' something or someone is represented by the dative case:

Augustinus <u>Paulo</u> amicus est.	*Augustine is friendly <u>to Paul</u> (or Augustine is Paul's friend).*
Non <u>culinae</u> sed <u>scholae</u> est Pauli oboedientia!	*Not <u>to the kitchen</u> but <u>to the school</u> is Paul's duty!*

The word in the dative is commonly an indirect, not direct, object of a verb:

Paulus <u>Benedicto</u> cibum vinumque portat.	*Paul is bringing food and wine for <u>Benedict</u>.*

Cibum vinumque is the object in the accusative, and **Benedicto** the indirect object in the dative.

	Nominative	Accusative	Genitive	Dative	Ablative
Sing.	silva	silvam	silvae	**silvae**	silva
	mulus	mulum	muli	**mulo**	mulo
	vinum	vinum	vini	**vino**	vino
Plural	silvae	silvas	silvarum	**silvis**	silvis
	muli	mulos	mulorum	**mulis**	mulis
	vina	vina	vinorum	**vinis**	vinis

The dative has a small overlap with the genitive in so far as the dative may also show possession. The genitive is generally attached to another noun (e.g. **magister <u>scholae</u>**), whereas the dative is affected by a verb (often the verb 'to be'). The genitive tends to emphasize the possessor, and where the dative is used, the emphasis is on the thing(s) possessed:

Sunt Benedicto unguenta.	*The perfumes are to/for Benedict (Benedict has perfumes).*

'To' or 'for' will help you find the meaning of the dative, but these prepositions are sometimes not appropriate in a final English version. A word in the dative should be taken closely with the verb – be this an indirect object, possessive or whatever.

▶ Augustinus

Mox Stephanus e culina revenit. 'Paulus non in culina laborat sed in silvis vacat.'

'Ex oppido revenit,' inquit Augustinus, qui Paulo est amicus. 'Paulus cibum vinumque ex oppido portat.'

'Cibum vinumque? Quis iussit Paulum ad oppidum ire et cibum vinumque emere?'

'Et oleum et ova et unguenta,' inquit Augustinus.

'Unguenta? Sumus monachi! Et ova? Hic multa sunt ova.'

'Non satis Benedicto, o Magister,' inquit Augustinus. 'Paulus Benedicto cibum vinumque semper dat. Paulus culinae servus est.'

'Neque coquo neque culinae sed magistro et scholae est Pauli oboedientia,' clamavit miser magister.

'Sed nunc Paulus Benedicto est servus,' inquit Augustinus, 'et in culina cum ancillis laborat.'

'In culina cum ancillis?'

'Etiam-ne nos possumus in culina laborare, Domine?'

'St! Tacete! Ad libros! Ubi eram?'

'In culina cum ancillis?' rogant discipuli.

'Me miserum! Ah ... in amphitheatro eram.'

clamavit	*wailed*
dat	*(s/he) gives, is giving*
emere	*to buy*
eram	*I was*
ire	*to go*
iussit	*(s/he) told, ordered*
miser-a-um	*wretched*
oboedientia-ae [f]	*duty*
possumus	*we are able, can*
satis	*enough*
servus-i [m]	*serf, slave*
St!	*Sssh!*
tacete!	*be quiet!*
vacat	*(s/he) is idle*

Practice (ii)

1 Add the missing forms to the tables:

	Singular			
Nominative				oleum
Accusative	agrum			
Genitive	agri		culinae	
Dative		coquo		
Ablative				oleo
	Plural			
Nominative				
Accusative				
Genitive			culinarum	oleorum
Dative		coquis		
Ablative	agris			

2 Put each noun in its correct form and translate:

(a) (Ancilla/Ancillae) (discipulos/discipulis) cibum portat.

(b) Discipulus non (episcopi/episcopo) sed (abbatissae/
abbatissa) unguentum dat.

3 Change the underlined words to the singular (other endings
should be changed if affected) and translate the new version:

(a) Episcopus historiam monasterii presbyteris mona-
chisque narrat.
(b) Discipuli ignavi Luciam spectant.
(c) Miser mulus sarcinas onerosas semper portat.
(d) Cur ancillae cum monachis laborare debent?

About Latin

Latin wanted – dead or alive?

After the Renaissance Latin survived as the language of scholars
and intellectuals, and with Greek was a fertile source for
scientists and innovators looking for new words and names. The
majority of these are unwieldy and obscure, though shorter ones
were also coined, sometimes for wider commercial impact. A
scientist will deliberately choose a long-winded word which has
little appeal to the rest of us because he has to be as precise as
he can. Any word which spills into everyday use, where it may
pick up further, figurative meanings (e.g. *magnet*, *radical*, *livid*),
will lose its specialist value.

Some Latin-derived words mean much the same as a native
English word, though tend to be more formal: someone who
admits he is 'culpable' is almost too clever to be given the blame
(*culpa*); to 'concur' (*concurrere*) is somehow not as supportive
as 'agree'. But this gives the wrong impression of the Latin

language, and not an entirely representative one of its influence on English. There are also countless shorter words derived from Latin, many via French, whose origins we hardly notice. Examples with Latin ancestors in the last few passages are: *vacant, data, servile, labour, wine, doctor, popular, spectator, unit, history, obscure* and *mural*. Some Latin words have been absorbed in their original form, e.g *aborigine, agenda, arena, computer, deficit, facsimile, genius, junior, miser, rabies, recipe, referendum, series, squalor, status, video* and *virus*.

The correct form of the plural of Latin-derived words remains debatable. For instance, Latin-derived words which end *-um* in the singular change to *-a* in the plural (e.g. *curriculum, curricula*); others are similar according to declension and form. The trouble with this rule is its inconsistency. Some loan-words like *circus* and *area* already had ordinary English plurals before the influx of further loan-words during the Renaissance. Others such as *affidavit* (*s/he has affirmed*) and *recipe* (*take...* i.e. ingredients, the first word of cooking instructions) are nouns now but in Latin were verbs. The plural of these can hardly be *affidaverunt* and *recipite*, which are the respective plural forms in Latin. Should we be receiving *boni* in place of *bonuses*? *Referendums* is heavier on the ear than *referenda*, but *agendum* is a rather unwieldy singular form of *agenda* (and though it may offend some, *agendas*, the 'plural of a plural', is now commonplace).

A number of Latin-derived words and phrases are current in legal and other technical uses of English. Recently there has been a move to rid the language of such obscure archaisms, but will the awkward phrases or forgettable acronyms which may replace them be an improvement? In any case, *ad hoc, status quo* and *et cetera* can scarcely be called Latin any more. These words and phrases are now part of English. And this is a good point to move on, for the purpose of this course is not to pick over Latin's lifeless present, but sample the living past.

Revision

1 Make a phrase which is current in English with these words:

(a) **initium-i** (*beginning*), **ab**
(b) **annus-i** (*year*), **dominus-i** (*lord, master*)
(c) **vita-ae** (*life*), **curriculum-i** (*course*)
(d) **ceterus-a-um** (*other, rest*), **et**

  (e) **nausea-ae** (*sickness*), **ad**
  (f) **infinitus-a-um** (*endless*), **ad**

2 Rewrite these sentences, changing the underlined words into the plural, and translate:

  (a) <u>Bestia</u>-ne <u>Christianum</u> in amphitheatro devorat?
  (b) <u>Monachus</u> bonus ludos saevos non amat.
  (c) Paulus-ne <u>coquo</u> cibum vinumque semper portat?
  (d) Cur discipulo <u>librum</u> magister dat?

3 Add the missing forms to the table:

Case	Singular		
	paganus-i [m] *pagan*	**oppidum-i** [n] *town*	**bestia-ae** [f] *animal*
Nominative			
Accusative			
Genitive		**oppidi**	**bestiae**
Dative			
Ablative	**pagano**		
	Plural		
Nominative			
Accusative		**oppida**	**bestias**
Genitive	**paganorum**		
Dative			
Ablative			

4 Translate into Latin:

  (a) Paul gives much food to the cook.
  (b) The student ought to walk not with the maids but with the monks.
  (c) The monks want to watch the games but have to work in the monastery.
  (d) Is Lucia able to work in the kitchen?

5 Check you know these words:

narrat	**dat**	**bestia-ae**
dominus-i	**domina-ae**	**populus-i**
miser-a-um	**qui**	**satis**
ancilla-ae	**abbatissa-ae**	

6 Look at the box overleaf. How many words can you make by matching the prepositions on the left with the stems on the right – e.g. *pre* + *fer* = prefer, preference, etc.?

ad	*(to)*	**dic-**	*(say)*
con-, com-, coll-	*(with, together)*	**duc-**	*(bring)*
contra-	*(against)*	**fer-**	*(carry, bear)*
de-	*(down, from)*	**habit-**	*(live)*
e(x)-	*(out, from)*	**iac-/jac-**	*(lie)*
in-, im-	*(in, on)*	**labor-**	*(work)*
per-	*(through)*	**mit-**	*(send)*
pre-	*(before)*	**port-**	*(carry)*
pro-	*(forward)*	**scrib-**	*(write)*
re-	*(back)*	**ven-**	*(come)*
sub-	*(under, beneath)*		
trans-	*(across)*		

▶ Living Latin

1 *Si monumentum quaeris circumspice.

(Epitaph of Christopher Wren in St Paul's Cathedral)

If you seek a memorial, look around you.

2 *Nihil est in intellectu quod non fuerit in sensu.

(Locke, 17th century)

Excipe: nisi ipse intellectus.

(Leibnitz, 17th/18th century)

There is nothing in the mind which exists separate from the senses. With one exception: the mind itself.

**3 *Floreas longum, America, o beata,
libera et felix vigeas in aevum.**

(Samuel Wilson c.18th century)

Blessed America, long may you flourish, and enjoy your freedom and good fortune far into the future.

4 *Inter Vietnamiam et Civitates Americae Unitas relationes diplomaticae coniunguntur. De ea re praesidens Bill Clinton oratione sollemni in Aedibus Albis die Martis habita nuntiavit.

(The Finnish Broadcasting Company, Nuntii Latini)

Diplomatic relations between Vietnam and the United States of America are being restored. On that matter President Bill Clinton made an announcement in a formal speech in the White House on Tuesday.

*post-classical

revision I
(units 01–06)

1 Identify the correct form of the nouns in brackets (the nominative and genitive forms are given):

(a) **Abbatissa (bestia-ae) sanctam timet.**

(b) **Ova in (episcopus-i) ignavum cadunt.**

(c) **Liber Augustini non (discipulus-i) furiosis sed (ancilla-ae) gratus est.**

(d) (Benedictus-i) gulosus
   unguenta (abbatissa-ae)
   odorae desiderat.

2 Rewrite these sentences, changing underlined words to the plural if they are singular, or to the singular if plural. Translate the new version.

   (a) <u>Monachus</u> muros monasterii videre potest.
   (b) Misera <u>ancilla</u> semper in <u>culina</u> laborat.
   (c) <u>Puer</u> <u>mulo</u> cibum dat.
   (d) Cur est <u>abbatissa</u> in bibliotheca?
   (e) Ludos <u>monachi</u> non spectant.
   (f) <u>Episcopi</u>-ne in <u>monasteriis</u> habitant?
   (g) <u>Monachus</u> <u>feminae</u> aquam dat.

3 What do these words mean?

saepe	igitur	ad
enim	cum	ubi
quod	nunc	ex
cur	nonne	per
semper	mox	hodie

4 Translate into Latin:

   (a) Are the students tired?
   (b) An evil monk cannot live in the monastery.
   (c) The furious master gives books to the wretched students.
   (d) The mistress's daughter is unable to work in the kitchen. Surely she ought not to walk with the students?
   (e) Can the horses hear the mule in the wood? He is bringing the horses' food to the monastery.

5 Fill the table with the correct forms of **magnus-a-um** *large, great*:

	Masculine	Feminine	Neuter
Singular			
Nominative			
Accusative			
Genitive			
Dative			
Ablative			
Plural			
Nominative			
Accusative			
Genitive			
Dative			
Ablative			

▶ 6 Pronounce the following words in the recommended classical manner:

bonus	miser	bona fide
data	Cicero	angelus
pater	mater	et cetera
alibi	circus	recipe
alias	pauper	veto
video	agenda	genius

7 **Vespa-ae** is (**a**) a wasp; (**b**) an abbreviated version of ancient evensong; (**c**) an early medieval form of bicycle.

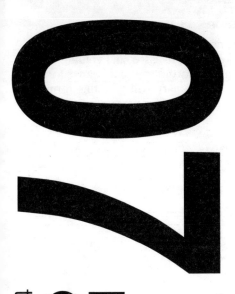

07

puer cum
diabolo ambulat

the boy walks with the devil

In this unit you will learn about
- third declension nouns

- and find out more about Roman gods in 'Di immortales'

Nouns: third declension

So far you have met the first declension (nouns like **silva**) and the second declension (nouns like **mulus**, **magister** and **vinum**). Now for the third. These nouns have many different nominative forms, but the genitive (remember a dictionary will give this form as well) of *all* third declension nouns is -is. The genitive will also show you the noun's stem as it appears in all cases other than the nominative, e.g.

abbas, abbatis (stem: **abbat-**) *abbot*
arbor, arboris (stem: **arbor-**) *tree*
pater, patris (stem: **patr-**) *father*
virgo, virginis (stem: **virgin-**) *maiden, girl*

		Singular		
Nom.	abbas	arbor	pater	virgo
Acc.	abbat-em	arbor-em	patr-em	virgin-em
Gen.	abbat-is	arbor-is	patr-is	virgin-is
Dat.	abbat-i	arbor-i	patr-i	virgin-i
Abl.	abbat-e	arbor-e	patr-e	virgin-e
		Plural		
Nom.	abbat-es	arbor-es	patr-es	virgin-es
Acc.	abbat-es	arbor-es	patr-es	virgin-es
Gen.	abbat-um	arbor-um	patr-um	virgin-um
Dat.	abbat-ibus	arbor-ibus	patr-ibus	virgin-ibus
Abl.	abbat-ibus	arbor-ibus	patr-ibus	virgin-ibus

Practice (i)

1 Translate the underlined nouns into Latin in their correct case:

   (a) with the <u>abbots</u>
   (b) in the <u>trees</u>
   (c) of the <u>maiden</u>
   (d) for the <u>father</u>
   (e) with the <u>abbot</u>
   (f) of the <u>trees</u>
   (g) with the <u>father</u>
   (h) for the <u>maidens</u>
   (i) the <u>father's</u>
   (j) he sees the <u>abbot</u>

2 Identify the English meanings of each noun (look them up in the back if necessary):

(a)

superstitio, superstitionis
sun

virtus, virtutis
love

pax, pacis
mind

mens, mentis   *peace*
virtue

sol, solis

amor, amoris   *superstition*

(b)

miles, militis
soldier   *ox*

homo, hominis
mother

bos, bovis

panis, panis   *man*   *king*

rex, regis

mater, matris   *bread*

3 Rewrite these sentences, changing underlined words to the plural if they are singular, or to the singular if plural. Translate the new version.

    (a) <u>Rex</u> in monasterio non habitat.
    (b) Monachus <u>bovem</u> in silva videre potest.
    (c) Virtutem <u>matris</u> laudant.
    (d) <u>Amicus</u>-ne <u>abbatis</u> <u>gratus</u> est <u>militi</u>?

▶ O di immortales! *Oh immortal gods!*

Shared endings key

-is	silvis, mulis, vinis: dat. pl. or abl. pl. **3rd declension: genitive**	**-e**	**3rd declension: ablative** mule, Paule: vocative
-i	muli: nom. pl.; muli: vini: genitive **3rd declension: dative**	**-um**	mulum: acc. vinum: nom. or acc. **3rd declension: gen. pl.**
-es	**3rd declension: nom. pl. or acc. pl.**		

Stephanus discipulis fessis Romae historiam adhuc narrabat. 'At Romanis erant multi dei deaeque. Iuppiter deus erat caeli, Diana silvarum et venationis, Mars belli et militum, Venus amoris, Neptunus aequoris, Apollo solis et carminum. Quomodo autem possumus, ut dicit unus ex sanctis, "commemorari omnia nomina deorum et dearum?" Quis vero sapiens piusque in tot deos credere potest?'

    'Liberum amo!' susurravit Augustinus.
    'Quid?'
    'Nihil, Magister.'
    'Quid dixisti?'
    'Librum amo.'

'Bene. Mox librum recitabis exscribesque. Ubi eram? ... Dei deaeque ergo in fabulis male se gerebant, et nunc nobis illae superstitiones sunt exempla turpitudinis. Neque enim virtutem laudabant neque animas hominum curabant. Deus tamen, creator terrae caelique hominumque bestiarumque, semper nos omnes curat. "Num," ut dicit sanctus Boethius, "Deus facere malum potest?" Nos sumus omnes semper carissimi Deo...'

'Magister, ecce Paulus!' Augustinus clamavit.

'... fortasse praeter Paulum. Ubi est ille delinquens?' inquit Stephanus, et ad fenestram festinavit. 'Nihil videre possum nisi boves ovesque.'

'Paulus sub arboribus cum virgine ambulat.'

'Cum virgine?' Stephanus Paulum et Luciam conspexit. 'Mehercule,' inquit, 'illa est virgo!' et statim discipuli libros reliquerunt et ad fenestram festinaverunt. 'Ad libros, o inepti, ad libros! Cibum vinumque scilicet! Paulus modo cum ancillis modo cum virgine vacat. O di immortales!'

adhuc	*still*
aequor-is [n]	*water, sea*
aliquis	*someone*
amo	*I love*
amor-is [m]	*love*
anima-ae [f]	*soul*
at	*but, yet*
autem	*however*
bellum-i [n]	*war*
bene	*fine*
caelum-i [n]	*heaven, sky*
carissimus-a-um	*very dear, special*
carmen-inis [n]	*song, poem*
clamavit	*(s/he) shouted*
commemorari	*to remember, relate*
conspexit	*(s/he) caught sight of*
creator-is [m]	*creator*
credere	*to believe*
curabant [+acc.]	*(they) cared for*
curat [+acc.]	*(s/he) cares for*
dea-ae [f]	*goddess*
deus-i (n.pl.: **di**) [m]	*god*
di immortales	*immortal gods*
dicit (dixisti)	*(s/he) says (you said)*
ecce	*look*

exemplum-i [n]	*example, proof*
exscribes	*you will write out*
facere	*to do, make*
fenestra-ae [f]	*window*
festinaverunt	*(they) hurried*
fortasse	*perhaps*
homo-inis [m]	*man*
illa	*that, she*
illae	*those*
ille delinquens	*that delinquent*
Iuppiter	*Jupiter*
laudabant	*(they) praised*
liber-bri [m]	*book*
Liber-i [m]	*Liber, god of wine*
male se gerebant	*(they) conducted themselves badly*
mehercule!	*well I be Hercules!*
miles-itis [m]	*soldier*
modo ... modo	*one minute ... the next*
narrabat	*(s/he) was recounting*
nihil	*nothing*
nisi	*except*
nomina [acc.] [n]	*names*
omnia [n.pl.]	*all*
pius-a-um	*pious, dutiful*
possum (possumus)	*I am able (we...)*
praeter [+acc.]	*except, besides*
quomodo	*how*
recitabis	*you will recite*
reliquerunt	*(they) left*
sapiens	*wise*
scilicet!	*my foot!*
sol-is [m]	*sun*
sub [+abl.]	*beneath*
superstitio-nis [f]	*superstition*
susurravit	*(s/he) whispered*
tot	*so many*
turpitudo-inis [f]	*disgraceful behaviour*
ut	*as*
vacat	*(s/he) idles*
venatio-nis [f]	*hunt*
virtus-tutis [f]	*courage, virtue*

The third declension: neuter nouns *-us*, *-en*

Like all neuter nouns, the nominative and accusative endings are the same, with the plural always -a. Do not confuse nouns like **mulus** with third declension neuter nouns like **tempus**. Having learned the ending **-um** to be the object ending of **-us,** you now have to recognize that **-us** may be an object ending itself! The genitive, dative and ablative endings are the same as those of other third declension nouns:

	tempus *time*	**carmen** *song, poem*
	Singular	
Nom.	**tempus**	**carmen**
Acc.	**tempus**	**carmen**
Gen.	**temporis**	**carminis**
Dat.	**tempori**	**carmini**
Abl.	**tempore**	**carmine**
	Plural	
Nom.	**tempora**	**carmina**
Acc.	**tempora**	**carmina**
Gen.	**temporum**	**carminum**
Dat.	**temporibus**	**carminibus**
Abl.	**temporibus**	**carminibus**

Practice (ii)

1 Identify the English meanings of each noun:

opus, operis
nomen, nominis
munus, muneris
corpus, corporis

gift   *body*
work   *name*

2 Translate into Latin:

    (**a**) the names of the abbots
    (**b**) mother's gifts
    (**c**) many tasks
    (**d**) the bodies of the beasts
    (**e**) the songs of the abbot
    (**f**) (with) pleasing songs

▶ Paulus cum diabolo ambulat *Paulus walks with the devil*

Shared endings key

-us   **tempus:** nom. or acc.   -a   **tempora, carmina:** nom. or acc. pl.
      mulus: nom.   **silva:** nom. or abl.
                               vina: nom. pl. or acc. pl.

In culina ancillae strenuae cenam magnam parant; nam hodie abbatem ex abbatum convocatione exspectant. Aliae igitur potiones aliae carnem aliae panem aliae crusta aliae fruges parant. Deinde operibus fessae in horto requiescunt.

Mox Paulum et Luciam conspexerunt. 'Quis est illa? Quid est puellae nomen?' rogavit una ex ancillis.

'Filia est Comitis Karoli, nomine Lucia,' inquit alia. Nunc ancillae possunt videre abbatissam abbatemque qui Luciam salutant. Interea Benedictus culinam intravit.

'Age, tempus fugit!' clamavit coquus. 'Ubi sunt unguenta vinaque? Ubi est ignavus servus?'

'Hic est puer, Pater Benedicte, nunc Paulus adest.'

'Dico vobis, puer ille ignavus cum diabolo ambulat .... Sancta Maria! Paulus cum abbatissa ambulat? Num abbatissa salutem dicit puero? Quid fit? Nunc puer abbati salutem dicit! Dic mihi, nam scire volo: quis est illa virgo? Est-ne puer nunc magnus et abbati amicus? Paulo gratiam et munera praebeo, sed quid ille puer Benedicto dat?'

'Ecce, nunc venit.'

'Videre est credere.'

Una ancillarum e culina ad Paulum festinavit. 'Age, Paule, Pater Benedictus sarcinas desiderat!'

Paulus 'ubi Patris Benedicti,' inquit, 'est temperantia?'

---

adest	*(s/he) is here*
age	*come on!*
alia	*another (person)*
aliae... aliae	*some... others*
amicus-i [m]	*friend*
caro, carnis [f]	*flesh, meat*
cena-ae [f]	*dinner*
comes-itis [m]	*count*
conspexerunt	*(they) caught sight of*
convocatio-nis [f]	*conference*
crustum-i [n]	*pastry, cake*
dat	*(s/he) gives*

diabolus-i [m]	devil
dic mihi	tell me
dico vobis	I tell you
exspectant	(they) wait for
festinavit	(s/he) hurried
frux-gis [f]	fruit
fugit	(s/he/it) flees, flies
gratia-ae [f]	favour
hic	here
hortus-i [m]	garden
ille [m], illa [f]	he/she, that
interea	meanwhile
intravit	(s/he) entered
Karolus-i [m]	Charles
nam	for
panis-is [m]	bread
parant	(they) prepare
possunt	(they) are able
potio-nis [f]	drink
praebeo	I give, offer
qui	who
quid fit?	what's going on?
requiescunt	(they) relax
salutant	(they) greet
salutem dicit	(s/he) says hello
scire	to know
strenuus-a-um	energetic
temperantia-ae [f]	restraint
volo	I want

▶ Living Latin

Di immortales *Immortal gods*

Countless stories from Greek mythology were unravelled in Latin and with them came their gods: Zeus, Aphrodite, Ares, Hephaistos and Artemis were absorbed and further embellished in Jupiter, Venus, Mars, Vulcan and Diana. These pagan gods were not only pagan, they were immoral. The stories about them were so appealing to the monks that after overcoming resistance they came to settle on monastic shelves as allegories, not heresies.

1 Vulcan, the god of the forge, finds his wife Venus is having a fling with Mars, the god of war. So using his skills, Vulcan sets a trap.

Ut venere torum coniunx et adulter in unum,
arte viri vinclisque nova ratione paratis
in mediis ambo deprensi amplexibus haerent.
Lemnius extemplo valvas patefecit eburnas
inmisitque deos; illi iacuere ligati
turpiter, atque aliquis de dis non tristibus optat
sic fieri turpis; superi risere diuque
haec fuit in toto notissima fabula caelo.

(Ovid, Metamorphoses iv, 182–9)

When his wife and her adulterer came together on the couch, by
his skill and with the chains which he had so cleverly set up, they
were both caught fast in each other's arms. Immediately the
Lemnian god opened the ivory doors and let in the other gods:
there the two lay in their shaming bondage – and one of the gods,
who were much tickled, wished he could be so ashamed. The
gods laughed, and for a long time this story went the rounds of
heaven.

2 In another story Venus gently brings her husband round to
her way of thinking.

Dixerat et niveis hinc atque hinc diva lacertis
cunctantem amplexu molli fovet. Ille repente
accepit solitam flammam, notusque medullas
intravit calor et labefacta per ossa cucurrit.

(Virgil, Aeneid viii, 387–90)

Venus finished speaking, and slipping her snow-white arms this
way and that, wraps him up in a cuddle. He hesitates. Then
suddenly he felt that familiar rush and recognized the glow as it
penetrated his innermost core flickering through his trembling
bones.

3 Lucretius, a poet-philosopher and contemporary of Cicero,
had little time for the gods.

Quippe ita formido mortalis continet omnis,
quod multa in terris fieri caeloque tuentur
quorum operum causas nulla ratione videre
possunt ac fieri divino numine rentur.

(Lucretius, De rerum natura i, 151–4)

There's no question all mortals are repressed by fear: they see
many phenomena on earth and in the sky which they are unable to
account for with any rational explanation, so they imagine them to
be the work of gods.

Revision

1   Fill the gaps:

Case	corpus, corporis [n] *body*	homo, hominis [m] *man, person*	potio, potionis [f] *drink*
		Singular	
Nominative	corpus		
Accusative		hominem	
Genitive			potionis
Dative	corpori		
Ablative			
		Plural	
Nominative			
Accusative	corpora		potiones
Genitive		hominum	
Dative			
Ablative			

2   Rewrite these sentences, making the underlined words plural:

(a) <u>Munus</u> discipuli dominae gratum est.
(b) Num magister in <u>superstitionem</u> credit?
(c) Augustinus <u>carmen</u> <u>virgini</u> recitat.
(d) <u>Monachus</u> pacem, <u>miles</u> bellum desiderat.

3   Translate into Latin:

(a) Who is the goddess of love? Is it Diana?
(b) The abbess walks with Father Benedict into the wood.
(c) Are the maiden's songs pleasing to the abbot?
(d) Why does Benedict always long for meat, bread and cakes?

4   Check you know these words:

abbas-atis	pax-cis	nomen-inis
amor-is	corpus-oris	nihil
arbor-is	tempus-oris	interea
virgo-inis	opus-eris	nam
pater-tris	munus-eris,	age!
mater-tris	superstitio-nis	
homo-inis	carmen-inis	

08

nos fortunatos!
how lucky we are!

In this unit you will learn about
- verbs: first and second conjugations

- and find out more about Latin authors in 'Brotherly love'

Present tense: *amo* I love, *amare* to love

For the different ways we express the present tense in English, see 'Verbs' on p. vii.

I love (am loving /do love)	**am-o**
you (singular) love (are loving /do love)	**am-as**
s/he, it loves (is loving /does love)	**am-at**
we love (are loving /do love)	**am-amus**
you (plural) love (are loving /do love)	**am-atis**
they love (are loving /do love)	**am-ant**

Practice (i)

1   All these verbs belong to the first conjugation, and have endings like **amo, amare**. Match each one to its English meaning (look in the vocabulary section if necessary):

(a)

ambulo-are	ask
desidero-are	greet
habito-are	live
laboro-are	long for*
paro-are	prepare
puto-are	think
rogo-are	walk
saluto-are	watch
specto-are	work

(b)

intro-are	enter
laudo-are	mutilate
monstro-are	praise
mutilo-are	recite
narro-are	recount/tell
oro-are	save/preserve
recito-are	show/point out
servo-are	tolerate
tolero-are	beg/pray

(c)

curo-are	care for/look after*
damno-are	condemn
do-are	eat
devoro-are	explain
equito-are	fly
explico-are	give
sto-are	stand
susurro-are	ride
volito-are	whisper

(d)

aestimo-are	hurry
canto-are	be empty/idle
castigo-are	estimate/value
clamo-are	preach
exspecto-are	punish
festino-are	shout
ostento-are	show off*
praedico-are	sing
vaco-are	wait for*

* These Latin verbs take an object in the <u>accusative</u> even though the English has a preposition to complete the meaning: e.g. **mulum curat** *s/he cares for the mule.*

2 Translate the underlined verbs into Latin:

  (a) They <u>wait for</u> the student.
  (b) We <u>praise</u> the monk.
  (c) He <u>is idle</u>.
  (d) You <u>are working</u>, boys.
  (e) I <u>am reciting</u> a poem.
  (f) They <u>whisper</u>.
  (g) He does not <u>ride.</u>
  (h) They <u>are preparing</u> dinner.
  (i) She <u>greets</u> Augustine.
  (j) Horses do not <u>fly</u>.
  (k) The bishop <u>is preaching</u>.
  (l) The cook <u>looks after</u> the wine.
  (m) Why are you <u>punishing</u> the student, Stephen?

Present tense: *moneo* I warn, *monere* to warn

The endings of verbs like **amare** and those like **monere** are very similar but for the 'a' and 'e'. **Amare** belongs to the first conjugation, **monere** to the second (there are five conjugations in all, the third, fourth and fifth all being fairly similar).

I warn (am warning /do warn)	**mon-eo**
you (singular) warn (are warning /do warn)	**mon-es**
s/he, it warns (is warning /does warn)	**mon-et**
we warn (are warning /do warn)	**mon-emus**
you (plural) warn (are warning /do warn)	**mon-etis**
they warn (are warning /do warn)	**mon-ent**

Practice (ii)

1 Match each verb to its English meaning:

(a)

debeo-ere	*have* *grieve*
doceo-ere	
doleo-ere	*lie*
habeo-ere	*order/tell*
iaceo-ere	*owe/ought*
iubeo-ere	*remain/stay*
maneo-ere	*teach*

(b)

respondeo-ere	*fear* *hold*
rideo-ere	
sedeo-ere	*reply*
taceo-ere	*laugh/smile*
teneo-ere	*see*
timeo-ere	*sit*
video-ere	*be silent*

2 Translate the underlined verbs into Latin:

(a) <u>We sit</u> in the field.
(b) <u>They fear</u> the woods.
(c) <u>She is warning</u> the maids.
(d) <u>Are you laughing</u>, students?
(e) <u>We stay</u> in the monastery.
(f) <u>Do they reply</u>?
(g) <u>Are you teaching</u> the students, Stephen?
(h) <u>They grieve</u> in the church.

▶ Quanti diligentiam aestimas? *What value do you put on diligence?*

Shared endings key			
-es	3rd declension : nom. pl. or acc. pl.	**-as**	1st declension: acc. pl. (silvas)
	mones : 'you...' (s.)		**amas** : 'you...' (s.)

'Sancti igitur,' inquit Stephanus, 'exempla nobis virtutum et pagani vitiorum monstrant. Sancti nos vitam bonam, pagani malam, docent. Carmina quidem Romana superstitionibus fabulisque deorum sunt plena; sed nonne poetae deos esse falsos putaverunt? Lucretius certe in illos non credidit et originem superstitionum sic explicat: *"Formido mortales continet omnes"*. Nunc poetarum opera magni aestimamus et in monasterii bibliotheca servamus: fabulas enim sicut allegorias tolerabimus nec damnabimus. Nos fortunatos! Nunc multos carminum libros in bibliotheca habemus. Nunc ergo ad legendum .... hoc opus, hic labor est.'

'Cur tibi soli mortui poetae sunt grati, o Pater Stephane?' inquit Augustinus. 'Poeta Martialis olim dicebat: *"Nec laudas nisi mortuos poetas"*.'

'Hodie, o pueri, opus non Martialis sed Vergilii recitabimus:
*"Aurora interea miseris mortalibus almam
extulerat lucem referens opera atque labores ...."* Quis est ille?'

'Ignoscas, Pater Stephane.'

'Paule? Nunc ades? O male discipule! Cur lascive in silvis vacas ubi in bibliotheca adesse debes? Dolebis certe, o puer, et te castigabo.'

'Magister, erat puella in silva.'

'Ita vero.'

'Saucia erat.'

'Saucia, puto, amore.'

'Ex equo cecidit, Magister.'

'Cecidit scilicet, puer. Unde? De caelo? Equus-ne in caelo volitabat? Ut poma de arboribus sic virgines de caelo cadunt?' Alii discipuli rident.

'Magister, vera tibi dico.'

'Vera? O tempora o mores! Putas-ne studia esse nugas? Quanti diligentiam aestimas?'

'Magni, Pater Stephane, magni.'

'O Paule, magister non saevus sum, sed diligentiam te docebo. Vides-ne hunc librum?'

'Video, Magister.'

'Hodie liber est exscribendus; etiam in noctem, si necesse est, laborabis.'

'Hodie?'

ad legendum	*to (our) reading*
agamus	*we should do*
alii	*the other* (pl)
allegoria-ae [f]	*allegory*
'Aurora...'	see Unit 1
cadunt	*(they) fall*
cecidit	*(s/he) fell*
certe	*at least, of course*
credidit	*(s/he) believed*
de [+abl.]	*from, about*
dicebat	*(s/he) said*
diligentia-ae [f]	*attentiveness*
ergo	*so, therefore*
exemplum-i [n]	*example, precedent*
exscribendus-a-um	*to be written out*
fabula-ae [f]	*story*
falsus-a-um	*false*
'formido...'	see Unit 7
fortunatus-a-um	*happy, lucky*
hoc... hic	*this... this*
hunc	*this*
in illos	*in them*
laborabis	*you will work*
labor-is [m]	*work*
lascive	*wantonly*
magni	*much, greatly*
mortuus-a-um	*dead*
nec	*and...not*
nugae-arum [pl.]	*trifles, nonsense*
o tempora o mores!	see Unit 1
olim	*once (upon a time)*

origo-inis [f]	*origin*
paganus-i [m]	*pagan*
plenus-a-um [+abl.]	*filled (with)*
poeta-ae [m]	*poet*
pomum-i [n]	*fruit*
putaverunt	*(they) thought*
quanti	*how much, at what value*
quidem	*in fact*
saucius-a-um	*wounded, smitten*
si	*if*
sic	*thus*
sicut	*just as, as if*
solus-a-um	*only, alone*
studium-i [n]	*study*
tibi [dative]	*(to) you*
tolero-are	*endure, support*
unde	*from where*
ut	*as*
vita-ae [f]	*life*
vitium-i [n]	*vice*
volitabat	*(s/he, it) was flying*

Future tense: *amo, amare; moneo, monere*

The future tense is expressed in English with the help of auxiliaries (*shall, will, going to*). In Latin there's only one word to cover the pronoun (I, *you*, *he*, etc.) and the tense itself. So, not so many words to remember, but once more the inevitable endings; at least they are the same for both verbs:

Future			
I shall love	**ama-bo**	*I shall warn*	**mone-bo**
you (s.) will love	**ama-bis**	*you (s.) will warn*	**mone-bis**
s/he, it will love	**ama-bit**	*s/he, it will warn*	**mone-bit**
we shall love	**ama-bimus**	*we shall warn*	**mone-bimus**
you (pl.) will love	**ama-bitis**	*you (pl.) will warn*	**mone-bitis**
they will love	**ama-bunt**	*they will warn*	**mone-bunt**

Practice (iii)

1 Identify the correct endings of **canto, cantare** and **iaceo, iacere**:

(a) Corpus in terra ____

(b) Pater Benedictus ____

2 Translate the underlined verbs into Latin:

(a) <u>She will warn</u> the abbot.
(b) <u>Will they love</u> the songs?
(c) <u>We shall praise</u> courage.
(d) <u>You</u>, boys, <u>will sit</u> in the garden.
(e) Paul, <u>will you sing</u> to me?
(f) <u>We shall order</u> the students to recite the songs.
(g) The abbot <u>will preach</u> in the church.
(h) Now <u>you will see</u> the bishop, Father Stephen.
(i) <u>We shall stay</u> in the monastery.

▶ Quis philosophus esse vult? *Who wants to be a philosopher?*

Lucia et abbatissa et episcopus prope portam monasterii stant, ubi equos raedamque exspectant. Mox abbas e monasterio venit et eis vale dicit; deinde duo famuli viatoribus equos et raedam e stabulo ducunt. Lucia tamen ipsa non equitabit quod adhuc convalescit, sed cum abbatissa in raeda sedebit. Nunc episcopus in equum ascendit et sub arbores cum raeda equitat.

Interea in bibliotheca Paulus et Augustinus adhuc laborant; duos enim Stephanus iussit regulam monachorum per totum diem exscribere. Nunc Augustinus e fenestra viatores monasterium relinquentes conspexit: 'Illic tua virgo monasterium relinquit. Eam-ne videre vis?'

'Num adhuc vacas, Augustine? Opus perficere debemus,' inquit Paulus.

'Scribere est lentum et difficile: *"Nam vigilare leve est, pervigilare grave est"*, ut dicit Martialis. Ecce illa virgo: est abbati abbatissaeque amica; etiam, puto, opulenta. Et tu, Paule, scientiam an pecuniam habere vis? an amorem?'

'Sst! Nunc est scribendum.'

'Quis philosophus vel theologus esse vult? Ego volo divitias habere:

> *Disputet philosophus vacuo cratere,*
> *sciat quia minus est scire quam habere.'*

amica-ae [f]	*girlfriend*
an	*or*
conspexit	*(s/he) caught sight of*
deinde	*then*
dicit	*(s/he) says*
per totum diem	*all day long*
difficile	*difficult*
disputet	*let (him/her) dispute*
divitiae-arum [pl.]	*riches*
ducunt	*(they) bring*
duos	*two*
eam	*her*
eis	*to them*
exscribere	*to write out*
famulus-i [m]	*attendant*
grave	*serious*
illic	*over there*
iussit	*(s/he) told, ordered*
leve	*unimportant*
Martialis-is	*Martial*
minus	*less*
opulentus-a-um	*well-heeled, rich*
pecunia-ae [f]	*money*
perficere	*to finish*
pervigilare	*to lie awake all night*
philosophus-i [m]	*philosopher*
porta-ae [f]	*gate*
prope [+acc.]	*near*
quam	*than*
quia	*that*
raeda-ae [f]	*carriage*

regula-ae [f]	*rule*
relinquentes	*leaving*
relinquit	*(s/he) leaves*
sciat	*let (him / her) know*
scientia-ae [f]	*knowledge*
scribendus-a-um	*should be written*
stabulum-i [n]	*stable*
sub [+acc./abl.]	*under*
theologus-i [m]	*theologian*
tuus-a-um	*your*
ut	*as*
vacuo cratere	*with an empty bowl*
vale dicit	*(s/he) says goodbye*
vel	*or*
viator-is [m]	*traveller*
vigilare	*to lie awake*
vis	*you want*

▶ Living Latin

Brotherly love

1 The 'republic' of ancient Rome was an oligarchy of aristocrats tempered by public elections of questionable influence. From time to time ambitious individuals upset the balance of this oligarchy, only for it to be restored by a concession or something underhand. However, in the first century BC, Julius Caesar and Octavian each gained supreme power having survived the efforts of Pompey to oppose one, and Mark Antony the other. Octavian defeated Antony (and Cleopatra) at the battle of Actium in 32 BC, and consolidated his authority, taking the name 'Augustus'. He was succeeded by Tiberius, Tiberius by Caligula, Caligula by Claudius, and Claudius by Nero, and so a dynasty of emperors was created.

Under the emperors the facade of republican government continued with elections, consulships and meetings of the senate, but a revolution of power had occurred, from oligarchy of nobles to an absolute ruler influenced by counsellors and favourites. Political rivalries within the republic had seldom been resolved without bloodshed, and although the absolute power of an emperor may not have pleased what was left of the old republican nobility, many less influential people will have welcomed the security and safety which a single authority brought.

Even the murder of Nero's step-brother, Britannicus, failed to excite much reaction beyond the walls of the dining-room where he was poisoned:

(Nero) ut erat reclinis et nescio similis solitum ita ait per comitialem morbum quo prima ab infantia adflictaretur Britannicus, et redituros paulatim visus sensusque. Ita post breve silentium repetita convivii laetitia. Nox eadem necem Britannici et rogum coniunxit, proviso ante funebri paratu, qui modicus fuit. In campo tamen Martis sepultus est adeo turbidis imbribus, ut vulgus iram deum portendi crediderit adversus facinus cui plerique etiam hominum ignoscebant, antiquas fratrum discordias et insociabile regnum aestimantes.

(Tacitus, Annals xiii, 16–17)

Nero just lay there feigning ignorance, and remarked that Britannicus had suffered from epilepsy since childhood and this was one of the symptoms; little by little, he told them, Britannicus would recover his sight and senses. And so, after a brief silence, the jollity of dinner was resumed. Britannicus meanwhile was buried the same night, since arrangements for the funeral – a rather modest one – had been taken care of. He was buried in the Field of Mars amid such a violent rainstorm that ordinary folk believed it to be a sign of the gods' anger. Most people condoned the murder, putting it down to age-old feuds of brothers and a power which could not be shared.

2 Worldly politics seem very distant to the poet Martial, who lived during Nero's reign. His problems start with his neighbour – a teacher:

Vicini somnum non tota nocte rogamus:
  nam vigilare leve est, pervigilare grave est.
Discipulos dimitte tuos. Vis, garrule, quantum
  accipis ut clames, accipere ut taceas?

(Martial, Epigrams ix, 68, 9–12)

We neighbours do not ask for sleep all night long: some loss of sleep is neither here nor there, but to lie awake the whole night is no joke. Dismiss your students. Tell me, you chatterbox, do you want to earn as much as you are paid to make your din – just to keep quiet?

3 Virgil, Horace and other poets were considered 'classics' almost while they were still alive. The 'dead poets' society' is something Martial is not quite ready to join:

Miraris veteres, Vacerra, solos
nec laudas nisi mortuos poetas.
Ignoscas petimus, Vacerra: tanti
non est, ut placeam tibi, perire.

(Martial, Epigrams viii, 69)

You like only the ancient poets, Vacerra, and give no acclaim
unless they are dead. Pray forgive me, Vacerra, but I don't wish to
die just to keep you happy.

Revision

1 Change the underlined verbs into the future tense and translate:

(a) Equi in caelo <u>volitant</u>.
(b) In ecclesia <u>sedeo</u>.
(c) Discipulos somnulentos <u>castigant</u>.
(d) Lucia mihi in ecclesia <u>susurrat</u>.

2 Change the underlined verbs into the present tense and translate:

(a) O Domina, cur <u>dolebis</u>?
(b) Philosophiam te <u>docebo</u>, o Paule.
(c) Labores in agris non <u>tolerabimus</u>.
(d) Nonne, o Virgo, Augustinum <u>amabis</u>?

3 Fill the gaps:

Case	munus [n] muneris *gift*	labor [m] laboris *toil*	allegoria [f] allegoriae *allegory*	deus [m] dei *god*
	Singular			
Nominative		labor	allegoria	deus
Accusative				deum
Genitive		laboris		
Dative			allegoriae	
Ablative	munere			
	Plural			
Nominative			allegoriae	dei (di)
Accusative	munera			
Genitive		laborum		
Dative				
Ablative				

4 Translate into Latin:

(a) The abbess will prepare a large dinner.
(b) Are the students still working in the library?
(c) What are you whispering, Lucia?
(d) They will grieve in the church.

5 Check you know these words:

susurro-are	curo-are	paro-are
recito-are	oro-are	canto-are
do-dare	debeo-ere	habeo-ere
doceo-ere	video-ere	timeo-ere
rideo-ere	si	nisi
ut	sicut	ergo
olim	deinde	fabula-ae
labor-is	studium-i	pecunia-ae
minus		

09

quis in silva ululat?

who is howling in the wood?

In this unit you will learn about
- adjectives like **omnis**
- verbal adjectives: **-ndus, -nda, -ndum** (gerundives)

- and find out more about Latin authors in 'Speculator amicae'

Third declension adjectives

Adjectives like **sanctus** have endings identical to the nouns **mulus**, **silva** and **vinum**, and agree with the noun they qualify. A noun and adjective in agreement may have matching endings, e.g. **mulus bonus** *a good mule*, but not always so, e.g. **virgo laeta** *a cheerful maiden*, or **magnum opus** *a great work*.

There are some adjectives which do not have endings like **sanctus**, but are similar to third declension nouns. The ablative usually ends -i, and the neuter singular -e, otherwise they are identical to the third declension. There is no difference between masculine and feminine forms:

Case	**omnis** *all, every* Masc./Fem.	Neuter
	Singular	
Nominative (+voc.)	**omn-is**	**omn-e**
Accusative	**omn-em**	**omn-e**
Genitive	**omn-is**	
Dative	**omn-i**	
Ablative	**omn-i**	
	Plural	
Nominative	**omn-es**	**omn-ia**
Accusative	**omn-es**	**omn-ia**
Genitive	**omn-ium**	
Dative	**omn-ibus**	
Ablative	**omn-ibus**	

Practice (i)

1   Match the Latin and English adjectives:

(a)

brevis	*disgraceful* *brief*
facilis	
fortis	*serious*
gravis	*soft*
humilis	*easy*
levis	*humble*
mollis	*trivial*
nobilis	*brave*
turpis	*noble*

(b)

crudelis	*slender*
difficilis	*sweet*
gracilis	*cruel*
mirabilis	*terrible*
terribilis	*sad*
tristis	*useful*
utilis	*marvellous*
dulcis	*difficult*
fidelis	*faithful*

2 Translate into Latin:

(a) (with) all the students
(b) a brief song
(c) difficult tasks
(d) of humble monks
(e) a disgraceful superstition
(f) a soft tunic
(g) for the brave soldiers
(h) a sweet mistress

▶ Regula monachorum *The rule of the monks*

Augustinus de Lucia adhuc cogitat: 'Tua amica monasterium reliquit, et ex oculis evanuit,' Paulo inquit Augustinus.

'Illa non amica est mea.'

'Non tua vero? Bene. Ego virginem salutabo. Quis scit? Fortes Fortuna adiuvat, ut dicunt poetae.'

'O satis poetarum, Augustine; opus perficere debes.'

'Dulcis amica, tu es mirabilis, et me Cupido inflammat amore. Carmina tibi, Lucia, dedicabo ... vel hoc Propertii: *Dum nos fata sinunt oculos satiemus amore.* Vel hoc Catulli: *Vivamus mea Lucia atque amemus.*'

'Satis carminum, amice! Nunc exscribendum, si tibi placet, silentio.'

'Ignoscas si tibi sum molestus,' inquit Augustinus, et librum spectat. Omnes paginae sunt abbatum monachorumque regulis plenae. Stephanus discipulos duos monachorum regulas exscribere iusserat omnes. 'Num totum librum exscribere debeo?' rogavit Augustinus.

'Ita vero,' respondit Paulus, et Augustinus tandem scribere incipit: *I... Dominum Deum diligere. II... Non occidere. III... Non adulterare. IV... Non facere furtum. V... Mortuum sepelire. VI... Iniuriam non facere. VII... Inimicos diligere. VIII... Non falsum testimonium dicere. IX... Nudum vestire. X... Infirmum visitare. XI... Non esse superbum. XII... Invidiam non exercere. XIII... Castitatem amare. XIV... Non esse vinolentum...* 'Io Benedicte!' et cantat: *'Bibat ille, bibat illa, bibat servus et ancilla.'*

adiuvat	*(s/he) helps*
amemus	*let us love*
bibat	*let [him/her] drink*
castitas-tatis [f]	*chastity*
Catullus-i	*Catullus*
cogito-are	*think*
Cupido-inis	*Cupid*
diligere	*to love*
dum	*while, as long as*

evanuit	*(s/he) has vanished*
fatum-i [n]	*fate*
furtum-i [n]	*theft*
hoc	*this*
incipit	*(s/he) begins*
infirmus-a-um	*sick*
inflammo-are	*inflame*
inimicus-i [m]	*enemy*
iniuria-ae [f]	*harm*
invidia-ae [f]	*grudge, jealousy*
iusserat	*(s/he) had ordered*
meus-a-um	*my*
molestus-a-um	*troublesome*
occidere	*to kill*
oculus-i [m]	*eye*
pagina-ae [f]	*page*
placeo-ere	*please*
Propertius-i	*Propertius*
reliquit	*(s/he) has left*
rogavit	*(s/he) asked*
satiemus	*let us fill*
satis	*enough*
scit	*(s/he) knows*
sepelire	*to bury*
silentium-i [n]	*silence*
sinunt	*(they) allow*
superbus-a-um	*proud*
tandem	*at last*
tu [nom.]	*you*
tuus-a-um	*your*
vestire	*to clothe*
vinolentus-a-um	*fond of booze*
vivamus	*let us live*

Adjectives ending -ndus, -nda, -ndum

The girl's name 'Amanda' comes from the Latin for 'to-be-loved':

Virgo amanda   *a girl to be loved*

Amandus-a-um is an adjective with the same endings as **sanctus-a-um**. It is formed from a verb (**amo, amare**) but behaves exactly like an adjective, agreeing with its noun in number, case and gender. It is called a 'gerundive', and usually carries a sense of obligation ('should', 'ought', 'must'):

| Virgo amanda est. | *The girl is to be loved (ought to be loved).* |
| Stephanus monendus est. | *Stephen is to be warned (should be warned).* |

A gerundive is always <u>passive</u>. This means the subject is 'done to', not the 'doer' (i.e. in the examples above, **virgo** is loved, not doing the loving, and Stephanus is to be warned, not doing the warning).

The first conjugation (-**are** verbs) end -**andus**, all the remainder -**endus**:

amandus-a-um
monendus-a-um
agendus-a-um, etc.

Practice (ii)

1 Match the Latin phrases to their English meanings:

---

a monk to be praised; a maid to be admired; an abbess to be revered; an abbot to be revered; gifts to be distributed; a song not to be heard; tasks to be done; words to be added

carmen non audiendum
abbatissa reverenda
opera agenda
monachus laudandus
munera dividenda
verba addenda
abbas reverendus
ancilla miranda

---

2 Identify the correct form of the gerundive, and translate:

e.g. **Ancilla (laudo, laudare, laudandus-a-um) est.**
Ancilla <u>laudanda</u> est. *The maid should be praised.*

(a) **Abbas (audio, audire audiendus-a-um) est.**

(b) Milites non (amo, amare, amandus-a-um) sunt.

(c) Opus (perficio, perficere, perficiendus-a-um) est.

▶ Ohe, libelle! *Whoa, little book!*

Nunc Paulus opere perfecto abiit, sed Augustinus adhuc scribit:

... XXVII... diem iudicii timere. XXVIII... veritatem ex corde et ore proferre. XXIX... nihil amori Christi praeponere. XXX... honorare omnes homines. XXXI... dolum in corde non tenere. XXXII... contentionem non amare... '...scribere est difficile,' inquit, et carmen Martialis murmurat: *'Ohe, iam satis est, ohe, libelle,'* nec multo post obdormit.

'Eho! Ubi est regula?' clamat Stephanus, 'Dormis-ne, Augustine?' et e somno Augustinum excitat.

'Regula? Immo, o Domine, non dormio.'

'Nunc regula est perficienda!'

'Ita vero Pater Stephane. Cogitabam de regulis.'

'Cogitabas an dormiebas?'

'Ignoscas, Domine. Ego fessus sum.' Subito Stephanus et Augustinus horrendum clamorem audiunt. Unus ex monachis in monasterio magna voce ululare incipit.

'Quis est ille? Audivisti-ne?' Stephanus ad fenestram festinavit. 'Illic Theodorus e silva currit. Cur Theodorus territus est?' et Stephanus celeriter bibliothecam reliquit.

abiit	*(s/he) went away*
audivisti	*you heard*
clamor-is [m]	*shout, cry*
cogitabam, cogitabas	*I was thinking, you ...*
contentio-nis [f]	*dispute, competition*
cor-dis [n]	*heart*
currit	*(s/he) runs*
de [+abl.]	*about*
dolus-i [m]	*deceit*
dormiebas	*you were sleeping*
dormio, dormis	*I am sleeping, you ...*
excito-are	*wake, arouse*
honoro-are	*honour*
horrendus-a-um	*fearful, to be feared*
iam	*now, already*
immo	*no, on the contrary*
iudicium-i [n]	*trial, judgment*
libellus-i [m]	*little book*
murmuro-are	*murmur*
nec multo post	*not long afterwards*
obdormit	*(s/he) falls asleep*
ohe	*whoa*
opere perfecto	*with the task completed*
os, oris [n]	*mouth*
praeponere	*to prefer*
proferre	*to put forward*
scribit	*(s/he) writes*
somnus-i [m]	*sleep*
ululo-are	*howl*
veritas-tatis [f]	*truth*
vox, vocis [f]	*voice*

▶ Living Latin

Speculator amicae *One who spies on his mistress*

The earliest erotic poetry which has survived is the work of Catullus, whose ill-starred passion for Lesbia fills his lyrics with hungry love mixed with bitter reproaches. Then we have the impassioned seriousness of Propertius, whose rough and tumble with Cynthia delighted the men and women of ancient Rome; so too the elegies of his contemporary Tibullus, whose yearning submission to his mistress makes him as loving as any of the poets. Last, and possibly most popular of all, comes Ovid: his sometimes frivolous and leering wit disguises a poet who was, he tells us, happily married and unpromiscuous.

1 Propertius spies on his mistress:

Mane erat, et volui, si sola quiesceret illa,
  visere: at in lecto Cynthia sola fuit.
Obstipui: non illa mihi formosior umquam
  visa, neque ostrina cum fuit in tunica,
ibat et hinc castae narratum somnia Vestae,
  neu sibi neve mihi quae nocitura forent:
talis visa mihi somno dimissa recenti.
  Heu quantum per se candida forma valet!
'Quid? tu matutinus,' ait, 'speculator amicae?
  Me similem vestris moribus esse putas?
Non ego tam facilis: sat erit mihi cognitus unus,
  vel tu vel si quis verior esse potest.
Apparent non ulla toro vestigia presso,
  signa volutantis nec iacuisse duos.
Aspice ut in toto nullus mihi corpore surgat
  spiritus admisso notus adulterio.'
Dixit, et opposita propellens savia dextra
  prosilit in laxa nixa pedem solea.
Sic ego tam sancti custos retrudor amoris:
  ex illo felix nox mihi nulla fuit.

(Elegies ii, 29B)

It was early, and I desired to see her, to see if she slept alone: but there was Cynthia by herself in bed. I was taken aback: never has she looked more stunning, not even when she went in her purple gear to chaste Vesta to report her dreams, in case they might bring harm to her or me: this is how she looked freshly arisen from sleep. What power such natural beauty holds!

'Oh?' she says, 'do you lark about spying on your mistress? Do you judge me by your standards? I'm not so free and easy: one lover is plenty, yourself maybe, or another if there's one more true. You'll find no trace of rough and tumble in this bed, no sign of a couple's frolicsome contortions. See for yourself: my body is quite calm without the adulterer's breathless panting flagrante delicto.' With that, she waved away my lunging kisses, slipped into loose sandals and was gone. Thus am I, the guardian of so heavenly a love, rejected: since then I've not had a single happy night.

2 Catullus reflects on his girl's faithlessness:

> **Nulli se dicit mulier mea nubere malle**
> **quam mihi, non si se Iuppiter ipse petat.**
> **Dicit: sed mulier cupido quod dicit amanti,**
> **in vento et rapida scribere oportet aqua.**

(Poems lxx)

My girl says she wants to marry no one other than me. Not even if Jupiter himself should ask. That's what she says. But what a girl says to an eager lad is best inscribed in the breeze and swift-flowing streams.

3 The piece below is part of a letter written in the twelfth century by Héloise to her former tutor, lover, and husband, Abelard. Her uncle had taken violent and cruel exception to their match (Abelard was castrated), and Héloise lived the remainder of her life in a nunnery.

*Missam ad amicum pro consolatione epistolam, dilectissime, vestram ad me forte quidam nuper attulit. Quam ex ipsa statim tituli fronte vestram esse considerans, tanto ardentius eam coepi legere, quanto scriptorem ipsum charius amplector, ut cuius rem perdidi, verbis saltem tanquam eius quadam imagine recreer.

(From *Mediaeval Latin*, ed. K.P. Harrington,
University of Chicago Press, 1997)

Dearest, a letter you sent to a friend pouring out your feelings happened recently to fall into my hands. I knew it was yours the moment I saw your writing on the envelope, and a desire to read it seized me, much as I desire to have its author in my arms. I may not have him in person, but at least his words give some sort of picture to refresh me.

*post-classical

Revision

1 Rewrite these sentences, changing underlined words to the plural, if they are singular, or to the singular if plural. Translate the new version.

(a) **Magna <u>cena</u> in culina paranda est.**
(b) **Dulces <u>dominae</u> semper audiendae sunt.**
(c) **Turpis <u>discipulus</u> excitandus est.**
(d) **Humiles <u>servi</u> etiam laudandi sunt.**
(e) **Cur <u>abbates</u> reverendi sunt?**

2 Translate into Latin:

(a) We will dedicate the song to the brave soldiers and the humble maid.

(b) I grieve, because Lucia will inflame me with love but will not love me.

(c) Now the girl will sing a sweet song, and the boys will relate the history of the monastery.

3 Write out all the endings, singular and plural, masculine, feminine and neuter of (a) **dulcis** (b) **agendus**.

4 Check you know these words:

omnis	brevis	facilis
gravis	turpis	mirabilis
tristis	dulcis	oculus-i
somnus-i	tandem	

10 lacrimae in monasterio

tears in the monastery

In this unit you will learn about
- third, fourth and mixed conjugations
- irregular verbs: **sum, possum, volo**

- and find out more about Latin authors in 'Miserabile corpus'

Present tense: third, fourth and mixed conjugations

The third and fourth conjugations are quite similar. A 'mixed' conjugation which shares endings with both the third and fourth conjugations only has a few verbs, though these are frequently used (e.g. **capio**, **capere** and compounds, **recipio**, **accipio**, etc.; and **facio**, **facere** and compounds, **perficio**, etc.).

	third **mitt-ere** *to send*	fourth **aud-ire** *to hear*	mixed **cap-ere** *to take, capture*
I	**mitt-o**	**aud-io**	**cap-io**
you (s.)	**mitt-is**	**aud-is**	**cap-is**
s/he, it	**mitt-it**	**aud-it**	**cap-it**
we	**mitt-imus**	**aud-imus**	**cap-imus**
you (pl.)	**mitt-itis**	**aud-itis**	**cap-itis**
they	**mitt-unt**	**aud-iunt**	**cap-iunt**

Practice (i)

1 Translate the underlined verbs into Latin:

(a) She <u>sends</u> a gift.
(b) We <u>capture</u> the soldier.
(c) They <u>hear</u> a song.
(d) I <u>capture</u> the beast.
(e) They <u>send</u> a book.
(f) You <u>are hearing</u> the abbot, students.
(g) We <u>send</u> money.
(h) Do you <u>hear</u> Paul, Augustine?

2 Match each verb to its English meaning (look them up if necessary):

(a)

third conjugation:

curro-ere		write		leave
dico-ere				
duco-ere		lead		say
lego-ere				
rego-ere				read
relinquo-ere		rule		
scribo-ere			run	

(b)

third conjugation:

ascendo-ere			live
credo-ere		climb	
bibo-ere			believe
cado-ere		drink	
emo-ere			fall
ago-ere	buy		
vivo-ere			do

(c)

fourth conjugation:		
venio-ire	bury	know
dormio-ire		
scio-ire		open
sentio-ire	sleep	
sepelio-ire		come
aperio-ire	feel	

(d)

mixed conjugation:		
facio-ere	flee	make
fugio-ere		
incipio-ere	complete	
perficio-ere		regain/accept
recipio-ere		begin

3 Translate the underlined verbs into Latin:

   (a) I <u>am reading</u> Augustine's book.
   (b) <u>Are they running</u> into the church?
   (c) The abbot <u>writes</u> all the rules.
   (d) We <u>are beginning</u> to live!
   (e) <u>Are they burying</u> a monk?
   (f) Why <u>are they fleeing</u> from the monastery?
   (g) <u>Are you drinking</u> wine in the kitchen, maids?
   (h) Who <u>is coming?</u>
   (i) They do not <u>hear</u> the abbess.

▶ Miserabile corpus *The pitiable corpse*

> **Shared endings key**
>
> **-is** silvis, mulis, vinis: dat. pl. or abl. pl.
>   3rd declension: genitive
>   **mitti(ti)s, audi(ti)s, capi(ti)s: 'you...'**
>
> **-o** mulo: dat. or abl.
>   **all verbs: 'I...'**

Post Theodori mortem – fortuitam, ut dicit abbas, sed quis potest scire? – multae erant lacrimae. Theodorus enim fuerat monachus pius et omnibus amicus. Timor autem per monasterium agrosque vulgatus est. Monachi multos dies erant pavidi tacitique.

    Nunc in schola discipulis pauca verba de Theodori morte Stephanus dicit. Postea magister tristis e Vulgato legit:

    'Hoc autem dico, fratres, quoniam caro et sanguis regnum Dei possidere non possunt ...'

    Paulus per fenestram spectat et mortem Theodori contemplat. Quis eum occidere voluisset? Fuerat amicus omnibus, vir pius et humilis. Erat rumor. Dani? Num Dani Theodorum trucidaverunt? Dani in regione iam viginti annos non visi erant.

    ...Ubi est, mors, victoria tua? Ubi est, mors, stimulus tuus?'
Stephanus campanam per monasterium resonantem audit et legere desinit. 'Nunc corpus Theodori sepeliemus, o pueri,' inquit, 'et vos unam horam sine me laborabitis et opera perficietis,' et per genas lacrimas fundens bibliothecam relinquit.

annus-i [m]	*year*
campana-ae [f]	*bell*
caro, carnis [f]	*flesh*
Danus-i [m]	*Dane, Viking*
desino-ere	*leave off, abandon*
dies [nom./acc.]	*days*
fortuitus-a-um	*accidental*
frater-tris [m]	*brother*
fuerat	*(s/he) had been*
fundens	*pouring*
genae-arum [f]	*cheeks*
hora-ae [f]	*hour*
lacrima-ae [f]	*tear*
mors, mortis [f]	*death*
paucus-a-um	*few*
pavidus-a-um	*fearful*
possideo-ere	*occupy*
post [+acc.]	*after*
postea	*afterwards*
quoniam	*since*
regio-nis [f]	*region*
regnum-i [n]	*kingdom*
resonantem	*resounding*
rumor-is [m]	*rumour, gossip*
sanguis-inis [m]	*blood*
sine [+abl.]	*without*
stimulus-i [m]	*sting*
tacitus-a-um	*silent, quiet*
timor-is [m]	*fear*
trucidaverunt	*(they) murdered*
tuus-a-um	*your*
unus-a-um	*one*
verbum-i [n]	*word*
victoria-ae [f]	*victory*
viginti	*twenty*
vir-i [m]	*man*
visi erant	*(they) had been seen*
voluisset	*had wanted*
Vulgatum-i [n]	*the Vulgate*
vulgatus est	*was spread abroad*

Accusative of duration

The accusative case is used to express a length of time. Thus above we have **multos dies** *for many days*, **viginti annos** *for twenty years* and **unam horam** *for one hour*. Most numbers have fixed endings, like **viginti**; a few have endings which change (e.g. **unus, una, unum; duo, duae; tres, tria**).

Future tense: third, fourth and mixed conjugations

The future of the first two conjugations have the endings **-bo, -bis, -bit**, etc. The third, fourth and mixed are different, all sharing the letter **e** in the ending:

	mitt-ere *to send*	**aud-ire** *to hear*	**cap-ere** *to take, capture*
I	mitt-am	audi-am	capi-am
you (s.)	mitt-es	audi-es	capi-es
s/he, it	mitt-et	audi-et	capi-et
we	mitt-emus	audi-emus	capi-emus
you (pl.)	mitt-etis	audi-etis	capi-etis
they	mitt-ent	audi-ent	capi-ent

Irregular verbs: *sum, possum, volo*

It is one of the laws of language that rules and regular forms have exceptions. Irregular verbs are amongst the most commonly used:

	esse *to be*	**posse** *to be able*	**velle** *to want*
		Present	
I	sum	possum	volo
you (s.)	es	potes	vis
s/he, it	est	potest	vult
we	sumus	possumus	volumus
you (pl.)	estis	potestis	vultis
they	sunt	possunt	volunt
		Future	
I	ero	potero	volam
you (s.)	eris	poteris	voles
s/he, it	erit	poterit	volet
we	erimus	poterimus	volemus
you (pl.)	eritis	poteritis	voletis
they	erunt	poterunt	volent

The compound forms of **esse** (**abesse, adesse**) share the same irregular endings.

Practice (ii)

1 Translate the underlined verbs into Latin:

(a) She <u>will send</u> a gift.
(b) We <u>shall capture</u> the beasts.
(c) They <u>will hear</u> a song.
(d) She <u>is sitting</u> in the church.
(e) <u>Will you hear</u> the abbot, students?
(f) They <u>will be able to see</u> us.
(g) Do you <u>want to come</u>, Paul?
(h) We <u>shall be present</u> in the monastery today.

How to recognize a conjugation

Conjugation	first person	infinitive	How to recognize the conjugation
first	**am-o**	**am-are**	*the infinitive ending -are*
second	**mon-eo**	**mon-ere**	*the infinitive -ere, and the e in the present*
third	**mitt-o**	**mitt-ere**	*same infinitive as **monere** but no e in the present*
fourth	**aud-io**	**aud-ire**	*the i in the present, with infinitive -ire*
mixed	**cap-io**	**cap-ere**	*the i in the present, with infinitive -ere*

Practice (iii)

1 To which conjugation do the following verbs belong?

(a) aperio-ire
(b) oro-are
(c) incipio-ere
(d) dico-ere
(e) satio-are
(f) retineo-ere
(g) bibo-ere
(h) scio-ire
(i) perficio-ere
(j) video-ere
(k) laudo-are
(l) vivo-ere

▶ Hic iacet Theodorus *Here lies Theodorus*

'Miserum Theodorum,' inquit Paulus, per fenestram exsequias Theodori spectans. Pluit; monachi miserabile corpus Theodori ex ecclesia portant et abbas exiguam pompam ducit.

Discipuli libros relinquunt et per fenestram pompam spectant. 'Ecce, Theodorum sepelient sub arborem ubi nobis fabulas narrabat,' inquit unus. 'Cur omnes monachi non adsunt? Cur eum tam cito sepeliunt?' rogavit alter. 'Quis Theodorum occidit?' rogavit tertius.

'Quis scit?' respondit Paulus.

'Quando sciemus?' rogavit Augustinus.

'Abbas proxima nocte eum vidit,' inquit Paulus. 'Fortasse Stephano dicet.'

'Soles occidere et redire possunt. Nobis cum semel occidit brevis lux, Nox est perpetua una dormienda,' murmurat Augustinus, e Catulli libello recitans.

> HIC IACET THEODORUS
> MONASTERII HUIUS
> MONACHUS QUI IN
> ANNO VICESIMO ET
> QUINTO MORTUUS
> NUNC CUM DEO IN
> PACE REQUIESCIT

'O miserum Theodorum!' inquit Paulus. Ecce, nunc corpus in terram demittunt.' Nunc aliquis flere incipit.

Mox abbas et monachi in ecclesiam reveniunt praeter Stephanum qui prope sepulcrum orat. Adhuc pluit; mox vocem Stephani iterum iterumque gementem audiunt.

aliquis	*someone*
alter	*another*
cum semel	*as soon as*
demitto-ere	*lower*
eum	*him*
exiguus-a-um	*slender, scant*
exsequiae-arum	*funeral*
fleo-ere	*weep*
gementem	*groaning*
huius	*of this*
iterum	*again*
libellus-i [m]	*book*
lux-cis [f]	*light, life*
miserabilis-e	*pitiable*
murmuro-are	*murmur*
nox, noctis [f]	*night*
occidit	*(s/he) kills/killed* or *falls/fell*
occido-ere	*fall*
occīdo-ere	*kill*
perpetuus-a-um	*unending*
pluit	*it is raining*
pompa-ae [f]	*procession*
praeter [+acc.]	*except, besides*
proximus-a-um	*nearest, previous*
quando	*when*
redeo-ire [irreg.]	*return*

rogavit	(s/he) asked
sepulcrum-i [n]	grave
sol-is [m]	sun, day
spectans	watching
tam cito	so quickly
tertius-a-um	third
vicesimo et quinto	in the twenty-fifth

▷ Living Latin

Miserabile corpus *The pitiable corpse*

1 The Aeneid of Virgil is regarded by many as the Latin poem with the most breadth and range, reaching all corners of the soul with moments of love, friendship, loyalty, suffering, fulfilment and despair. In this scene below, the Trojans bring the corpse of Pallas back to his father, Evander:

At non Evandrum potis est vis ulla tenere,
sed venit in medios. Feretro Pallanta reposto
procubuit super atque haeret lacrimansque gemensque,
et via vix tandem vocis laxata dolore est:
'Non haec, o Palla, dederas promissa parenti,
cautius ut saevo velles te credere Marti.
Haud ignarus eram quantum nova gloria in armis
et praedulce decus primo certamine posset.
Primitiae iuvenis miserae bellique propinqui
dura rudimenta, et nulli exaudita deorum
vota precesque meae!'

(Virgil, Aeneid xi, 148–58)

Nothing could restrain Evander who came out into the middle of the throng. The bier was put down and he knelt over Pallas. He clung to him, and wept and groaned, and hoarse with grief could barely speak:

'O Pallas, are these the promises you gave your father, that you take care of yourself in the savage fighting? I was all too aware of the lure of honour in a man's first battle, and the first sweet taste of glory in untried combat. What a wretched coming-of-age, what a cruel start to a war so close to home. Not one of the gods listened to my prayers or vows!'

2 Life is short, so let's make it sweet, says Catullus:

> **Vivamus, mea Lesbia, atque amemus,**
> **rumoresque senum severiorum**
> **omnes unius aestimemus assis.**
> **Soles occidere et redire possunt:**
> **nobis cum semel occidit brevis lux,**
> **nox est perpetua una dormienda.**
> **Da mi basia mille, deinde centum,**
> **dein mille altera, dein secunda centum,**
> **deinde usque altera mille, deinde centum.**

(Poems v, 1–9)

Come my Lesbia, let's live, let's love, and never mind the chatter of old frowning bores – they're not worth tuppence. The sun may go down and return, but for us when our brief peep of light goes out, a single night awaits of unbroken sleep. So give me a thousand kisses, then a hundred, then I'll take another thousand, and another hundred, and then yet another thousand, and one more hundred.

Revision

1 Change the underlined verbs to the future tense, and translate:

(a) **Monachus mulum in silvam ducit.**
(b) **Hodie discipuli labores perficiunt.**
(c) **Monasterium-ne relinquimus?**
(d) **Augustinum audire non possum.**

2 Change the underlined verbs to the present tense, and translate:

(a) **In superstitiones non credam.**
(b) **Me amica inflammabit amore.**
(c) **Carmina-ne Augustini audies?**
(d) **Discipuli e Vulgato legent.**

3 Translate into Latin:

(a) The maids always want to hear Augustine's songs!
(b) Lucia is already able to read, sing and work in the fields.
(c) We shall care for the souls of both humble serfs and great kings.
(d) Why are the monks fleeing out of the wood?

4 Write out these nouns, all cases, singular and plural: **opus, operis; nox, noctis** (gen.pl.: **noctium**); **fabula, fabulae; sepulcrum, sepulcri; annus, anni.**

5 Check you know these words:

dico-ere	facio-ere	scio-ire
scribo-ere	duco-ere	credo-ere
ago-ere	vivo-ere	incipio-ere
bibo-ere	mors-tis	verbum-i
regnum-i	iterum	

libera nos a malo

deliver us from evil

In this unit you will learn about
- imperfect tense
- adjectives: -ens
- present participles

- and find out more about Latin in 'Yaysoos in chaylo'

Past tense: imperfect

The present tense describes this moment or current period, the future tense is for a future event, and all the remaining tenses are past ones. The imperfect tense describes a past event which was habitual, recurrent or lasting for a while. The name 'imperfect' means unfinished:

Discipuli ante cenam in ecclesia <u>cantabant</u> sed Augustinus carmina <u>legebat</u>.	*Before dinner the students <u>used to sing/were singing</u> in the church, but Augustine <u>would read/was reading</u> his poetry.*

There are different ways to express this tense in English: 'used to sing', 'were singing', 'was reading' and 'would read' may all be used to represent the imperfect. A simple past might do as well, as in 'Every day the students <u>sang</u> in the church'.

The endings of this tense are common to all verbs:

	am-are *love*	mon-ere *warn, advise*	mitt-ere *send*
I	ama-bam	mone-bam	mitte-bam
you (s.)	ama-bas	mone-bas	mitte-bas
s/he, it	ama-bat	mone-bat	mitte-bat
we	ama-bamus	mone-bamus	mitte-bamus
you (pl.)	ama-batis	mone-batis	mitte-batis
they	ama-bant	mone-bant	mitte-bant

	aud-ire *hear*	cap-ere *take, capture*
I	audie-bam	capie-bam
you (s.)	audie-bas	capie-bas
s/he, it	audie-bat	capie-bat
we	audie-bamus	capie-bamus
you (pl.)	audie-batis	capie-batis
they	audie-bant	capie-bant

Exceptions are **sum, esse** (and compounds: **adsum, absum, possum**):

I was	eram	*I was able/could*	poteram
you (s.) *were*	eras	*you* (s.) *were able/could*	poteras
s/he, it was	erat	*s/he, it was able/could*	poterat
we were	eramus	*we were able/could*	poteramus
you (pl.) *were*	eratis	*you* (pl.) *were able/could*	poteratis
they were	erant	*they were able/could*	poterant

▶ In ecclesia *In church*

Nec multo post Theodori exsequias, multi in ecclesia aderant. Ecclesia candelis incensique fragrantia plena erat. Abbas ipse cum monachis missam celebrabat. Lucia iuxta matrem in primis˘ subselliis inter magnas familias sedebat. Post nobiles erant peregrini et agricolae et pueri et ancillae et servi. Abbas ad aram in veste purpurea splendens stabat et monachi discipulique post aram in choro cantabant.

'Pater noster, qui es in caelis…' cantare abbas incipiebat. Omnes discipuli cantabant praeter Augustinum, qui dormiebat quod Stephanus eum per totam noctem epistulas sancti Pauli ad Corinthios exscribere iusserat. Augustinus poenas dabat quod in schola carmina Catulli, non epistulas sancti Pauli, legebat.

'Et ne nos inducas in tentationem, sed libera nos a malo,' abbas cantabat.

agricola-ae [m]	*farmer*
ara-ae [f]	*altar*
candela-ae [f]	*candle*
celebro-are	*celebrate*
chorus-i [m]	*choir*
Corinthi-orum	*Corinthians*
epistula-ae [f]	*letter*
eum	*him*
exscribo-ere	*write out*
familia-ae [f]	*family*
fragrantia-ae [f]	*odour*
incensum-i [n]	*incense*
inter [+acc.]	*among*
ipse	*himself*
iusserat	*(s/he) had ordered*
iuxta [+acc.]	*next to*
libera	*free, deliver*
missa-ae [f]	*mass*
ne... inducas	*do not lead us into*
noster	*our*
peregrinus-i [m]	*foreigner, pilgrim*
poenas do-are	*to pay the penalty, be punished*
primus-a-um	*first*
purpureus-a-um	*purple*
qui	*who*
splendeo-ere	*be bright, resplendent*
subsellium-i [n]	*pew, bench*
tentatio-nis [f]	*temptation*
vestis-is [f]	*clothing*

Practice (i)

1 Translate the underlined verbs into Latin (all verbs should be in the imperfect):

(a) She <u>used to love</u> the student.
(b) They <u>were listening</u> to their mother.
(c) We <u>would send</u> food to the slaves.
(d) Where <u>were</u> you, Paul?
(e) I <u>could</u> see all the students in the church.
(f) She always <u>warned</u> us.
(g) All the poems of Catullus <u>were</u> in the book.

2 Put the underlined verbs into the imperfect and translate:

(a) <u>Pluit</u>. (pluit, pluere)
(b) Miserabile corpus in terra <u>iacet</u>. (iaceo-ere)
(c) Carmina Catulli <u>legimus</u>. (lego-ere)
(d) Monachum prope ecclesiam <u>sepeliunt</u>. (sepelio-ire)
(e) Virgo <u>flet</u>. (fleo-ere)

Adjectives ending -*ens*

You have already met adjectives like **sanctus** and **omnis**. You will also come across adjectives like **omnipotens** or **prudens**. These are third declension adjectives, similar to **omnis**. Most of the cases have a 't' and extra syllable:

Case	prudens *wise*		
	Masc./fem.		Neuter
	Singular		
Nominative	**prud-ens**		**prud-ens**
Accusative	**prud-entem**		**prud-ens**
Genitive		**prud-entis**	
Dative		**prud-enti**	
Ablative		**prud-enti**	
	Plural		
Nominative	**prud-entes**		**prud-entia**
Accusative	**prud-entes**		**prud-entia**
Genitive		**prud-entium**	
Dative		**prud-entibus**	
Ablative		**prud-entibus**	

Present participles

A participle is a cross between an adjective and a verb. It has the function of an adjective but is formed from a verb:

Augustinus viatores monasterium <u>relinquentes</u> vidit.	*Augustine saw the travellers <u>leaving</u> the monastery.*	

Relinquentes agrees with **viatores**. Unlike an ordinary adjective, a participle can have an object of its own, here **monasterium**:

A present participle can be translated in different ways:

> *Augustine saw the travellers <u>who were/as they were leaving</u> the monastery.*

These participles all share the endings of **prud-ens**. Participles of verbs from the first conjugation, like **amare**, have an **a** in place of the **e** in the ending:

amo-are	**am-ans**	*loving*
moneo-ere	**mon-ens**	*advising, warning*
mitto-ere	**mitt-ens**	*sending*
audio-ire	**audi-ens**	*listening (to), hearing*
capio-ere	**capi-ens**	*taking, capturing*

Adjectives as nouns

The traditional 'parts of speech' (i.e. nouns, verbs, adjectives, etc.) from time to time adopt each other's roles. If your grasp of these is still a little shaky, pursue them on p. vii and through the **Index of grammar support** on p. viii.

It is not uncommon for journalists and others to use nouns as adjectives in English (e.g. 'Government sex scandal cover up'). Conversely we use adjectives as nouns: 'The good, the bad, and the ugly'.

Latin adjectives (and participles) also act as nouns:

<u>Nobiles</u> in ecclesia sedent.	*The <u>nobles</u> are sitting in the church.*
Ille qui proximus <u>dormienti</u> stat.	*He who is standing next to <u>the one-who-sleeps</u>.*

▶ Insolentes monachi *The insolent monks*

In ecclesia Lucia Paulum et Augustinum, qui adhuc dormiebat, conspexit. Iam Augustinus stertere incipiebat. Paulus Augustinum excitare volebat quod Stephanum eum spectantem videre poterat.

In primis subselliis Egberta filiam furtim spectantem unum ex discipulis qui in choro cantabant conspexit.

'Lucia, quid spectas?' susurravit Egberta.

'Nil, praeter illum, qui dormit, discipulum,' Lucia respondit.
Iam Paulus etiam Luciam spectabat.

'Quis est ille puer qui te spectat?' rogavit mater.

'Quis puer?'

'Puer ille qui proximus dormienti stat,' inquit Egberta ridens. 'Eho, nunc abbas praedicabit.' Egberta tamen ridere desiit ubi Benedictum se ipsam spectantem conspexit. 'Insolentissimos monachos!' susurravit Egberta, et Karolus, coniunx, eam audiens rogavit: 'Mea carissima, vales-ne?'

Interea Stephanus Augustinum dormientem adhuc stertentemque spectabat. Paulus Stephanum spectabat et 'Cave, Augustine!' susurravit, 'nunc est cantandum.'

'Abi!' respondit magna voce Augustinus. 'Volo dormire.' Omnes in ecclesia vocem eius audire poterant.

'Ora pro nobis peccatoribus,' cantabat abbas, palmas ad caelum tendens.

abi	*go away!*
carissimus-a-um	*dearest*
cave	*look out*
coniunx-gis [m/f]	*husband/wife*
conspexit	*(s/he) caught sight of*
desiit	*(s/he) stopped*
eam	*her*
eius	*his/her*
furtim	*secretly*
illum [acc.]	*that one, him*
ipsam	*her(self)*
nil (nihil)	*nothing*
nunc est cantandum	*it is time to sing*
ora pro nobis peccatoribus	*pray for us sinners*
palma-ae [f]	*palm*
proximus-a-um	*next, nearest*
quis	*who, which*
respondit	*(s/he) replied*
se	*her(him/them)self*
sterto-ere	*snore*
te [acc.]	*you*
tendo-ere	*stretch*
valeo-ere	*to be well*
volebat	*(s/he) wanted*

Practice (ii)

1 Choose the correct form for each gap from: **praedicans, praedicantem, praedicantes, dormiens, dormientem, dormientes**:

(a) Discipuli abbatem in ecclesia _____ audiebant.

(b) Omnes monachi discipulos _____ videre poterant.

2 Change the underlined word to the plural if singular, or singular if plural, and translate:

(a) Egberta <u>ova</u> e sarcina cadentia videt.
(b) Lucia <u>monachos</u> in ecclesia cantantes audiebat.
(c) Paulus cum <u>discipulo</u> stertenti sedebat.
(d) Abbatissa cibum <u>monachis</u> dormientibus non dabit.
(e) Benedictus <u>ancillam</u> in culina susurrantem audiebat.
(f) <u>Femina</u> Theodorum in silva currentem videre poterat.

▶ Living Latin

'Yaysoos in chaylo'

Latin was finally dropped from Catholic liturgy in the 1960s, ending an unbroken line of Latin from the Church's earliest days. The pronunciation will have varied from country to country and priest to priest. Some of the clergy may have harboured a love for classical Latin, but the primary use of the language was to get the Christian message across to their local brethren. Each region of the Christian domain will have had its own mix of Latin and local speech habits, evolving over many centuries. In 1912 Pope Pius X, who wanted to create a uniform pronunciation of Latin, encouraged the clergy everywhere to adopt what was then the Italian pronunciation. Hence 'Yaysoos', 'bone-us' and 'chaylum' for **Jesus, bonus** and **caelum**. The pronunciation of the Latin used by the Church during the twentieth century has no foundation earlier than this point.

1 The Vulgate was the first full Latin version of the bible, translated by St Jerome at the end of the fourth century.

*Hoc autem dico, fratres, quoniam caro et sanguis regnum Dei possidere non possunt: neque corruptio incorruptelam possidebit. In momento, in ictu oculi, in novissima tuba: canet enim, et mortui resurgent incorrupti, et nos inmutabimur. Oportet enim corruptibile hoc induere incorruptelam: et mortale hoc induere inmortalitatem, tunc fiet sermo qui scriptus est: Absorta est mors in victoria. Ubi est, mors, victoria tua? Ubi est, mors, stimulus tuus?

(St Paul, Corinthians i, 15; 50, 52–5)

This I tell you, brothers, that flesh and blood cannot inherit the kingdom of God: neither will the perishable possess immortality. In a moment, in the twinkling of an eye, at the last call of the trumpet: for it will sound, and the bodiless dead will rise, and we shall be changed; for this matter must lose its perishability, and this mortality become immortal; then the saying which is written will come to pass: 'Death is swallowed up in victory. Where, death, is your victory? Where, death, is your sting?'

2 St Benedict was a contemporary of Jerome. His order has survived centuries of religious conflict, and there are now monasteries all over Europe.

*Cellerarius monasterii eligatur de congregatione sapiens, maturus moribus, sobrius, non multum edax, non elatus, non turbulentus, non iniuriosus, non tardus, non prodigus, sed timens Deum, qui omni congregationi sit sicut pater.

(Regula sancti Benedicti, xxxi)

A procurator for the monastery should be picked from the community, a prudent fellow of mature character, sober, without a great appetite, with no pretensions, not a trouble-maker, not one who causes harm, punctual, parsimonious, and fearing the Lord; a man who may be a father to the community.

3 Monks of the middle ages were not too immersed in pious abstinence and godly spirituality to overlook the pleasures of life. Refuge from the rigours of monasticism was found in the bottle, with girlfriends, and with the pen. Many anonymous verses have survived, some of which were parodies of formal, ecclesiastical Latin:

> ***Bibat ille, bibat illa,**
> **bibat servus et ancilla,**
> **bibat hera, bibat herus:**
> **ad bibendum nemo serus.**

Let him drink and her drink, and the serf have one, the maid too, and the mistress, and the master – no one's too late for a jugful.

*post-classical

Revision

1 Write a sentence with:

    (a) the present participle of **devoro-are;**
    (b) the present participle of **ululo-are;**
    (c) the present participle of **bibo-ere;**
    (d) the gerundive of **audio-ire.**

2 Translate into Latin:

    (a) Augustine was sleeping for twelve hours.
    (b) Wise teachers always used to drink with students.
    (c) Lucia, could you hear the mule drinking in the field?
    (d) The students were watching the abbot leading a procession out of the church.

3 Fill each gap with the corresponding form in the correct tense:

	Infinitive	Present	Future	Imperfect
love	amare	amamus	amabimus	amabamus
hear	audire	audit	audiet	audiebat
work	laborare		laborabitis	laborabatis
send		mitto		mittebam
		venis	venies	veniebas
write			scribent	
take		capit		
	timere		timebis	
give		dat		
open		aperio		
		vident		
		laudamus		
do	facere			faciebat
teach		docetis		

4 Check you know these words:

    agricola-ae   **epistula-ae**   **peregrinus-i**
    post   **praeter**   **iubeo-ere**
    n(ih)il   **quis**   **primus-a-um**

12

in manus tuas commendo spiritum meum

into your hands I commend my spirit

In this unit you will learn about
- perfect tense
- personal pronouns: ego, tu, nos, vos
- meus, tuus, noster, vester (*my, your, our, your* [pl])

- and find out more about Latin in 'The murder in a cathedral'

Past tense: perfect

The perfect ('finished', 'perfected') is a past tense describing an action which is more momentary or instantaneous than that of the imperfect. In general the imperfect points us to the action itself, the perfect to the completion of the action (and therefore what comes next). In the two examples below, the same English verbal phrase is used to translate both tenses. But in one, the 'hurrying' is a singular, momentary, completed event, and in the other a recurring one.

Perfect

Stephanus ad fenestram festinavit.

Stephen hurried to the window.

Imperfect

Stephanus ad fenestram saepe festinabat.

Stephen often hurried (used to hurry) to the window.

Perfect endings

	am-are *love*	**mon-ere** *warn, advise*	**mitt-ere** *send*
I	**amav-i**	**monu-i**	**mis-i**
you (s.)	**amav-isti**	**monu-isti**	**mis-isti**
s/he, it	**amav-it**	**monu-it**	**mis-it**
we	**amav-imus**	**monu-imus**	**mis-imus**
you (pl.)	**amav-istis**	**monu-istis**	**mis-istis**
they	**amav-erunt**	**monu-erunt**	**mis-erunt**
	aud-ire *hear*	**cap-ere** *take, capture*	
I	**audiv-i**	**cep-i**	
you (s.)	**audiv-isti**	**cep-isti**	
s/he, it	**audiv-it**	**cep-it**	
we	**audiv-imus**	**cep-imus**	
you (pl.)	**audiv-istis**	**cep-istis**	
they	**audiv-erunt**	**cep-erunt**	

In the perfect tense the endings of the verbs are not the only parts to change. Some verbs have a different stem. Try to remember it when you look the verb up.

ambulo	ambulare	**ambulavi**	I (have) walked
laudo	laudare	**laudavi**	I (have) praised
habeo	habere	**habui**	I (have) had
video	videre	**vidi**	I saw, have seen
scribo	scribere	**scripsi**	I wrote, have written
dico	dicere	**dixi**	I (have) said
venio	venire	**veni**	I came, have come
facio	facere	**feci**	I (have) made, did, have done
sum	esse	**fui**	I have been, was

Practice (i)

1 Translate into Latin (in the perfect tense):

(a) He has walked.
(b) They saw.
(c) We have come.
(d) I have taken.

(e) You (s.) have warned.
(f) He heard.
(g) We have sent.
(h) She advised.

2 Change the underlined verbs to the corresponding perfect form, and translate:

(a) Monachus servo <u>dicit</u>.
(b) Ancillas in culina <u>laudamus</u>.
(c) Dani-ne omnia monasteria <u>capiunt</u>?
(d) Epistulam episcopo <u>scribis</u>?

▶ Si munimentum quaeris, circumspice *If you seek protection, look around you*

Adhuc abbas in ecclesia praedicabat: '... Hic, in ecclesia, ubi sedemus, ubi oramus, ubi Deum laudamus, est vestra securitas. Si igitur munimentum quaeritis, circumspicite. Ecce tectum! Ecce magni muri! Hic in ecclesia vos curavimus, nunc vos curamus, et post mortem animas vestras semper curabimus. Aedificatum lapidibus monasterium centum annos hic stetit et hic stabit annos mille! Hic sunt omnia tuta. Quod vestras animas illud vestras res custodire potest. Iterum vobis dico: in ecclesia non solum animae sed etiam res sunt tutae. Scitis-ne cur haec dicam? Rumores quosdam audivimus, non quidem confirmatos, sed tamen referendos. Nihil nos vidimus. Alieni-ne in silvis adfuerunt? Vidit-ne alienos in silva Theodorus? Quis nunc dicere potest? Theodorum miserum! Theodorus saltem in caelo cum angelis requiescit. Cras, ergo, si vultis esse securi, boves oves equi mulique in monasterii agros adducendi sunt. Si vobis placet, etiam res vestras in monasterio relinquatis. Vel autem, si mavultis, res vestras retinere licet, sed cavete.'

aedificatus-a-um	*built*
alienus-i [m]	*stranger*
angelus-i [m]	*angel*
bos-vis [m/f]	*ox*
cavete	*take care*
centum	*hundred*
circumspicite	*look around*
confirmatus-a-um	*confirmed*
cras	*tomorrow*
custodio-ire	*guard, watch over*
haec [n.pl.]	*these things*
hic	*here*
lapis-idis [m]	*stone*
licet	*it is permitted*
mavultis	*you prefer*
mille	*thousand*
munimentum-i [n]	*protection*
murus-i [m]	*wall*
non solum... sed etiam	*not only... but also*
ovis-is [f]	*sheep*
placet	*it pleases*
quaero-ere	*seek*
quidem	*indeed*
quod... illud	*that which... that...*
quosdam	*certain, unspecified*
refero, referre	*report*
relinquatis	*you may leave*
requiesco-ere	*rest*
res [f]	*things, possessions*
saltem	*at least*
securitas-tatis [f]	*peace of mind*
securus-a-um	*sure, secure*
sto-are, steti	*stand*
tectum-i [n]	*ceiling*
tutus-a-um	*safe*
vester-tra-trum	*your*
vos, vobis [dat.]	*you* (pl.)

Personal pronouns: *ego, tu, nos, vos*

They are only used in the nominative case for emphasis, because
subject pronouns are implied in the ending of a verb (if there is
no subject noun):

Danos non vidimus.   *We did not see the Danes.*
<u>**Nos**</u> **nihil vidimus.**   <u>*We*</u> *saw nothing.*

Pronouns are words used in place of nouns (**pro** is the Latin word for *in place of*):

	I/me	*you (s.)*	*we/us*	*you (pl.)*
Nom.	**ego**	**tu**	**nos**	**vos**
Acc.	**me**	**te**	**nos**	**vos**
Gen.	**mei**	**tui**	**nostri/nostrum**	**vestri/vestrum**
Dat.	**mihi/mi**	**tibi**	**nobis**	**vobis**
Abl.	**me**	**te**	**nobis**	**vobis**

The preposition **cum** *with* often follows rather than precedes a pronoun, and is attached to it: **nobiscum** *with us*, **mecum** *with me*.

'My', 'your', 'our'

The possessive adjectives **meus, mea, meum** *my*, **tuus, tua, tuum** *your* (s.) have endings like **sanctus-a-um**, as do the plural equivalents **noster, nostra, nostrum** *our* and **vester, vestra, vestrum** *your* (pl.) with the exception of the nominative masculine singular (**-er**):

my	**meus-a-um,** etc.
your (sing.)	**tuus-a-um,** etc.
our	**noster, -tra, -trum,** etc.
your (pl.)	**vester, -tra, -trum,** etc.

▶ Da mi basia mille *Give me a thousand kisses*

'Nunc, o amici, est optandum,' abbas adhuc praedicabat. 'Nos monachi, qui in monasterio habitamus, scientiae artium vitarum animarum sumus custodes. Deo volente, nos vigilantes capita bonaque vestra bene curabimus. Nunc, igitur, si dormire sine cura vultis, hodie in monasterium bona vestra capitaque adducenda sunt.' Abbatis vox e somno Augustinum excitavit.

'Dormire?' inquit Augustinus. 'Ego certe dormire sine cura volo.'

'St.' susurravit Paulus. 'Dani prope monasterium visi sunt.'

'Non credo!' inquit Augustinus. 'Cuius est fama?'

'Stephani.'

'Stephani? Si elephantus iuxta Stephanum sedeat, magister noster eum non agnoscat.'

'Immo. Theodorus ante mortem Danos in silvis ipse vidit et Stephano dixit.' Augustinus Paulum non audivit sed Luciam in primo subsellio spectabat: 'Da mi basia,' murmuravit Augustinus.

'Quid?'

'Da mi basia mille'.

'St. Taceas.'

'Deinde usque altera mille.'

'Equidem tibi nulla basia dabo,' ridebat Paulus.

'Eheu!' gemuit Augustinus, 'Illa te solum spectat, te solum amat. *Ille mi par esse deo videtur, ille, si fas est, superare divos.'*

'Quis est *ille*?' rogavit Paulus.

'Tu.'

'Ego?'

'Ita vero.' inquit Augustinus. 'Cupido est saevus. Me miserum. *Certas habuit puer ille sagittas.'*

'Io satis carminum!' exclamavit Paulus.

'Rosa veris, quae videris clarior quam lilium,' murmuravit Augustinus. Subito Pater Stephanus apparuit:

'Augustine et Paule, hodie ambo vos mecum ad Patrem Ricardum venietis,' inquit magister. 'Ille vos severissime verberabit.'

'Nos? Cur?' rogavit Augustinus.

'Semper in ecclesia estis garruli. Vos antea admonui. Nunc poenas dabitis.'

'Ignoscas nobis. Te oro, Magister, ne nos ducas ad Ricardum. Si tibi placet, rursum regulam monachorum exscribam.'

'O Sancta Maria!'

'Te oramus.'

'O molesti pueri .... esto. Sed si vos iterum susurrantes in ecclesia videbo, ambo verberandi eritis. Totus liber est exscribendus – hodie.'

'Ut vis, Magister.'

'St. Nunc cum ceteris discipulis cantandum est.'

Tandem abbas praedicare desiit. Omnes 'Deo gratias,' responderunt et cantare inceperunt.

agnoscat	*would recognize*
altera	*another*
ante(a)	*before(hand)*
appareo-ere-ui	*appear*
ars-tis [f]	*art, skill*
basium-i [n]	*kiss*
caput, capitis [n]	*head, capital*
certus-a-um	*sure, unerring*
clarior	*more lovely*

cuius	*whose*
cura-ae [f]	*anxiety, stress*
custos-dis [m/f]	*guardian*
da	*give!*
deinde	*then, next*
deo volente	*with God willing*
divus-i [m]	*god*
equidem	*indeed, to be sure*
esto	*so be it*
fama-ae [f]	*story, report*
fas	*not blasphemous*
garrulus-a-um	*talkative*
gemo-ere-ui	*groan*
illa [f]	*she, that*
ille [m]	*he, that*
immo	*no*
io	*hey*
ipse	*he himself*
lilium-i [n]	*lily*
molestus-a-um	*troublesome*
ne ducas	*do not take*
opto-are	*choose*
par	*equal*
quae videris	*you who seem*
quam	*than*
quid	*what*
rosa-ae [f]	*rose*
rursum	*again*
sagitta-ae [f]	*arrow*
scientia-ae [f]	*knowledge*
sedeat	*were to sit*
severissime	*very severely*
supero-are	*surpass*
usque	*and on to*
ver-is [n]	*spring*
verbero-are	*beat*
videtur	*(s/he) seems*
vigilans	*watchful*
visi sunt	*were seen*
vita-ae [f]	*life*

Practice (ii)

Rewrite the words in brackets in their correct forms:

(a) In ecclesia (nos) monachi (vester) pecuniam custodiemus.

(b) Ubi est (meus-a-um) vinum? Ancillae-ne vinum (vos) dederunt?

(c) (Meus-a-um) carmina (tu) dare volo.

(d) Gratias (tu), multas gratias.

▶ Living Latin

The murder in a cathedral

The sacrosanctity of a church in the middle ages was taken for granted. Refugees from the bloodiest conflicts might seek sanctuary in a church and even the least godfearing of soldiers would think twice before breaking it. The majority of people lived very parochial lives. The local church was one of the few stone buildings some might ever see. Here was a solid fortress for their protection, and a symbol of permanence and life everlasting. A church was, in both senses, a building you could have faith in.

Cathedrals were even more imposing, and some still stand out in today's urban skylines. How much more impressive when all around them lay wooden houses and thatched huts. Canterbury Cathedral was the scene of Thomas Becket's murder in the twelfth century, a shocking episode because an archbishop was hacked to death – in a cathedral.

This is an abbreviated version of the account by an eyewitness to Thomas' murder, William FitzStephen*:

1 The monks persuade Thomas to come into the church.

> **Quid nisi timor et tremor venerunt super nos monachos, clericos et socios archiepiscopi? Sed bonus ille Thomas contemptor mortis erat.**

Nothing but fear and trembling came over us monks, clerics, and companions of the archbishop. But the good Thomas was disdainful of death.

2 The assassins arrive.

Iturus ad aram superiorem, iam quattuor gradus ascenderat, cum ecce ad ostium claustri, quo veneramus, primus adest Reginaldus Ursonis loricatus, ense evaginato, et vociferans, 'Nunc huc ad me, homines regis!' Nec multo post adduntur ei tres socii eius, similiter loricis contecti corpora et capita praeter oculos solos, ensibus nudatis.

He was about to go up to the upper altar and had already gone up four steps, when there by the door to the cloister, where we had entered, stood the first of them, Reginaldus Ursonis, in full armour, sword drawn, shouting, 'Now follow me, men of the king!' A moment later his three accomplices joined him, their bodies and heads covered with armour except for their eyes alone, and their swords drawn.

3 'Where is the traitor?'

Clamavit aliquis, 'Ubi est proditor?' Ille: 'Ecce ego, non proditor, sed presbyter Dei; et miror, quod in tali habitu ecclesiam Dei ingressi estis. Quid placet vobis?' Unus sicarius, 'Ut moriaris.' At ille: 'Et ego in nomine Domini mortem suscipio, et animam meam et ecclesiae causam Deo et beatae Mariae et sanctis huius ecclesiae patronis commendo. Absit ut propter gladios vestros fugiam.'

One of them shouted: 'Where is the traitor?' He replied: 'Here I am, no traitor, but a priest of God; and I am surprised that you have entered the house of God in such attire. What is your business?' One of the murderers said: 'To kill you.' He replied: 'I embrace death in the name of the Lord, and I commend my soul and the cause of the church to God, to Blessed Mary and to the patron saints of this church. Don't think that I will run from your swords.'

4 His death.

Quidam eum plano ense caedebat inter scapulas, dicens, 'Fuge; mortuus es.' Ille immotus perstitit, et cervicem praebens, se Domino commendabat. 'In manus tuas, Domine, commendo spiritum meum.' Datur in caput eius ictus secundus. Super dextram cecidit, ad dextram Dei iturus.

*One of them whipped him across his shoulders with a flat blade,
saying, 'Run; you are a dead man.' He didn't budge but stood his
ground, and offering his neck he entrusted himself to the Lord.
'Into your hands, O Lord, I commend my spirit.' A second blow
struck his head. He fell to the right, on his way to the right hand
of God.*

*post-classical

Revision

1 Fill each gap with the corresponding form in the correct
tense:

	Infinitive	Present	Future	Imperfect	Perfect
walk	ambulare	ambulat			ambulavit
come	venire	venimus			venimus
			laudabitis		laudavistis
teach		doceo			docui
		dicis	dices		
				scribebant	
take			capiemus		
	videre		videbunt		
be			erit		fuit

2 Rewrite these sentences making underlined words plural (if
singular) and singular (if plural), and translate:

(a) O Augustine, mihi dulce <u>carmen</u> tuum leges?
(b) Miser Stephanus cum <u>discipulo</u> in bibliotheca semper
laborabat.
(c) Lucia-ne <u>peregrinos</u> in silva audivit?
(d) <u>Ancilla</u> nos monuit.

3 Translate into Latin (use the perfect for all past tenses):

(a) Students, did Theodorus walk with you in the wood?
(b) Augustine, did you hear the abbot preaching?
(c) I saw the abbess whispering to the cook.
(d) Paul, did you write a letter to Lucia?

4 Check you know these words:

centum	mille	annus-i
cura-ae	scientia-ae	vita-ae
deinde	rursum	subito
quidem		

revision II
(units 07–12)

1 Fill the gaps with the correct form (tense and person) of one of:

canto-are-avi   devoro-are-avi   dormio-ire-ivi
scribo-ere, scripsi   video-ere, vidi

(a) **Abbatissa nobis** ____ (future).

(b) **Monachi** ____ (present)
**quod multum cibum
vinumque** ____ (perfect).

Multos Danos in silva.....!

(c) **Multos Danos in
silva** ____ (perfect)!

(d) Paulus epistulam
Luciae ____ (present).

2 Identify the future, imperfect and perfect forms of the underlined verbs:

(a) In bibliotheca discipulus carmina <u>recitat</u>.
(b) Discipuli <u>rident</u>.
(c) O ancillae, Danos <u>auditis</u>?
(d) Epistulam Luciae <u>scribo</u>.

3 Choose the correct form of the gerundive:

(a) Peregrini multas linguas (doceo-ere) sunt.
(b) Nunc corpus miserabile est (sepelio-ire).
(c) Discipuli mali non (laudo-are) sunt.
(d) Epistula non in ecclesia sed in bibliotheca est (scribo-ere).

4 Choose the correct form of the present participle:

(a) Monachus in terram cecidit e silva (fugio-ere).
(b) Abbatem ex monasterio pompam (duco-ere) spectavi.
(c) Amicos nostros in ecclesia (sedeo-ere) vidimus.
(d) Discipulus virgines in horto (canto-are) audivit.

5 Write out the following nouns in all five cases, singular and plural:

annus-i, vita-ae, oppidum-i, potio-nis, clamor-is, tempus-oris

6 Translate into Latin:

(a) Did you hear the maiden's song, Father Stephen?
(b) The bishop was preaching to all the monks.
(c) Soon we shall bury the monk's pitiable corpse.
(d) The cook was drinking wine with the sad student all night long.

7 Group the English words with their Latin ancestor:

> **hospes, hospitis**   sure   dainty
>
> **caput, capitis**   predicate   dish   host
>
> **discus-i**   hotel   disco
>
>   fantasy
>
> **dignitas, dignitatis**   hospital   computer
>
>   cattle
>
> **phantasia-ae**   disk
>
>   secure   fancy
>
> **praedico-are**   hospice   chapter   count
>
> **blasphemo-are**   capital   discus   chattel
>
> **securus-a-um**   blaspheme   blame
>
> **computo-are**   hostel   dignity   preach

8 A **popina** is (a) an illegitimate daughter of a pope; (b) a small flower found in Rumania, which produces opium; (c) an ancient inn or take-away – a place to pop in for a quick snack?

13 Paulus sub aqua

Paulus under water

In this unit you will learn about
- past participles
- perfect passive (past participles with esse)
- participle phrases (including the ablative absolute)
- irregular verb: eo, ire (*to go*)

- and find out more about Latin in 'A winter's night'

Past participles: *desiderata*

So far you have met three core forms of a verb:

desidero	*I desire, long for*
desiderare	*to desire, long for*
desideravi	*I (have) desired, longed for*

There is a fourth and final form worth a look, the past participle:

cibus desideratus	*the desired food*
unguenta desiderata	*the desired perfumes*
libri desiderati	*the desired books*

The past participle is like the present one (see p. 112) in so far as it is an adjective formed from a verb. The endings, however, are not the same. The past participle has endings like **sanctus-a-um** (**mulus, silva, vinum**):

Ancilla in culinam <u>vinum</u> <u>desideratum</u> portavit.	*A maid carried the longed-for wine into the kitchen.*
Paulus <u>virgini</u> <u>desideratae</u> dicere volebat.	*Paul wanted to speak to the girl he longed for* (lit. *the longed-for girl*).

Practice (i)

Complete the table of the four main parts (or 'principal parts') of a verb. A fifth column is added for English words which have a similar form to the past participle.

Present ('I...')	Infinitive ('to...')	Perfect ('I have...')	Past participle (neuter)	Derivative
oro	orare	oravi	oratum	oration
narro	narrare	narravi	narratum	narrative
aestimo	aestimare		aestimatum	estimation
sto	stare	steti	statum	
saluto	salutare	salutavi		salutation
recito		recitavi	recitatum	recitation
vaco	vacare	vacavi		vacation
damno	damnare	damnavi	damnatum	
maneo	manere	mansi	mansum	
rideo		risi	risum	(de)rision
sedeo	sedere	sedi		session
teneo	tenere	tenui		(at)tention
video	videre	vidi	visum	
moneo		monui		(ad)monition

Present ('I...')	Infinitive ('to...')	Perfect ('I have...')	Past participle (neuter)	Derivative
dico	dicere	dixi		diction
duco		duxi		(in)duction
relinquo		reliqui	relictum	(de)reliction
scribo	scribere	scripsi		(de)scription
ascendo	ascendere	ascendi		ascension
ago	agere	egi		action
audio	audire	audivi		audition
venio	venire	veni		(in)vention
perficio	perficere	perfeci		perfection
recipio	recipere	recepi		reception

The past participle (**desideratus-a-um**) is usually passive, whereas the present participle is active:

| **mulus desideratus** | *the longed-for mule* | (passive) |
| **mulus desiderans** | *the mule, longing for...* | (active) |

So far you have met mostly active expressions, with the subject as the 'doer' and the object 'done to'. For examples of the passive, see pp. 93, 157.

Past participles with *esse*

With the appropriate part of **sum, esse**, the past participle becomes part of the verb itself, in the perfect passive:

| **Paulus ad oppidum missus est.** | *Paul was sent to the town.* |
| **Ancillae numquam laudatae sunt.** | *The maids were never praised.* |

Note that when the participle is used with **est** or **sunt**, the meaning is past (*was* sent, not *is* sent; and *were* never praised, not *are* never praised).

Practice (ii)

Complete each sentence with the past participle in its correct form, and translate:

(a) **Theodorus in agro (sepelio-ire-ivi, sepultum) est.**
(b) **Peregrini in silva (video-ere, vidi, visum) sunt.**
(c) **Mulus ab umbris (terreo-ere, terrui, territum) est.**
(d) **Virgo a patre (laudo-are-avi, laudatum) est.**

Past participles without *esse*

The verb 'to be' is sometimes left out (if a sentence appears to be without a verb, try **est** or **sunt**, as these are often left implied, or understood):

Unguenta a coquo desiderata, sed a mulo portata sunt. *The perfumes <u>were</u> desired by the cook, but were carried by the mule.*

A past participle is often used, not as the main verb, but in conjunction with it:

Iosephus et Maria a tabernis <u>reiecti</u> stabulum inveniunt. *Joseph and Mary, <u>(having been) rejected</u> by the inns, find a stable.*

The past participle **reiecti** describes an action which is completed before that of the main verb **inveniunt**. Hence it is a 'past' participle.

Practice (iii)

Pair a noun with a past participle, and translate:

carmen... mulus... cenam... discipuli...

e.g. ____ (auditus-a-um) ancillae omnes amaverunt.
<u>Carmen</u> <u>auditum</u> ancillae omnes amaverunt.

All the maids loved the poem having-been-heard (after they had heard it).

(a) ____ in silvam (ductus-a-um) umbras timet.

(b) ____ a Stephano (doctus-a-um) obdormiverunt.

(c) ____ ab ancillis (paratus-a-um) Benedictus devoravit.

◗ Natalis Christi dies *Christ's birthday*

Menses lente transibant. Hiems erat severissima et frigus monasterium invadit. Paulus Luciam videre solam non poterat, quod virgo semper cum matre ambulabat aut in ecclesia orabat. Infelix per longas gelidasque noctes per fenestram stellas spectans in cella iacebat.

Mox natalis Christi dies a monachis celebratus est. Karolus et Egberta et Lucia ad missas audiendas advenerunt et postea domum cum episcopo abbatissaque discesserunt. In monasterio Augustinus ceterique discipuli fabulam agebant: Iosephus et Maria a tabernis reiecti stabulum inveniunt. Omnes monachi ab Augustini fabula sunt exhilarati praeter abbatem qui eam iocosiorem vocabat. Multae vini amphorae exhaustae, multi anseres devorati sunt. Sic paucos dies omnes curae sublatae sunt.

Per multos menses monachi anxii fuerant, populus incertus. Media in hieme plurimi Danos propter frigus atque mare turbulentum non exspectabant; itaque res suas apud se tenebant. Vere tamen veniente res bovesque in monasterium adductae sunt. Primo thesaurus in ecclesia modicus erat quod exiguae pauperibus servisque res. Sed post paucos dies fictilia, fibulae, scuta, lintea et cetera in ecclesiam tradita sunt; thesaurus igitur gradatim crescebat.

adduco-ere-xi-ductum	*bring*
amphora-ae [f]	*jug*
anser-is [m]	*goose*
apud se	*at their homes*
aspicio-ere	*look at*
atque	*and*
aut	*or*
celebro-are-avi-atum	*celebrate*
cella-ae [f]	*cell, room*
Christus-i	*Christ*
cresco-ere	*grow*
discedo-ere-essi	*depart*
domum	*homewards*
eam	*her, it*
exhaurio-ire-ivi, exhaustum	*drain, empty*
exhilaro-are-avi-atum	*cheer*
exiguus-a-um	*scant, bare*
fibula-ae [f]	*brooch*
fictilia-ium [n]	*earthenware*
frigus-oris [n]	*chill, cold*
fuerant	*(they) had been*
gelidus-a-um	*cold*
gradatim	*gradually*
hiems, hiemis [f]	*winter*
iocosiorem	*too flippant*
linteum-i [n]	*linen cloth*
mare-is [n]	*sea*
medius-a-um	*mid-, middle of*
mensis-is [m]	*month*
modicus-a-um	*modest, small*
natalis dies [m]	*birthday*
pauper-is [m]	*pauper*
plurimi	*most people*

postea	*afterwards*
propter [+acc.]	*because of*
reicio-ere-eci-ectum	*reject, refuse*
scutum-i [n]	*shield*
severissimus-a-um	*very severe, hard*
stabulum-i [n]	*stable*
stella-ae [f]	*star*
sublatae sunt	*were raised, lifted*
suus-a-um	*their/his/her own*
taberna-ae [f]	*inn*
thesaurus-i [m]	*store*
trado-ere-didi-ditum	*hand over*
transeo-ire	*pass, go by*
ver-is [n]	*spring*

Participles: subject phrases and object phrases

A participle agrees with its noun, as any adjective does, and that noun may be the subject, object or indirect object of the main verb:

Subject:

<u>Iosephus</u> et <u>Maria</u> a tabernis <u>reiecti</u> stabulum inveniunt.

Joseph and Mary, <u>(having been) rejected</u> by the inns, find a stable.

Object:

<u>Multos</u> in agris <u>laborantes</u> spectabat.

He watched <u>many (people) working</u> in the fields.

Indirect object:

Paulus <u>visum</u> ad <u>stagnum</u> mulum flectebat.

Paul turned the mule towards a <u>pool having-been-seen</u>.

Ablative absolute

You will find many noun-and-participle phrases in the ablative. These expressions are almost detachable from the core of the sentence. They work as extra clauses, and are neither subject nor object of the main verb:

Monachi <u>Theodoro sepulto</u> in monasterium revenerunt.

The monks, <u>with Theodorus having been buried</u>, came back into the monastery. (The monks, after burying Theodorus, ...)

<u>Visis mulis aliis</u> mulus Pauli rudere incepit.	*<u>With other mules having-been-seen</u>, Paul's mule began to bray. (Upon seeing other mules ....)*
<u>Vere veniente</u> monachi in agros redierunt.	*<u>With spring coming</u> the monks returned to the fields. (At the arrival of spring....)*

(The ablative of the present participle ends **-ente**, not **-enti**, when it is used in an ablative absolute. Otherwise the endings of the present participle are the same as those of **prudens** – see p. 198).

Practice (iv)

Choose the correct word and translate:

(a) **Paulus, Augustino Tibulli carmina (legente/legentia), regulam monasterii exscribebat.**

(b) **Theodorus alienos in silva (susurranti/susurrantes) vidit.**

(c) **Multo cibo (devoratus/ devorato) Benedictus obdormivit.**

Irregular verb: *eo, ire, ii (ivi), itum* to go

No language course would be complete without some space devoted to irregular verbs. They are 'irregular' because they do not conform to the patterns of the main conjugations, adopting their abnormal shape partly from breadth of use (words which are confined to grammarians, lexicographers and crossword buffs may keep their shape for generations, but those which enjoy widespread use can be affected by any number of things); and partly from evolving as a fusion of different roots. Consider for example our verb 'to go' and its different forms: 'go', 'going', 'gone', 'went', 'been'. The French for 'to go' also has radically different forms: the Latin words **ambulo, ambulare, vado, vadere,** and **eo, ire** are all roots of *aller* (*je vais, j'irai*).

ire *to go*	Present	Future	Imperfect	Perfect
I	**eo**	**ibo**	**ibam**	**ii**
you (s.)	**is**	**ibis**	**ibas**	**isti**
s/he, it	**it**	**ibit**	**ibat**	**iit**
we	**imus**	**ibimus**	**ibamus**	**iimus**
you (pl.)	**itis**	**ibitis**	**ibatis**	**istis**
they	**eunt**	**ibunt**	**ibant**	**ierunt**

Compound forms: **abeo-ire** *to depart*, **redeo-ire** *to return*, **adeo-ire** *to approach/go to*, **exeo-ire** *to go out*.

Practice (v)

Translate:

(a) We depart.
(b) They will return.
(c) We were approaching.

(d) They have departed.
(e) She goes out.
(f) They go out.

▶ Castellum Comitis Karoli *Count Charles' castle*

Paulus, aestate adveniente, ad oppidum rediit. Die aestuoso sub arbores frondescentes cum mulo per iter insolitum ambulabat; nam Luciae villam spectare volebat. Post tria milia e silvis venerunt et Paulus videre poterat magnum castellum in quo Lucia cum matre Egberta et patre Karolo, viro nobili et ditissimo, habitabat. Comes Karolus regionem totam regebat. Abbas Laurentius et Comes Karolus erant duo in regione potentissimi.

Paulus multos in agris prope castellum laborantes spectabat. Alii herbam metebant, alii faenum in praedium portabant. Subito visis mulis aliis mulus rudere incepit. 'Eheu, tace!' clamavit Paulus habenas quatiens et celeriter mulum in silvam duxit. Prope silvam Paulus visum ad stagnum adiit ubi multam aquam mulus sitiens bibit. Deinde, mulo arbori in silva ligato, Paulus ad stagnum revenit et veste deposita in aquam frigidam se immersit: sub aquam natavit et rediens ad aequor exhalavit. 'Utinam hic maneam per totum diem,' suspiravit Paulus, et otiosus in aequore innavit caelum contemplans. Haud multo post mulum rudentem audivit. 'Quid est tibi, mule? Tace, improba bestia!'

aequor-is [n]	*surface*
aestas-tatis [f]	*summer*
aestuosus-a-um	*hot*
depono-ere-sui-situm	*put down*
ditissimus-a-um	*very rich*
faenum-i [n]	*hay*
frondesco-ere	*put forth leaves*
habena-ae [f]	*rein*
haud multo post	*not long afterwards*
herba-ae [f]	*grass*
improbus-a-um	*troublesome*
inno-are-avi	*swim, float*
insolitus-a-um	*unusual, unfamiliar*
iter-ineris [n]	*way, route*
ligo-are-avi-atum	*tie, bind*
meto-ere	*gather, reap, mow*
nato-are-avi	*swim*
otiosus-a-um	*lazy*
potentissimus-a-um	*most powerful*
praedium-i [n]	*store, barn*
quatio-ere	*shake*
quid est tibi?	*what's the matter with you?*
sitiens	*thirsty*
stagnum-i [n]	*pond, lake*
suspiro-are-avi	*sigh*
tria milia	*three miles*
utinam maneam	*if only I might stay*

▶ Living Latin

A winter's night

1 No room in the inn:

> *Exiit edictum a Caesare Augusto, ut describeretur universus orbis. Haec descriptio prima facta est praeside Syriae Quirino: et ibant omnes ut profiterentur singuli in suam civitatem.

Ascendit autem et Ioseph a Galilaea de civitate Nazareth, in Iudaeam civitatem David, quae vocatur Bethleem: eo quod esset de domo et familia David, ut profiteretur cum Maria desponsata sibi uxore praegnate. Factum est autem cum essent ibi, impleti sunt dies ut pareret. Et peperit filium suum primogenitum, et pannis eum involvit: et reclinavit eum in praesepio, quia non erat eis locus in diversorio.

(St Luke ii, 1–7)

A formal command was issued by Caesar Augustus that there should be a census of the whole world. This census first took place when Quirinus was governor of Syria: each and every person went to his own town to be registered. And Joseph went up from Galilee, from the town of Nazareth, into Judaea, to the town of David which is called Bethlehem: he went there, since he belonged to the house and line of David, to register with his wife, Mary, who was heavy with child. And during the time they were there, the day arrived when she gave birth. And she bore a son, her firstborn, and wrapped him in swaddling clothes, and laid him in a manger as there was no room for them in the inn.

2 Refusal of entry is a stock convention of ancient comedy and love poetry. Languishing outside his mistress's house, a lover may have to contend with the door, doorkeeper, dog, husband and bad weather.

Nam posita est nostrae custodia saeva puellae,
　　clauditur et dura ianua firma sera.
Ianua difficilis domini te verberet imber,
　　te Iovis imperio fulmina missa petant.
Ianua, iam pateas uni mihi victa querellis,
　　neu furtim verso cardine aperta sones.
Et mala si qua tibi dixit dementia nostra,
　　ignoscas; capiti sint precor illa meo.
Te meminisse decet quae plurima voce peregi
　　supplice cum posti florida serta darem.
Tu quoque ne timide custodes, Delia, falle.
　　Audendum est: fortes adiuvat ipsa Venus.

(Tibullus, Elegies i, 2, 5–16)

A tight security has been put on my girl, and the thick door is closed with an uncaring bolt. You, door, belong to an unfeeling master, and I pray the rain lash you, I pray Jupiter aim his lightning down upon you. Now look here, door, won't you be won over by my pleas and open up just for me? Quietly turn your hinges and don't make a sound as you open. Forgive me if I ever spoke ill of you – I was unhinged. May my curses rebound on my own head.

Better you recall my many moments of suppliant pleading when I laid flowery wreaths about your post. And you too, Delia, be fearless and evade your guards. Be bold: Venus herself looks well on the brave.

*post-classical

Revision

1 Translate into Latin and include a <u>present</u> participle in each sentence:

  (a) Theodorus, fearing the pilgrims, went out of the wood.
  (b) For a long time the cook was watching the maidservants working in the garden.
  (c) Father Stephen sat in the church, grieving.
  (d) While Paul was swimming in the pond, the pilgrims were approaching the wood.

2 Translate into Latin and include a <u>past</u> participle in each sentence. Remember that they are passive (e.g. (a) 'The Danes having-been-heard, ...')

  (a) Upon hearing the Danes, Lucia returned to the monastery.
  (b) The meal was prepared by the maids and devoured by the monks.
  (c) The letter was written by the monk and handed over to the count.
  (d) After the horse had been tied to a tree, the student swam in the pond.

3 Complete the table, which includes a column for derivatives similar to the present/infinitive forms:

Present ('I...')	Infinitive ('to...')	Derivative
efficio	efficere	efficient
relinquo	relinquere	relinquish
delinquo	delinquere	
rideo		(de)ride
duco		(pro)duce
scribo	scribere	
recipio	recipere	

4 How would you account for the ending of **desiderata**?

14

venatrix in silva

a huntress in the wood

In this unit you will learn about
- fourth declension nouns
- fifth declension nouns
- pluperfect tense

- and find out more about Ovid's story of Diana and Actaeon in 'A hunting moral'

Nouns: fourth declension

These are similar to nouns of the second declension, although the ending **-us** is not limited to the nominative singular: **-us** could also indicate a genitive singular, nominative plural or accusative plural:

	arcus (m) *bow, arch*	
	Singular	Plural
Nominative	**arc-us**	**arc-us**
Accusative	**arc-um**	**arc-us**
Genitive	**arc-us**	**arc-uum**
Dative	**arc-ui**	**arc-ibus**
Ablative	**arc-u**	**arc-ibus**

Practice (i)

1 Match each noun to its meaning:

(**a**)

metus	*spirit*
impetus	*chance*
casus	*verse*
gradus	*fear*
spiritus	*step*
versus	*attack*

(**b**)

gemitus	*hunt* *hand*
tumultus	
vultus	*noise*
exercitus	*face/expression*
manus	*army*
venatus	*groan*

2 Translate into Latin:

(**a**) with a sad expression   (**e**) of the holy spirit
(**b**) by chance   (**f**) with a groan
(**c**) pleasing verses   (**g**) the count's armies
(**d**) by hand   (**h**) the maiden's bow and arrows

Prepositions with the ablative

The prepositions **in** *in*, **ex** *out of, from*, and **ab** *by, from*, and **cum** *with, in the company of* are all used with the ablative. The ablative is also used without a preposition, for example explaining how or with what something is done:

Gemitu dixit.	*He spoke with a groan.*
Metu pavidus...	*Quaking with fear...*

Pluperfect tense

The pluperfect is another past tense, whose English equivalent uses the auxiliary 'had'. It is a further step into the past:

Numquam abbatem audiveramus.	*We had never heard the abbot.*
Peregrini nos viderant.	*The pilgrims had seen us.*

The stem of the pluperfect is the same as that of the perfect, the endings are those of **esse** in the imperfect:

	Pluperfect	
I had...	**vid-eram**	**audiv-eram**
you had... (s.)	**vid-eras**	**audiv-eras**
s/he had...	**vid-erat**	**audiv-erat**
we had...	**vid-eramus**	**audiv-eramus**
you had... (pl.)	**vid-eratis**	**audiv-eratis**
they had...	**vid-erant**	**audiv-erant**

▶ Luciae venatus *Lucia's chase*

Shared endings key

-us mulus : nom.
tempus : nom. or acc.
arcus : nom., gen., nom. pl., acc. pl.

Interea Lucia venatu, qui fuerat longus et sine praemio, fessa erat. Equus eius quoque erat calidus fessusque. Illa igitur in stagno natare constituerat et nunc per silvam ad stagnum adibat. Gemitu tamen muli audito 'Heus, ecquis hic est?' dicens circumspexit. Nullo ergo respondente, sagitta e pharetra erepta, equum lente ad sonitum duxit. In silva mulum atque relictam Pauli vestem agnoscens, ex equo descendit et arcum sagittamque manu tenens furtim ad stagnum adibat.

Paulus, qui mulum audiverat, adhuc caelum contemplabat. Subito vocem 'Tolle manus tuas!' audivit. 'Qu... qu... qu... quis es?' metu balbus rogavit, 'Quid vis?'

'Tu-ne anas?' inquit Lucia ridens, simul et arcum sagittamque tenens ex arboribus venit.

'Lucia! Ego Paulus. Nonne me agnoscis?'

'Paulus?'

'Ita vero. Salve, salve! Eheu, tumultu perterritus sum! Vis-ne natare? Age, tibi arcum deponere licet.'

'Cur in hoc loco ades?'

'Natare volui. Si tibi placet, arcum deponere licet.'

'Semper arcum teneo,' respondit illa.

'Tu es sagittaria?' rogavit ille.

'Ita certe sum. Pater me tela conicere docuit. Et tu, quo vadis?'

'Ad oppidum. Ignoscas mihi si non licet natare in hoc stagno.'

'Manere tibi licet.'

'Gratias tibi. In quid arcum intendis?'

'In arborem illam,' inquit Lucia arborem in ulteriore ripa demonstrans.

'Numquam illam percuties!' Paulus risit. Luciae tamen telum per auras stridens eundem in arborem adhaesit. Paulus balbus 'Incredibile ... mirabile,' inquit. 'Tu vera es venatrix. Animalia saepe interficis?'

'Non numquam,' inquit Lucia ridens et stagnum ad sagittam recuperandam circumvenit. 'Hodie tamen nihil cepimus.'

'Nisi me!' risit Paulus.

'Nisi te. Sed bestias multo saeviores quam te vidi.'

'Ego bestias omnes amo nec umquam interficio. Sub caelo omnes vivimus, animalia hominesque....'

'Hssh, taceas, quis est ille?' inquit Lucia.

'Quem dicis?'

'Voces audire possum. Ecce quidam ad stagnum adeunt.'

adhaereo-ere-si	*stick*
agnosco-ere	*recognize*
anas-atis [f]	*duck*
animal-is [n]	*animal*
balbus-a-um	*stammering*
calidus-a-um	*warm*
conicio-ere	*throw*
constituo-ere-ui	*decide*
depono-ere	*put down*
ecquis?	*who?*
eius	*her, his*
eripio-ere-ripui-reptum	*take out, snatch*
eundem [acc.]	*same*
heus	*hey!*
illa(m)	*she, her, that* (fem.)
intendo-ere	*aim*
interficio-ere	*kill*
licet	*it is permitted*
locus-i [m]	*place*
multo saeviores	*much more savage*

non numquam	*sometimes*
nullus	*not any, no one*
per auras	*through the air*
percutio-ere	*strike, hit*
perterritus-a-um	*thoroughly scared*
pharetra-ae [f]	*quiver*
praemium-i [n]	*reward*
quam	*than*
quem	*whom*
quidam [nom.]	*some (men)*
quo	*where (to)*
quoque	*also*
recupero-are	*recover*
ripa-ae [f]	*bank*
sagittaria-ae [f]	*archeress*
simul	*at the same time*
strideo-ere	*hum, whistle*
telum-i [n]	*missile*
tolle!	*raise, lift!*
ulterior	*far*
umquam	*ever*
vado-ere	*go*
venatrix-icis [f]	*huntress*

Nouns: fifth declension

This is the last of the declensions, and there are not many nouns belonging to this one. They are very similar to the third declension, with the exception of the genitive singular:

	res (f.) *thing, matter*	
	Singular	Plural
Nominative	**res**	**res**
Accusative	**rem**	**res**
Genitive	**rei**	**rerum**
Dative	**rei**	**rebus**
Ablative	**re**	**rebus**

Practice (ii)

Match each noun to its meaning:

dies	*faith*	
facies		*day*
fides	*hope*	
spes		*face*

Compound verbs

These are verbs such as **venire**, **facere**, **capere** with prefixes which add to the essential meaning. See p. 26 for the changes to the root syllable of compound verbs (e.g. f**a**cere, ref**i**cere), and p. 62 for English derivatives.

Practice (iii)

Fill the gaps in the following table, adding a prefix from the list below to the left-hand column:

Prefixes: **a(b), ad, circum, cum, de, e(x), in, per**

Prefix	Simple verb		Compound	
ad	ire		adire	*go to, approach*
		go		*go out*
	esse			*be absent*
		be	adesse	
	mittere	*send*	amittere	*send away, lose*
ad	capere	*take*		*receive, welcome*
		come	circumvenire	
		call	convocare	*call together*
		send	demittere	*send down, lower*
	facere	*make*	afficere	*treat, afflict*
	putare	*think*	computare	*sum up, reckon*
		take, snatch	eripere	*snatch out*
	ruere	*rush*	irruere	*rush in*
	venire		invenire	*come upon, find*
per	facere	*make*		*make thorough, finish*

▶ Peregrini ad stagnum *Strangers at the lake*

> ### Shared endings key
>
> **-i** second declension : muli : nom. pl.; muli, vini : gen.
> third declension : dat.
> **fifth declension : gen., dat.**
> first person, perfect (I have ...)

'Qui sunt illi?' rogavit Paulus.
'Nescio. Numquam eos vidi.'
'Ocius, in aquam, ocius!' Lucia celeriter se immersit in aquam et ambo inter calamos se celaverunt. Mox peregrini ad stagnum advenerunt.

'...Postero die pecora et aurum rapiemus,' inquit quidam. 'Immo,' inquit alius, 'aurum est non rapiendum.... sola pecora. Ecclesiae est aurum. Omnes res rapiendae sunt, praeter aurum et argentum.'

Paulus, voce agnota, attonitus 'Est Pater Ricardus!' exclamavit, 'cellerarius noster qui in nostro monasterio habitat!'

'Ssst!' susurravit Lucia ponens manum ad os eius; quam Paulus basiavit et virgo removit.

'Quid facit Ricardus in hoc loco?' Paulus in animo volutabat. 'Qui sunt socii eius? Mercatores?' Facies hominum videre non poterant; multas voces alias audierunt sed non agnoverunt. Equos virorum quoque bibentes audire poterant. Subito mulus Pauli in silva rudivit.

'Quid est illud?' clamavit quidam. 'Ne timeas,' respondit alter, 'ecce muli in agris.' Nec multo post viri abierunt.

'Mulus tuus est loquax!' inquit Lucia ex aqua resurgens.

'Quo abis? Nonne natare vis?'

'Minime! Illae voces erant Danorum.'

'Illi viri erant Dani? Cum Ricardo? Nonne erravisti?'

'Certa sum. Olim Danos hospites in nostro castello accepimus. Age, illi statim sequendi.'

'Statim? Sed vestes induere debeo.'

'Ergo festina, ne eos amittamus!'

agnosco-ere-ovi-otum	*recognize*
ambo	*both*
animus-i [m]	*mind*
argentum-i [n]	*silver*
aurum-i [n]	*gold*
basio-are-avi	*kiss*
calamus-i [m]	*reed*
cellerarius-i [m]	*procurator*
eos	*them*
erro-are-avi	*make a mistake*
hospes-itis [m]	*host, guest*
illi	*those men*
immo	*on the contrary*
induo-ere	*put on*
loquax	*noisy*
mercator-is [m]	*trader*
ne amittamus	*lest we lose*
ne timeas	*don't be afraid*
nescio-ire	*do not know*
ocius	*quick!*
olim	*once (upon a time)*

os, oris [n]	mouth
pecus-oris [n]	herd, flock
postero die	on the next day
quam	which
resurgo-ere	reappear
se celo-are-avi	hide oneself
sequendus-a-um	to be followed
socius-i [m]	colleague, associate
voluto-are	ponder, turn

▶ Living Latin

A hunting moral

In his Metamorphoses Ovid recounts many tales from Greek mythology, each one included by virtue of a 'metamorphosis', a change of form. There are characters who turn into trees, into stone, into animals.

The story of Actaeon and Diana is an example of the kind of divine justice dished out by the ancient gods. It was not so much a set of universal moral values which you might conform to or transgress, but rather a personal affair between worshipper and god. Offend the deity and you were in a spot of bother...

1 Diana bathes in a forest pool, attended by her nymphs. Meanwhile Actaeon and his hunting friends have decided to rest a while before renewing their sport. He takes a walk through the forest and chances upon the pool.

> **Ecce nepos Cadmi dilata parte laborum**
> **per nemus ignotum non certis passibus errans**
> **pervenit in lucum: sic illum fata ferebant.**
> **Qui simul intravit rorantia fontibus antra,**
> **sicut erant, nudae viso sua pectora nymphae**
> **percussere viro subitisque ululatibus omne**
> **implevere nemus circumfusaeque Dianam**
> **corporibus texere suis; tamen altior illis**
> **ipsa dea est colloque tenus supereminet omnis.**

Uh oh! Cadmus' grandson, enjoying a break from hunting makes his way through the unfamiliar wood, uncertain of his course, and reaches the grove: thus the fates guided him. As soon as he stepped into the grotto bedewed with fountain spray, the nymphs saw him and just as they were, naked, beat their breasts, and filling the whole wood with their sudden cries thronged around Diana and obscured her with their bodies; the goddess herself, however, was taller than they, and stood out head and shoulders above them all.

2 Diana turns the luckless intruder into a stag. He escapes, but sees his reflection in some water.

'Me miserum!' dicturus erat: vox nulla secuta est!
Ingemuit: vox illa fuit, lacrimaeque per ora
non sua fluxerunt; mens tantum pristina mansit.
Quid faciat? Repetat-ne domum et regalia tecta
an lateat silvis? Pudor hoc, timor impedit illud.
Dum dubitat, videre canes, primique Melampus
Ichnobatesque sagax latratu signa dedere.

'I'm done for ...' he tried to say, but no words followed! He groaned – the limit of his speech – and tears flowed down his strange face; only his mind remained from before. What should he do? Make his way back home to the royal palace, or hide in the woods? He is afraid to try one, and ashamed of the other. While he dithered his hounds caught sight of him: Melampus and keen-scented Ichnobates were first to give the signal with their cry.

3 Actaeon's hounds surround him, eager to finish him off.

Heu! Famulos fugit ipse suos. Clamare libebat:
'Actaeon ego sum: dominum cognoscite vestrum!'
Verba animo desunt; resonat latratibus aether.

Oh no! He flees his own retainers. He wanted to shout: 'I am Actaeon: recognize your own master!' But words fail his will; and the air resounds with their baying.

(Metamorphoses iii, 174–82, 201–5, 229–31)

Revision

1 Write out all the endings, singular and plural, in all cases:
   (a) gradus, gradus; corpus, corporis; monachus, monachi;
   (b) dies, diei; miles, militis; sagitta, sagittae

2 Translate into Latin:

   (a) The maiden had never swum in the pond.
   (b) After much food had been devoured (*use an ablative absolute*), the pilgrims left the monastery.
   (c) We had found neither food nor water, but we never lost hope.
   (d) The students sitting on the steps of the church were listening to the verses of Augustine.
   (e) The monks had written all the books by hand.

15

audire est intellegere
to hear is to understand

In this unit you will learn about
- hic, ille, is
- se, ipse
- the passive

- and find out more about Latin in 'All's fair in philosophy, love and war'

Third person pronouns: *ille, hic* and *is*

Latin has several equivalents of the third person pronoun (*he, she, it, they, him, her, them*):

he	*she*	*it*	
hic	**haec**	**hoc**	*(this one here)*
ille	**illa**	**illud**	*(that one there)*
is	**ea**	**id**	

In classical Latin, **is** is a less emphatic pronoun than **ille** 'that person' or **hic** 'this person'. This distinction grows weaker in post-classical Latin, when all three pronouns are almost interchangeable. See pp. 196–7 for all pronoun endings.

The equivalent of our 'it' may also be masculine or feminine in Latin, according to the gender of the noun it represents, e.g. **ea** (f) for **silva** *a wood*.

Practice (i)

1 Choose a noun to replace a pronoun, and translate:

   vinum, ancillarum, Luciae, monachi

   (a) **Vultus <u>eius</u> tristis erat.**
   (b) **Cibus <u>harum</u> a Benedicto devoratus est.**
   (c) **<u>Illi</u> in monasterio habitant.**
   (d) **<u>id</u> ab abbate desideratum est.**

2 Replace each underlined word with the correct form of the pronoun in brackets, and translate:

   (a) **Filia <u>Comitis</u> <u>Karoli</u> in castello habitat.** (ille)
   (b) **Abbatissa in ecclesia cum <u>Lucia</u> orabat.** (hic)
   (c) **Paulus semper cibum <u>mulo</u> dabat.** (is)
   (d) **<u>Peregrini</u> in silva cum <u>monachis</u> visi sunt.** (ille / hic)

Hic, ille and *is* as adjectives

Hic, ille and is as described above are pronouns, words used in place of nouns. If, however, one is used with a noun, not in place of it, it is an adjective:

   <u>hic</u> mulus   *this* mule
   <u>illa</u> silva   *that* wood

Hic can also mean 'here':

   hic vivo, hic moriar   *here I live, here may I die*

A development in later Latin is the use of **ille** as a definite article (*the*):

bonus ille Thomas   *the good Thomas*

Ille is the ancestor of the words for both *s/he* and *the* in the Romance languages:

	French	Spanish	Italian
s/he	**elle, il**	**ella, él**	**lei, lui**
the (m/f)	**le, la**	**el, la**	**il, la**

Practice (ii)

1 Translate using **hic, haec, hoc,** etc.:

   (**a**) this wood
   (**b**) these perfumes
   (**c**) of these students

2 Translate using **ille, illa, illud,** etc.:

   (**a**) that mistress
   (**b**) those songs
   (**c**) I see that mule

3 Translate using **is, ea, id,** etc.:

   (**a**) that letter
   (**b**) with those monks
   (**c**) that is

se and *ipse*: *himself, herself, themselves*

One kind of the *-self* pronouns is reflexive, i.e. it refers back to the subject (Latin: **se**):

Lucia se celat.	*Lucia hides herself.*
Captivi se liberant.	*The captives free themselves.*

There are only four cases: **se** (accusative or ablative), **sui** (genitive) and **sibi** (dative). There is no separate plural form as **se** can be either singular or plural (or masculine or feminine) – it depends on the verb's subject.

The other kind of *-self* pronoun is used for emphasis (Latin: **ipse**):

Abbas ipse Ricardum vidit.	*The abbot himself saw Richard.*
Luciam ipsam sed non patrem amo.	*I love Lucia herself, but not her father.*

Occasionally **ipse** is used similarly to **is, ea, id**, i.e. as an ordinary third person pronoun (*s/he, him, her*, etc.) – see p. 197 for all the forms.

Practice (iii)

Fill each gap with the correct form of **se** or **ipse**:

(a) **Mulus in stagno ____ vidit et attonitus est.**

(b) **Abbatissa ____ sarcinas portabat.**

▶ In dumis se celant *They hide in the thickets*

Peregrini per silvam ad monasterium iter faciebant, sequentibus furtim Lucia et Paulo. Mox peregrini prope monasterium constiterunt, et aliis Ricardus ecclesiam monstravit. Itaque Lucia et Paulus ad eos audiendos se in dumis celaverunt.

'Ecce ecclesia,' vocem Ricardi audire potuerunt, 'Nunc abite quod in hoc loco estis non conspiciendi. Valete.'

'Ille est proditor,' murmuravit Paulus, 'Pater Ricardus est proditor. Malus, turpis, ignavus, saevus, crudelis, scelestus ...'

'Sst,' iterum illa ad os eius manum posuit, iterum eam Paulus basiavit.

'Desine! Cave ne peregrini nos audiant.'

'Quid est agendum?' rogavit Paulus.

'Pete fideles amicos quibus omnia referas. Cui monachorum credis?'

'Magistro Stephano, qui est aliquando austerus sed vero benignus.'

'Huic ergo refer; i, in monasterium festina! Eho, siste! Mulus ducendus.' His dictis Lucia in equum ascendit.

'Et tu,' respondit ille, 'Quid in animo habes?'

'Ego Ricardum observabo. Nunc abeundum!' Lucia eum cum mulo ad monasterium lente euntem spectavit; deinde ipsa, equo citato, abiit.

abite	*depart, go away!*
aliquando	*sometimes*
audiant	*(they) may hear*
benignus-a-um	*kind*
cave ne...	*be careful lest...*
cito-are-avi-atum	*rouse / stir*
consisto-ere-stiti	*stop*
credo-ere [+dat.]	*believe, trust*
cui [dat.]	*whom*
dumus-i [m]	*thicket*
euntem	*him as he went*
fidelis	*loyal*
i!	*go!*
in animo habeo-ere	*have in mind, intend*
iter facio-ere	*make one's way*
observo-are	*watch*
peto-ere	*seek*
pono-ere-sui-situm	*place, put*
proditor-is [m]	*traitor*
quibus	*to whom*
refer	*tell, report!*
referas	*you may report*
scelestus-a-um	*wicked*
sequens	*following*
siste	*stop!*

Passive forms

So far almost all the verbs you have met have been <u>active</u>, e.g.:

Mulus silvam spectat.	*The mule watches the wood.*
Silva mulum spectat.	*The wood watches the mule.*

In the passive voice, the verb is not a 'doing' word but 'done-to'. If you want to make a verb passive and keep the same meaning, the object of the active verb becomes the subject of the passive one:

Silva a mulo spectatur.	*The wood is watched by the mule.*
Mulus a silva spectatur.	*The mule is watched by the wood.*

The subject of the active verb has become an 'agent' in the ablative, while the previous object is now the subject. When a verb is passive, it is the subject, not the object, which is on the receiving end. If a verb is active, it's in the active 'voice', if passive, then passive voice.

The passive form of the third person, singular or plural, has -**ur** added to the active ending, whether present, future or imperfect.

Practice (iv)

Fill in the gaps:

Active		Passive	
s/he watches	**spectat**	**spectatur**	*s/he is watched*
they were watching	**spectabant**	**spectabantur**	*they were being watched*
s/he will love	**amabit**		*s/he will be loved*
they will see		**videbuntur**	*they will be seen*
s/he was hearing		**audiebatur**	
		capietur	*s/he will be captured*

You have already encountered the passive in both gerundives (e.g. **agendus** *to be done*) and the past participle (e.g. **actus** *having been done*). You have also met the perfect passive with **esse**:

duxit	*s/he led* (active)
ductus est	*he was led* (passive)
amavit	*s/he loved* (active)
amata est	*she was loved* (passive)

Practice (v)

1 Fill the gaps with the corresponding active or passive forms:

Active		Passive	
she sent	**misit**	**missa est**	*she was sent*
they led		**ducti sunt**	
he heard			*he was heard*
she captured			*she was captured*
he advised			*he was advised*

2 Rewrite each sentence making the verb passive, and translate (and look out for singular subjects being replaced by plural ones, and vice versa):

e.g. **Discipuli librum legunt** (*the students are reading the book*)
Liber a discipulis legitur (*the book is being read by the students*)

(a) **Pater Ricardus discipulos in schola castigat.**
(b) **Mulus ex oppido omnes sarcinas portabat.**
(c) **Augustinus amicis carmen Catulli recitavit.**
(d) **Paulus virginem matri dicentem vidit.**

3 Rewrite each sentence making the verb active, and translate:

(a) **Cibus a Benedicto devoratus est.**
(b) **Virgo in silva a Paulo est visa.**
(c) **Historia monasterii a monachis narrabitur.**
(d) **Corpus in horto a Danis sepultum est.**

▶ Credere est intellegere *To believe is to understand*

Discipuli in schola theologiam a Stephano docebantur.

'O discipuli, non quaero intellegere ut credam, sed credo ut intellegam. Praeterea,' inquit Stephanus, 'philosophiam per dialecticam scimus sed veritatem ipsam agnoscimus gratia Dei. Scribitis-ne? Nunc est scribendum.'

'Veritatem-ne autem agnoscere possumus per dialecticam?' rogavit Augustinus.

'Minime,' respondit magister. 'Cur tu semper contradicis, Augustine? Maioribus numquam credis?'

'Nonne autem, ut dixit Socrates, homo veritatem per dialecticam agnoscere potest?'

'Cave ne blasphemes,' admonuit Stephanus, 'Graeci quidem sapientes erant, sed nos sapientiores sumus quod Dei sapientiam illorum eruditioni additam habemus. Veritatem iam habemus. Per veritatem opus Dei in terra revelatur. Nunc est scribendum: credere est scire, scire est intellegere, intellegere est credere....'

'Videre est spectare bellissimam!' exclamavit Augustinus.

'Quid dixisti?' rogavit Stephanus.

'Illic est amica Pauli,' exclamavit Augustinus per fenestram spectans.

'O Augustine, nisi tacebis, Pater Ricardus ad vos docendos reveniet.'

'Ibi quoque ipse est Paulus! Ducens mulum in monasterium,' inquit Augustinus.

'Paulus? Num Paulus iam adest?' inquit Stephanus ad fenestram festinans. 'Eheu, ecce coquus est iratus. Paulus nihil emisse videtur.'

Mox Paulus e culina fugiens in scholam irruit et Stephano 'Pater, Pater!' clamavit, 'Pater Stephane ... Pater Ricardus ... Pater Ricardus ...' inquit Paulus balbus.

'Pater Ricardus non adest. Quid tibi cum Patre Ricardo est? Dic mihi.'

addo-ere-idi-itum	*add*
bellissimus-a-um	*most beautiful*
contradico-ere	*contradict*
dialectica-ae [f]	*discussion, argument*
dic	*tell, say*
emisse	*to have bought*
eruditio-nis [f]	*learning*
gratia-ae [f]	*favour, grace*
ibi	*there*
intellego-ere	*understand*
maiores-um	*betters, ancestors*
praeterea	*besides*
quaero-ere	*seek*
quid tibi .... est	*what is your problem ...*
sapientia-ae [f]	*wisdom*
sapientiores	*wiser*
ut credam	*that I may believe*
veritas-tatis [f]	*truth*
videtur	*is seen, seems*

▶ Living Latin

All's fair in philosophy, love and war

1 Cicero was inspired by the philosophy of Socrates and other Greeks:

O vitae philosophia dux, o virtutis indagatrix expultrixque vitiorum!

(Tusculan Disputations v, 5)

O Philosophy, guide of life, you bring us to right and rid us of wrongs.

2 Propertius' philosophy was guided by hedonism. A good life meant a good time:

Qualem si cuncti cuperent decurrere vitam
  et pressi multo membra iacere mero,
non ferrum crudele neque esset bellica navis,
  nec nostra Actiacum verteret ossa mare,
nec totiens propriis circum oppugnata triumphis
  lassa foret crines solvere Roma suos.
Haec certe merito poterunt laudare minores:
  laeserunt nullos proelia nostra deos.

(Elegies ii, 15, 41–8)

*I wish everyone desired to lead this life and relax their limbs heavy
with draughts of wine, then there'd be no cruel steel, no warship,
and the bones of our people would not be churned about on the
sea of Actium, and Rome would not be overwhelmed with so
many victories over her own subjects and be weary of loosening
her hair in grief. Truly will this deserve posterity's praise: our
skirmishes have not injured any gods.*

3 Ovid saw common ground between lover and soldier. Both
may suffer from battle-fatigue:

Quis nisi vel miles vel amans et frigora noctis
  et denso mixtas perferet imbre nives?
Mittitur infestos alter speculator in hostes:
  in rivale oculos alter, ut hoste, tenet.
Ille graves urbes, hic durae limen amicae
  obsidet. Hic portas frangit, at ille fores.

(Amores i, 9, 15–20)

*Who but a soldier or lover will endure the chill of night and snow
and driving rain? As one is sent to spy on the dangerous enemy,
the other keeps an eye on his rival, as he would on an enemy. The
soldier camps outside hostile cities, the lover outside the door of
an unfeeling girlfriend. The former breaks down gates, the latter
the door.*

4 The heat of battle brings a case of passion-fatigue for
Tibullus:

Hic mihi servitium video dominamque paratam:
  iam mihi, libertas illa paterna, vale.
Servitium sed triste datur, teneorque catenis,
  et numquam misero vincla remittit Amor,
et seu quid merui seu nil peccavimus, urit.
  Uror, io, remove saeva puella faces.

(Elegies ii, 4, 1–6)

Here I see enslavement and mistress ready for me. Now farewell, freedom, which was my family's right, farewell. Bleak slavery lies ahead, and I am held in chains. Love is never one to loosen a wretched prisoner's knots. He burns me whether I've deserved it or done no wrong. I'm on fire! Oh! You cruel girl, take away those brands.

Revision

1 Identify the past participles of these verbs, add the right endings, and translate:

   (a) **Multae epistulae Luciae ab Augustino (scribo-ere) sunt.**
   (b) **Monasterium a peregrinis (relinquo-ere) est.**
   (c) **Corpus monachi (sepelio-ire) est.**
   (d) **Libri in bibliotheca (pono-ere) sunt.**

2 Translate into Latin:

   (a) Soon the students will free themselves.
   (b) Do the monks themselves teach? Are they taught to teach?
   (c) Paul and Lucia were seen walking out of the wood (*if there is a 'mixed gender plural' the masculine tends to prevail*).
   (d) Paul hid himself in the pond as the pilgrims approached (*'as... approached': the present participle of* **adeo-ire** *is irregular:* **adiens,** *then* **adeunt-**).
   (e) Many beasts were captured by the maiden herself.
   (f) The oxen were being guarded by an army of Danes.

16

quis in monasterio conspirat?

who is plotting in the monastery?

In this unit you will learn about
- the subjunctive
- wishes and commands
- ut, ne, cum

- and find out more about the Roman historian, Tacitus

More about verbs: the subjunctive (present)

Verbs can be categorized in several different ways. There's the *tense*, (present, future, etc.), the *person* (who's doing it, 'I', 'you', 'he', etc.), the *voice* (i.e. active or passive), and now finally what linguists call the *mood*.

So far we have been dealing with the indicative mood, that is to say dealing with actual actions, things which happen (or have happened or are about to happen).

The subjunctive mood deals with potential, with hope, with what might happen (or might have happened). There are four tenses, active and passive. The endings are common across all five conjugations with the exception of the present subjunctive:

amare	monere	mittere
am-em	**mone-am**	**mitt-am**
am-es	**mone-as**	**mitt-as**
am-et	**mone-at**	**mitt-at**
am-emus	**mone-amus**	**mitt-amus**
am-etis	**mone-atis**	**mitt-atis**
am-ent	**mone-ant**	**mitt-ant**
capere	audire	
capi-am	**audi-am**	
capi-as	**audi-as**	
capi-at	**audi-at**	
capi-amus	**audi-amus**	
capi-atis	**audi-atis**	
capi-ant	**audi-ant**	

The second, third, fourth and fifth columns all have the same endings, but verbs in the first column (**-are**) have an 'e' in place of the 'a'.

Practice (i)

Fill the gaps:

Present indicative		Present subjunctive	
we live	**vivimus**	**vivamus**	*may we live*
s/he (it) stands	**stat**		*may s/he (it) stand*
we love		**amemus**	*may we love*
		ignoscas	*may you forgive*
s/he is careful	**cavet**		*may s/he be careful*
we rejoice		**gaudeamus**	
	laudamus		
		bibat	
	taces		*may you be quiet*

Orders and encouragement (imperative)

The most direct way to tell someone what to do is to use the imperative:

(to one person)				
ama!	mone!	mitte!	audi	cape
(to more than one)				
amate!	monete!	mittite!	audite!	capite!

Audite me, o molesti discipuli!	*Listen to me, you lazy students!*
Sede!	*Sit!*

The imperative is the most direct, urgent and potentially offensive form of encouragement. In ancient times no doubt it was the standard idiom for addressing menials, dependants and children, but perhaps unwise for anyone old enough, big enough – and not hampered by the bonds of servitude – to clock you one. The subjunctive was a more polite idiom of encouragement, expressing a wish rather than an order:

Audiatis me, o amici.	*May you hear me, friends.*
Sedeas.	*May you be seated.*

Practice (ii)

Choose the appropriate form:

(a) **(Festinate/Festinetis), o miseri servi!**

(b) **Si vobis placet, in ecclesiam (festinate/festinetis), o milites.**

(c) O discipuli,
(tacete/taceatis).

(d) O Abbatissa,
(tace/taceas).

▶ Lucia in trabibus celata *Lucia hidden in the beams*

> **Shared endings key**
>
> **-e(n)t** present : mone(n)t (second conjugation)
> future : mitte(n)t, audie(n)t, capie(n)t (third, fourth and mixed conjugations)
> **present subjunctive : ame(n)t (first conjugation)**
>
> **-a(n)t** present : ama(n)t (first conjugation)
> imperfect : -ba(n)t (all verbs)
> pluperfect : -era(n)t (all verbs)
> **pres. subj. : monea(n)t, mitta(n)t, audia(n)t, capia(n)t (second, third, fourth and mixed conjugations)**

Interea Lucia, Ricardum in monasterium euntem observans, in claustri tectum ascenderat ubi in pueritia saepe se celabat; Comes Karolus enim eam matremque ad monasterium adducere solebat. Despiciens igitur Lucia de trabibus Ricardum solum sedentem videre poterat. Tandem aliquis ad Ricardum adiit.

'Ubi sunt nostri hospites?' inquit advena. 'Salvi-ne?'

'Salvi sunt,' respondit alter.

'Omnia-ne parata sunt?'

'Ita vero, Domine Abba.'

Lucia est obstupefacta. Abbas! Omnia verba eorum audire non poterat quod duo monachi susurrabant. 'Tace!' dicebat abbas.

'Advenit aliquis, ergo in ecclesiam abi...' et Ricardus abiit. 'Ah Pater Stephane, salve.'

'Te saluto, Domine Abba,' respondit Stephanus, 'Ignoscas mi, sed tibi nuntios graves refero, mirabiles quidem, sed veros.'

'Quos nuntios dicis? Dic mihi, Stephane.'

'Unus ex discipulis meis, puer sapiens, honestus, fidelis ...'

'Quis ex tuis discipulis?'

'Paulus. Hodie cum ad oppidum ambularet, conspirantes in silva Danos conspexit ex quibus unum agnovit. Pater Ricardus in silva cum Danis!'

'Pater Ricardus in silva? Hodie? Sed Ricardus non est Danus. Ille puer elephantum ex musca facit.'

'Ille autem cum Danis erat.'

'Discipulo erranti credis, Pater?' inquit abbas. 'Nonne autem Paulus erat ille discipulus qui frustra filiam Comitis Karoli amabat? Ignoscas mihi sed puer fervidus amore est,' risit abbas. 'Ille Veneris discipulus non Christi esse videtur – eho Magister? Nos ne fabulas eius audiamus, sed tu eum saepius verberes. *Percute puerum tuum virga,* ut dixit sanctus Benedictus, *et liberabis animam eius a morte.* Regula XXVIII.'

'Ut vis, Domine, ut vis. Rumorem tamen ad te referendum esse putavi.'

'Sane, Pater. Ecce, nunc Ricardus adit: eum ipsum interrogemus ... Pater Ricarde, adsis.'

'Semper tibi pareo libens, o Domine...'

Lucia adhuc in trabibus immota omnia, quae homines infra dicebant, audire non poterat. Mox dicere desierunt et Stephanus Ricardusque abierunt.

abi!	*go away!*
advena-ae [f]	*newcomer*
anima-ae [f]	*soul*
claustrum-i [n]	*cloister*
conspiro-are	*conspire, plot*
credo-ere [+dat.]	*believe, trust*
cum ... ambularet	*when he was walking*
despicio-ere	*look down*
dic	*tell*
euntem (iens, euntis)	*going*
fervidus-a-um	*burning, impetuous*
frustra	*in vain, to no avail*
honestus-a-um	*decent, honourable*
immotus-a-um	*stationary*
infra	*below*

libens	*gladly*
musca-ae [f]	*fly*
nuntii-orum [m]	*news*
obstupefactus-a-um	*stupefied*
pareo-ere [+dat.]	*be obedient to*
percutio-ere	*strike, beat*
pueritia-ae [f]	*childhood*
saepius	*more often*
salve	*hello*
salvus-a-um	*safe*
sane	*certainly*
trabs-bis [f]	*beam*
virga-ae [f]	*rod*

Ut and *ne*

Ut with the indicative usually means *as*, or *when*. With the subjunctive **ut** is often used to express a wish or intention (negative **ne**).

Practice (iii)

Pair the Latin sentences with the corresponding English ones:

Cave ne audiant.   *May you be quiet!*

Credo ut intellegam.   *If only you'd be quiet!*

Ne silvam timeas.   *If only he'd believe us!*

Taceas!   *Do not be afraid of the wood.*

Ut nobis credat!   *Careful lest they hear.*

Ut taceas!   *I believe so that I may understand.*

The words which **ut** and **ne** introduce are often part of a larger sentence. The customary English equivalents are *that*, *so that*, or *in order that*:

Monent eum _ut_ nobis credat.	*They advise him to believe us (that he should believe us).*
Monent eum _ne_ abbati credat.	*They advise him not to believe the abbot (that he should not believe the abbot).*
In dumis se celant _ne_ a Danis videantur.	*They hide themselves in the thickets so that they may not be seen by the Danes.*

Sometimes **ut** + subjunctive introduces a result or consequence:

Tam celeriter currebant <u>ut</u> ad ecclesiam ante noctem pervenirent.

They used to run so fast <u>that</u> they would reach the church before nightfall.

Imperfect and pluperfect subjunctive

The three most used tenses are: the present, the imperfect, and the pluperfect.

The imperfect subjunctive is easy to recognize because the stem is the verb's infinitive. The pluperfect has the ordinary stem of the perfect with '**iss**' as part of the ending:

Imperfect subjunctive		
amare	-m	**amarem**
monere	-s	**moneres**
mittere	-t	**mitteret**
audire	-mus	**audiremus**
capere	-tis	**caperetis**
esse	-ent	**essent**

Pluperfect subjunctive		
amav-i	-issem	**amavissem**
monu-i	-isses	**monuisses**
mis-i	-isset	**misisset**
audiv-i	-issemus	**audivissemus**
cep-i	-issetis	**cepissetis**
fu-i	-issent	**fuissent**

It helps to be able to recognize a subjunctive; for instance the meaning of **ut** varies according to whether it's used with the indicative or subjunctive:

...ut credimus   *as we believe*
...ut credamus   *so that we may believe*

For all the forms of the subjunctive, including those of **sum, esse**, see p. 203.

Practice (iv)

Choose the correct form and translate:

(a) **Bibo ut (intellegam/intellego).**

(b) Lucia in stagnum se immersit ut se (celaret/celabit).

(c) Discipuli, ut Stephanus (dicit/dicat), theologiam docentur ut opus Dei (intellegunt/intellegant).

(d) Augustinus nos monuit ut carmina sua (audiremus/ audiemus).

Cum

The preposition **cum** *with* is followed by a noun in the ablative. Cum is also used as a conjunction, meaning *when* (sometimes *since* and occasionally *although*). It is usually followed by a verb in the subjunctive:

Paulus, cum in silva <u>ambularet</u>, monachorum voces audivit.

When Paul was walking in the wood he heard the voices of the monks.

Lucia, cum abbatem in claustro <u>vidisset</u>, attonita erat.

When Lucia had seen the abbot in the cloister she was astonished.

◘ Mulus et plaustrum *The mule and the cart*

Interea Paulus, cum Stephanus ut abbatem quaereret scholam reliquisset, ipse abiit ut Luciam inveniret. Paulus Augustinum et ceteros subvenire volentes ut manerent in schola monuit, ne a Ricardo aut consociis viderentur. Nec multo post Paulus, cum per monasterium solus ambularet, campanas ad monachos in ecclesiam convocandos resonantes audivit. Itaque, cum ipse adesse in ecclesia deberet, furtim e claustro in hortum ibat, ubi mulum plaustro vinctum vidit. 'Io mule, quo nunc vadis? Quo hoc plaustrum trahis? Quid hic habemus?' Deinde Paulus cum in plaustro omnes res quae in ecclesia erant custodiendae conspexisset valde attonitus erat 'Mehercule! Cur haec in plaustro?' murmuravit.

Prope plaustrum erat magna sarcina. 'Eheu!' gemuit ille, 'Vae! Vae! Miserrimum Stephanum!' corpore magistri caesi in sarcina invento. 'Propter me, o Magister, trucidatus es. Ut in schola remansisses!' flebat iuvenis. 'Statim abbati ut omnia referam ibo,' et gemitu in monasterium effugit.

caedo-ere, cecidi, caesum	*kill, cut*
campana-ae [f]	*bell*
consocius-i [m]	*associate*
furtim	*secretly*
miserrimus-a-um	*most wretched*
plaustrum-i [n]	*cart, wagon*
remaneo-ere-si-sum	*remain*
traho-ere	*pull, drag*
trucido-are-avi-atum	*slaughter*
vae	*alas, woe*
valde	*very much*

◘ Living Latin

Friends, Romans ... and family

Of the Roman historians, Tacitus is perhaps the most compelling. His contemporaries tell us he was a lawyer, and a good one (unlike Virgil who could not cope with the forum and retreated to a quieter life of reading and writing). His work is full of rhetorical cleverness, of withering irony interspersed with mischievous asides and occasional blasts of front-on invective.

1 After poisoning his stepbrother, Britannicus, Nero decided it was his mother's turn to die. Agrippina had been instrumental in helping Nero to power, and was almost as ruthless; but she later lost influence over him. First there was a botched job with a collapsing boat, from which she escaped to her villa. Then, after she sent Agerinus to Nero to tell him she had survived an attempt on her life, Nero confirmed her worst suspicions by sending assassins to finish her off.

Cubiculo modicum lumen inerat et ancillarum una, magis ac magis anxia Agrippina quod nemo a filio ac ne Agerinus quidem: aliam fore laetae rei faciem; nunc solitudinem ac repentinos strepitus et extremi mali indicia. Abeunte dehinc ancilla 'tu quoque me deseris' prolocuta respicit Anicetum trierarcho Herculeio et Obarito centurione classiario comitatum: ac, si visendum venisset, refotam renuntiaret, sin facinus patraturus, nihil se de filio credere; non imperatum parricidium. Circumsistunt lectum percussores et prior trierarchus fusti caput eius adflixit. Iam in mortem centurioni ferrum destringenti protendens uterum 'ventrem feri' exclamavit multisque vulneribus confecta est.

(Annals xiv, 8)

The room was dimly lit with only one maid for company. Agrippina became more and more fretful – no news from her son, no sign even of Agerinus. If all were well things would look otherwise; now there was loneliness and a sudden din, which pointed towards extreme danger. Her maid got up to go and she started to speak 'You're leaving me too...' when she saw Anicetus and the commander Herculeius and warrant officer Obaritus. 'If you have come to visit me,' she said, 'you may report that I am recovering. But if you are here to kill me, I believe my son has nothing to do with it – he would not order his mother's death!' The assassins stood round her couch. First the captain hit her on the head with a staff. Then as the lieutenant drew his sword to finish her off, she pointed to her womb and shouted 'Strike here!' After several blows she died.

2 Tacitus' picture of humanity is a desolate grey purpled by the lust of ambition, weakness or cruelty. The story of Octavia is an oasis of human innocence and virtue, and her murder shows to what lengths a cruel tyrant will go. Historians might have given their attention to less melodramatic material, such as the rise or fall in interest rates, achievements of engineering, or social statistics garnered from different corners of the empire – but this never occurred to the writers, or their readers.

Octavia was the sister of Britannicus, and the daughter of the emperor Claudius. She was also Nero's wife. She was murdered in her twentieth year to make way for Nero's mistress, Poppaea.

Restringitur vinclis venaeque eius per omnis artus exolvuntur; et quia pressus pavore sanguis tardius labebatur, praefervidi balnei vapore enecatur. Additurque atrocior saevitia quod caput amputatum latumque in urbem Poppaea vidit.

(Annals xiv, 64)

She was bound and veins in all her limbs were cut; and then because the flow of blood was checked by her panic, she was put in a very hot bath and finished off by its stifling heat. More appalling cruelty was to follow: her severed head was taken to Rome for Poppaea to see.

Revision

1 Change the underlined clauses into ablative absolutes without significantly changing the meaning:

e.g. **Augustinus cum virginem conspexisset diu per fenestram spectabat.**

Answer: **Augustinus virgine conspecta diu per fenestram spectabat.**

(a) **Mulus cum sarcinas omnes vidisset gemuit.**
(b) **Paulus cum Ricardum audivisset in monasterium festinavit.**
(c) **Stephanus cum corpus amici sepelivisset in ecclesiam abiit.**
(d) **Coquus cum cibum devoravisset in silvam ambulavit.**

2 Translate into Latin:

(a) May they capture all the Danes!
(b) May the abbot not see your book of poems, Augustine!
(c) Drink the wine, friends! May everyone drink the wine!
(d) The abbot advised him to leave the monastery (that he should leave – **ut** + *imperfect subjunctive*).

3 Write out the:

(a) present tense of **gaudeo-ere;**
(b) future tense of **scribo-ere;**
(c) present subjunctive of **laudo-are.**

17 peior quam diabolus

worse than the devil

In this unit you will learn about
- more passive forms
- deponent verbs
- *more* and *most*

- and find out more about the philosopher Boethius

More passive forms

The third persons of the present, future and imperfect passive have **-ur** added to the active ending. Other passive forms are on pp. 201–2.

Practice (i)

Identify the corresponding *passive* form of the bracketed verb and translate:

(a) Me felicem!
a mea domina (laudo).

(b) A virgine in
trabibus sedente (audimus).

(c) O sceleste puer, a magistro
(castigabis).

Deponent verbs: passive verbs with active meanings

There are quite a large number of verbs which have passive endings, but are active in meaning. These are called 'deponent' verbs. In this list of some of the more common deponent verbs, note the three principal parts, not four, as the past participle is part of the perfect form:

Present	Infinitive	Perfect
sequor *I follow*	**sequi** *to follow*	**secutus-a sum** *I (have) followed*
loquor *I speak*	**loqui** *to speak*	**locutus-a sum** *I (have) spoke(n)*
progredior *I advance*	**progredi** *to advance*	**progressus-a sum** *I (have) advanced*
miror *I admire, wonder at*	**mirari** *to admire*	**miratus-a sum** *I (have) admired*

These verbs should be translated like active ones, despite their passive endings.

Practice (ii)

Identify the correct form of the verb in the tense as directed, and translate:

(a) Lucia Ricardum in
monasterium (sequor,
sequi, secutus sum).
perfect

(b) Omnes homines mea
carmina (miror, mirari,
miratus sum).
future

Their passive form but active meaning extends to past participles:

| **secutus-a-um** | *having followed* | <u>not</u> *having been followed* |
| **miratus-a-um** | *having admired* | <u>not</u> *having been admired* |

But gerundives of deponent verbs remain passive, like other verbs:

| **sequendus-a-um** | *to-be-followed* |
| **mirandus-a-um** | *to-be-admired* |

▶ Gravis in discipulo stupor *The pupil is out of his mind*

Shared endings key

-or   third declension nominative: stupor, amor, etc.
         passive first person *('I ...')*

Paulus igitur, Lucia in trabibus adhuc celata, in claustrum irruit ut abbatem quaereret, 'Pater, Pater,' exanimatus clamans, 'Pater Abba!' Lucia vocem eius audire poterat et anxia erat.

'Quid est tibi, puer?' rogavit abbas.

'Stephanus est mortuus.'

'Deliras.'

'Sincerus vero loquor!'

'O stulte puer! Cur semper vanis de somniis loqueris? Sed tibi iam pro certo dico: Pater Stephanus nuper abiit et in ecclesiam ingressus est. Patrem Ricardum ceterosque in ecclesiam ad vesperas parandas sequebatur.'

'Ricardum?'

'Ita vero.'

'Pater, si tibi placet, e fenestro specta ut sarcinam videas quae corpus Stephani continet – in pace requiescat.'

'Nullam sarcinam videre possum.'

'Sequere me, Pater, ut eam ipse videas.'

Haud multo post duo homines redierunt Paulo dicente, 'Crede mihi, o Domine, corpus Stephani illa in sarcina fuerat!'

'Iam satis rumorum. Hoc tempore nos in ecclesia, ut vesperas dicamus, adesse debemus. Tu, o puer, amore es captus. Ah, ecce, Pater Ricarde,' inquit abbas adeunte Ricardo. 'Pater Ricarde, gravis in hoc discipulo stupor esse videtur; itaque ad medicum statim est ducendus.'

'Libenter eum ducam, mi Domine,' respondit Ricardus.

'Immo! vera dico,' clamavit Paulus.

'Puer sane est inops animi.'

Subito saeviens, furiosissima, exanimataque, irruit Lucia.

---

contineo-ere	*contain, hold*
deliro-are-avi	*be silly, insane*
exanimatus-a-um	*breathless*
haud	*not*
ingredior-i, ingressus sum	*enter*
inops animi	*out of his mind*

libenter	gladly
medicus-i [m]	doctor
nuper	recently
pro certo	for certain
saevio-ire	rage
sequere	follow!
somnium-i [n]	dream, fantasy
stultus-a-um	foolish
stupor-is [m]	senselessness
vanus-a-um	empty, false

Comparative adjectives: 'more ...'

An adjective qualifies a noun. Sometimes an adjective is used to make a comparison between two nouns: 'the dog is <u>bigger</u> than the cat'. This form of an adjective is called the comparative, and the English adjective either ends '-er' (big<u>ger</u>) or is preceded by 'more' – 'Latin is <u>more exciting</u> than space travel'. The Latin equivalent of the comparative form has the syllable **'ior'** in most endings. See **maior** on p. 198 for all the forms. The Latin for 'than' is **quam**.

Practice (iii)

1 Match legends to pictures and translate:

(a) Ancilla furiosior quam monachus est.

(b) Discipuli ignaviores quam ancilla sunt.

(c) Abbatissa sanctior quam milites est.

(d) Equus celerior quam mulus est.

2 With **quam**, the two things compared are always in the same case. Sometimes the ablative is used for the second element, without **quam**: e.g. **Ancilla furiosior monacho est**. Rewrite (b), (c) and (d) above, using the ablative and without using **quam**.

Superlative adjectives: 'most ...'

The comparative form of Latin adjectives means 'more...' or occasionally 'quite...', 'rather...'. The comparative deals with a comparison between <u>two</u> things: 'My dog is bigger than yours'. The superlative is for three or more: 'My dog is the <u>biggest</u> in the street'. The English adjective either ends '-est', or is preceded by 'most': 'That film was the <u>most exciting</u> I have ever seen.' The Latin equivalent is easily detected, for most superlative forms have the ending **-issimus-a-um** attached to the simple adjective:

	Comparative (of two)	Superlative (of three or more)
furios-us	**furios-ior**	**furios-issimus**
furious	*more furious*	*most/very furious*

Practice (iv)

1 Identify the correct forms of the superlative of each of the adjectives and translate:

(a) **Abbas-ne (sanctus-a-um) ex omnibus monachis est?**
(b) **Benedicti unguenta (suavis-e) sunt.**
(c) **Filia Karoli in terra (bellus-a-um) est.**

2 Here are some irregular ones. See how many gaps you can fill:

Meaning	Adjective	Comparative	Superlative	Derivative
good		**melior**	**optimus-a-um**	
	malus	**peior**		pessimist
great, large		**maior**		maximum
small	**parvus**	**minor**		minimum

▶ Puer turpissimus! *The boy is quite scandalous!*

> **Shared endings key**
>
> **-or** third declension nominative : pudor, amor, etc.
> passive first person ('*I.....*')
> **Comparative form of an adjective: sanctior**

'Domina Lucia? Quid tibi est in hoc loco?' rogavit abbas e solio surgens.

'Ille est peior quam diabolus!' exclamavit illa, gestu in Paulum attonitum furiosissimo.

'Si vis, o virgo, placidior sis,' inquit abbas.

'Semper mihi versus lascivos mittit. Tacere volui sed me pudor vetat.'

'Versus? Cuius versus?'

'Catulli carmina amatoria.'

'Catulli? In hac ecclesia? Quid dicis, puer?'

'Immo, numquam huic virgini versus Catulli misi,' inquit Paulus iam ipse anxius.

'Ecce liber,' inquit virgo, simul et abbati librum quem ex Augustino petiverat tradens. Tum ore Pauli manu percusso, 'Ille,' inquit Lucia, 'est scelestus et turpissimus!'

'Mea carissima, desiste,' inquit abbas, mollire eam conans.

'Ignoscas mi, Pater Abba!' et illa flere incepit.

'Crimina, o puer, audivisti. Quid dices?' Iam plurimi monachi aderant.

'Nescio, Domine, nescio.'

'Tu ergo poenas valde dabis, miserrime!' et Paulo secundum ictum dedit.

'Desiste, Pater Abba!' exclamavit Lucia.

'Rogas ut desistam? Ille tamen castigari debet!'

'Certe poenas dabit, sed Comes Karolus ipse iudicare vult. Reus ad castellum statim in vinclis ducendus.'

'Illum videre volet Comes Karolus?'

'Certe. Ille filiam suam curat.'

'Esto,' inquit abbas, 'Peregrini quidam hodie monasterium relinquent qui vos ad castellum comitentur,' sic locutus librum Augustini in ignem iniecit. Deinde cum monachi reum deduxissent, omnibus praeter se ipsum atque Ricardum digressis, 'Impera ut puerum virginemque trucident,' susurravit abbas.

castigari	to be punished
comitor-ari	accompany
conor-ari-atus sum	try, attempt
crimen-inis [n]	charge, crime
cuius	whose
digredior-i, digressus sum	depart
esto	so be it
gestus-us [m]	gesture
ictus-us [m]	blow
ignis-is [m]	fire
impero-are	order, instruct
inicio-ere, inieci, iniectum	throw in
iudico-are	try, adjudicate
lascivus-a-um	wanton
miserrimus-a-um	very wretched
mollio-ire	soften, calm
placidus-a-um	calm
plurimi	several
pudor-is [m]	shame
quem	which
reus-i [m]	defendant
secundus-a-um	second
solium-i [n]	seat
surgo-ere	rise
suus-a-um	his/her/their own
veto-are	forbid
vinclum-i [n]	chain

▶ Living Latin

The Consolation of Philosophy

Boethius (c.480–524) has been described as the last of the Roman philosophers and the first of the scholastic theologians.

In more senses than one his life represents something of a gateway, a passing point between the two worlds of ancient Rome and medieval Europe, between philosophical fatalism and Christian promise, between Roman pluralism and the one God. He was among the last of the Stoics and first of the martyrs.

A statesman and philosopher under the emperor Theodoric, Boethius fell from favour, was wrongly condemned and imprisoned in Pavia, where he wrote *The Consolation of Philosophy*. The central figure of the *Consolation* is the 'Lady Philosophy', a pagan presence in a Christian world. She visits his cell and encourages him to look beyond his immediate suffering and to recognize the manipulations of Fortuna, for whose fair-weather charms she urges caution.

The Stoics shared with Christians an inclination to confront life's hardships without demur, but viewed the causes of their suffering differently. Fortuna was a hazard of life, who had to be tolerated; she was the most worshipped deity in the ancient world. Christians, on the other hand, were inspired by an omniscient and benign God, and Boethius – a born Christian but with the education of a Stoic – wrestles with the reconciliation of human suffering and divine goodness. His *Consolation* was one of the most prized and influential books of the middle ages, and was translated into English by Alfred the Great some three hundred years later. Boethius died under torture in prison.

1 Philosophy reaches Boethius' cell to find him writing poetry under the influence of the Muses, whom she immediately dismisses:

*Quis has scenicas meretriculas ad hunc aegrum permisit accedere quae dolores eius non modo nullis remediis foverent, verum dulcibus insuper alerent venenis?

Who let these thespian tarts visit this sick fellow? They have no treatment for his condition – only sweet poisons to make it worse.

2 She asks the nature of his complaint:

*Si operam medicantis exspectas, oportet vulnus detegas.

If you wish to have the attention of a doctor, then you must lay bare your wound.

3 Boethius says he has been a good philosopher-politician.

*Haecine praemia referimus tibi obsequentes? Atqui tu hanc sententiam Platonis ore sanxisti: beatas fore res publicas, si eas vel studiosi sapientiae regerent vel earum rectores studere sapientiae contigisset. Tu eiusdem viri ore hanc sapientibus capessendae rei publicae necessariam causam esse monuisti, ne improbis flagitiosisque civibus urbium relicta gubernacula pestem bonis ac perniciem ferrent.

Are these the rewards we earn for our loyalty to you? After all it was your idea you put into the mouth of Plato: that those political states which were ruled by philosophers – or by kings who had experience of studying philosophy – would be happy. Through the same man you said there was an inevitable case for a republic to be guided by philosophers, to prevent the business of government falling into the hands of unprincipled and wicked characters which would bring ruin and destruction upon good people.

4 Boethius cannot understand how evil can succeed.

*Non ita sensus nostros maeror hebetavit ut impios scelerata contra virtutem querar molitos, sed quae speraverint effecisse vehementer admiror. Nam deteriora velle nostri fuerit fortasse defectus, posse contra innocentiam, quae sceleratus quisque conceperit inspectante deo, monstri simile est.

(i, 1–4)

My grief has not so blunted my senses that I should complain about those no-good sorts who try to topple virtue with their wicked schemes, but that they should have succeeded in their ambitions is frankly a shock. For we all have it in us to be less than perfect, but in full view of God, the wicked overcoming innocence? – it's appalling.

5 Philosophy says Boethius has mistakenly courted Fortuna:

*Fortunae te regendum dedisti; dominae moribus oportet obtemperes. Tu vero volventis rotae impetum retinere conaris?

(ii, 1)

You allowed yourself to be ruled by Fortuna; so your mistress's ways must be accommodated. Are you really going to try to stop the momentum of her turning wheel?

*post-classical

Revision

1 Change each underlined verb into the perfect tense, and translate:

   (a) Discipuli Danos in silvam <u>sequuntur</u>.
   (b) Lucia in ecclesiam <u>progreditur</u>.
   (c) In silva <u>loquimur</u>.
   (d) Augustinus filiam comitis <u>miratur</u>.

2 Change each underlined verb into the present tense, and translate:

   (a) Lucia peregrinos in monasterium <u>secuta est</u>.
   (b) De gravissimis rebus <u>locutus sum</u>.
   (c) Peregrini in silva conspirantes <u>visi sunt</u>.
   (d) Augustini-ne carmen <u>miratus es</u>?

3 Translate into Latin:

   (a) Are horses lazier than mules?
   (b) Is Augustine the best student?
   (c) Paul, have you ever seen a holier abbess?
   (d) Richard was more cruel than the Danes themselves.

18

versus Catulli combusti sunt!

the verses of Catullus have been incinerated!

In this unit you will learn about
- 'if' clauses
- direct and reported speech

- and find out more about the story of Dido and Aeneas

'If' clauses

The Latin for 'if' is **si** ('if...not': **nisi**). For something which could happen (or have happened) as easily as not, the verb is in the indicative:

Si e monasterio effugiemus, ad castellum ibimus.	*If we escape from the monastery, we will go to the castle.*
Si haec putas, stultus es.	*If you think this, you are foolish.*
Si haec putavisti, stultus fuisti.	*If you thought this, you were foolish.*

For a more remote possibility, or for musing on what-might-have-been, the subjunctive is used:

Stephanus, si viveret, nobis subveniret.	*If Stephen were alive (now), he would be helping us.*
Si in Hispaniam ambules, stultus sis.	*If you were to walk to Spain, you'd be a fool.*
Si Benedictum vidisses, risisses.	*If you had seen Benedict, you would have laughed.*

Practice (i)

Match pictures to sentences, and translate:

(a) **Si mulus opulentus esset, plaustra non traheret.**

(b) **Si effugere conabitur, eum occide!**

(c) **Si magister in schola mansisset, nunc viveret.**

(d) **Si bellus esses, te amarem.**

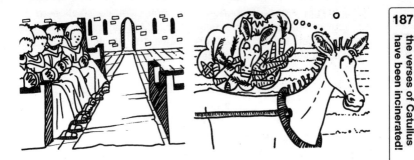

▶ Vale Augustine! *Farewell, Augustinus!*

Augustinus ad cellam in qua Paulus erat vinctus furtim adiit. 'Psst, Paule,' susurravit amicus, 'adsum ego. Si fortuna tibi favebit mox eris liber!'

'Augustine!'

'St; ne custodes excites. Tandem Lucia librum meum accepit. Me-ne quoque amat? Quid putas? Si antea cognovissem, iam rivalis tuus essem. Donum, quod Luciae dedi, erat solum exemplar Catulli.'

'Eheu, malos tibi nuntios refero,' susurravit Paulus.

'Quid dicis?'

'Liber ille est combustus.'

'Catulli liber?'

'Ita vero.'

'Combustus? A quo? Num Lucia versus Catulli delevit?'

'Abbas librum in ignem iniecit.'

'Non ita.'

'Vero.'

'Vae! Vae! Me miserrimum!' magna voce gemuit Augustinus.

'Taceas, ne custodes veniant.'

'Illi erant soli Catulli versus in bibliotheca, in monasterio, in terra! Quid agam?'

'Si potes omnes versus eius revocare, alium librum exscribas. Nunc mi ignoscas, amice, sed ego maiore in periculo sum quam tu.'

'Quid? Vero. Dico tibi, Paule: tu es fortunatus.'

'Vero? Num felix in vinclis?'

'Ecce, accipe hunc librum.'

'Alium librum?'

'De Philosophiae Consolatione.'

'O Augustine, quid agis? Boethius, cum Consolationem scripsisset, in vinclis trucidatus est. Ego non consolationem sed auxilium desidero!'

'Si librum leges,' respondit Augustinus, 'et consolationem et auxilium invenies. Lucia consilium cepit. Mox te iuvabit in teneris dominae iacere lacertis. Vale Paule,' inquit Augustinus librum, in quo Lucia epistulam scripserat, tradens.

'Vale amice.'

a quo	*by whom*
antea	*beforehand*
auxilium-i [n]	*help*
cognosco-ere-ovi	*discover*
combustus-a-um	*incinerated*
consilium-i [n]	*plan*
consolatio-nis [f]	*consolation*
deleo-ere-evi-etum	*destroy*
donum-i [n]	*gift*
excito-are	*wake, arouse*
exemplar-is [n]	*copy*
faveo-ere [+dat.]	*favour*
felix	*fortunate, happy*
iuvabit	*it will please, delight*
lacertus-i [m]	*arm*
liber-a-um	*free*
periculum-i [n]	*danger*
revoco-are	*recall*
rivalis-is [m]	*rival, competitor*
tener-a-um	*tender*

Direct and reported speech

An author can use direct speech (*"..."*) to show what his characters say. However, it is far more common in Latin for the words of a character to be expressed indirectly, with the help of a construction called the 'accusative and infinitive'. This gives us not the exact words spoken, but a report of what was said:

Dixit Paulum vivere.   *She said Paul to be alive (that Paul was...).*

The accusative (**Paulum**) is the subject, and the infinitive (**vivere**) the verb, of the original statement: **"Paulus vivit"**, what she or he actually said.

The accusative and infinitive is used for reported thoughts as well as spoken words:

| **Paulus credidit Stephanum pium sed abbatem scelestum esse.** | *Paul believed Stephen to be pious but the abbot wicked (that Stephen was...).* |

You will meet this construction all the time in Latin texts. If, however, the reported words are a question rather than statement, then a question word (e.g. **quid, cur**) is used with a verb in the subjunctive:

| **Virgo rogavit cur in stagno natarem.** | *The maiden asked why I was swimming in the pond.* |
| **Nescio quid sit amor.** | *I do not know what love is.* |

If the reported words are a command or piece of advice, then **ut** is used with the subjunctive (negative **ne**):

| **Abbas nobis imperavit ne scholam relinqueremus.** | *The abbot ordered us not to leave the school.* |
| **Paulus virginem monuit ut in stagno se celaret.** | *Paul advised the maiden to hide in the pond.* |

Practice (ii)

1 Write down the actual words or thoughts:

e.g. Dixit Paulum vivere.
    'Paulus vivit.'

(a) Paulus credidit Stephanum pium esse.
(b) Augustinus dixit abbatem scelestum esse.
(c) Stephanus discipulis imperavit ut in monasterium festinarent.
(d) Virgo rogat ubi peregrini sint.

2 Complete the sentences reporting what was said:

(a) 'Scelestus puer poenas dare debet.'
    Abbas dixit _____.
(b) 'Corpus magistri in sarcina est.'
    Paulus abbati dicit _____.
(c) 'Ubi sunt versus Catulli?'
    Augustinus rogat ubi _____.

▶ In antro *In the cave*

Eodem igitur die ad castellum septem Dani et Lucia et Paulus et mulus, qui plaustrum trahebat, e monasterio profecti sunt. Mox, cum omnes obscuram per silvam iter facerent, Paulus vinctus plaustrum sequens 'Io mule, lente, lente!' susurrare incepit. Unus Danorum anxius perturbatusque 'Sst, puer!' inquit, arbores umbrasque circumspiciens. Subito exclamavit Lucia 'Ecce aliquis in arboribus! Illum-ne vidistis?'

'Ubi?' respondit unus ex Danis.

'Credo alios pravos in animo habere illum liberare,' inquit virgo, cui alius se videre nihil posse respondit. Tertius socios rogavit ut festinarent dicens 'Silvam hanc non amo'.

'Vos hic remanete dum illos quaero,' inquit virgo.

'Immo vero! Absit ut nos relinquas.' Omnes Luciam obsecrabant ut maneret; quae tamen, equo citato, mediam in silvam evanuit. Ceteris diu moratis, stridens ex arboribus per auras sagitta plaustro adhaesit. Dani, cum se opprimi vidissent, attoniti paulisper ex equis descenderunt et se in dumis celaverunt. Deinde illum, qui Paulum custodiebat, gladio stricto ut captivum trucidaret, alia sagitta per auras stridens transfixit. Inde Paulus gladio Dani vulnerati rapto se liberavit et 'Io! Io!' magna voce equos Danorum adeo terruit ut non solum illi sed etiam mulus ipse quam celerrime densas in arbores effugerint.

'Vae! Plaustrum, plaustrum!' gemuit quidam et e latebra desiluit ut mulum sisteret; frustra. Mulus iam mediam in silvam abierat secum plaustrum atque praedam Danorum trahens. 'Et ubi est noster captivus?' rogavit alius. Dani tamen animis collectis Paulum nusquam invenire poterant.

Interea Lucia et Paulus mediam per silvam iter faciebant, et tandem defessa pluviaque madida 'Ohe caballe, ohe caballe!' inquit Lucia. 'Ecce antrum!'

'Hoc antea numquam vidi,' inquit Paulus ex equo descendens. In antro Paulus aquam e facie virginis tergens 'Tu es mirabilis,' susurravit, 'Bellissima Lucia, te amo.'

'Ergo da mi basia.'

'Quidquid imperas, labor est suavis.'

'Impero ut taceas.'

Nec multo post tumultu excitati e spelunca furtim exierunt ut quis adesset cognoscerent. Primo nihil viderunt; deinde conspexerunt Lucia atque Paulus plaustrum et res omnes, quas Dani ex ecclesia rapuerant, et placidum sub arboribus pascentem mulum.

absit ut [medieval]	*far be it that*
adeo	*so much, to such an extent*
antea	*before*
antrum-i [n]	*cave*
captivus-i [m]	*prisoner*
colligo-ere-egi-ectum	*recover*
cui	*to whom*
desilio-ire-ui	*leap out*

dum	*while*
effugerint [perf. subj.]	*(they) fled*
eodem [abl.]	*same*
evanesco-ere, evanui	*disappear*
gladius-i [m]	*sword*
latebra-ae [f]	*hiding-place*
madidus-a-um	*soaked*
moror-ari-atus	*delay, wait*
nusquam	*nowhere*
obsecro-are	*implore*
ohe!	*whoa!*
opprimi [passive infin.]	*to be attacked*
pascor-i	*graze, eat*
paulisper	*a little while*
pluvia-ae [f]	*rain*
praeda-ae [f]	*loot*
pravus-a-um	*wicked*
proficiscor-i, profectus	*set out*
quam celerrime	*as quickly as possible*
quas [acc.f. pl.]	*which*
quidquid	*whatever*
septem	*seven*
sisto-ere	*stop*
spelunca-ae [f]	*cave*
stringo-ere-nxi-ctum	*draw (sword)*
tergo-ere	*wipe*
terreo-ere-ui-itum	*frighten*
tertius-a-um	*third*
vulnero-are-avi-atum	*wound*

▶ Living Latin

Love in the rain

1 The story of Dido and Aeneas is one of the most celebrated in literature. Aeneas lands in north Africa, a fugitive from Troy, and is looked after by the queen of Carthage, Dido, who falls in love with him. During his stay, she and her fellow Carthaginians entertain Aeneas and his Trojans to a hunt in the forest.

> **Tandem progreditur magna stipante caterva**
> **Sidoniam picto chlamydem circumdata limbo;**
> **cui pharetra ex auro, crines nodantur in aurum,**
> **aurea purpuream subnectit fibula vestem.**

Nec non et Phrygii comites et laetus Iulus
incedunt. Ipse ante alios pulcherrimus omnis
infert se socium Aeneas atque agmina iungit.

Now at last Dido steps out, a great throng all around her. She
wears a Sidonian habit with a colourful hem, and a quiver of gold
and her hair tied back in a golden pin, and gold is the brooch
which fastens her purple cloak. There too come the Trojans, and
cheerful Iulus. Aeneas himself, the most handsome of all, rides up
to her side and brings the two parties together.

2 A thunderstorm brings Dido and Aeneas alone together.

Interea magno misceri murmure caelum
incipit, insequitur commixta grandine nimbus.
Et Tyrii comites passim et Troiana iuventus
Dardaniusque nepos Veneris diversa per agros
tecta metu petiere; ruunt de montibus amnes.
Speluncam Dido dux et Troianus eandem
deveniunt. Prima et Tellus et pronuba Iuno
dant signum; fulsere ignes et conscius aether
conubiis, summoque ulularunt vertice Nymphae.

(Aeneid iv, 136–42, 160–8)

Before long there was a loud rumbling in the sky, and there
followed a downpour of rain with hailstones. The young men of
Troy and their Carthaginian friends and he of Dardan's line,
grandson of Venus, all scattered helter-skelter across the fields in
fright, looking for cover, while torrents of water sweep down from
the hill-tops. Dido and Aeneas, the prince of Troy, happen upon
the same cave. Mother Earth – she's first – and Juno in nuptial
attendance give the signal; lightning flickers, heaven witnesses
their coupling, and on peak-tops the Nymphs wail in ecstasy.

Revision

1 Rewrite these sentences making the underlined words plural,
and translate:

(a) Si <u>ille discipulus</u> Danos non timeret, stultus esset.
(b) Stephanus <u>mihi</u> dixit cucullum monachum non facere.
(c) Qui ab <u>amico</u> amatur est felix.
(d) <u>Monachus</u>, si avaritia non movetur, laudandus est.

2 Translate:

(a) I believe that Augustine is a good friend to Paul.
(b) Stephen, if you find (*use the future*) Richard, ask (*imperative*) him to come (*pres. subj.*) to the cloister.
(c) The students say that Lucia is the most beautiful of all the maidens.
(d) Surely we do not believe that the daughter of the count loves the humble student?

Reference tables

Nouns: five declensions

	First declension		Second declension		
	wood	*mule*	*master*	*boy*	*wine*
	Singular		**Singular**		
nom.	silva	mulus	magister	puer	vinum [n]
acc.	silvam	mulum	magistrum	puerum	vinum
gen.	silvae	muli	magistri	pueri	vini
dat.	silvae	mulo	magistro	puero	vino
abl.	silva	mulo	magistro	puero	vino
	Plural		**Plural**		
nom.	silvae	muli	magistri	pueri	vina
acc.	silvas	mulos	magistros	pueros	vina
gen.	silvarum	mulorum	magistrorum	puerorum	vinorum
dat.	silvis	mulis	magistris	pueris	vinis
abl.	silvis	mulis	magistris	pueris	vinis

Nouns: five declensions – *continued*

Third declension

	father	*abbot*	*maiden*	*song, poem*	*time*
			Singular		
nom.	pater	abbas	virgo	carmen [n]	tempus [n]
acc.	patrem	abbatem	virginem	carmen	tempus
gen.	patris	abbatis	virginis	carminis	temporis
dat.	patri	abbati	virgini	carmini	tempori
abl.	patre	abbate	virgine	carmine	tempore
			Plural		
nom.	patres	abbates	virgines	carmina	tempora
acc.	patres	abbates	virgines	carmina	tempora
gen.	patrum	abbatum	virginum	carminum	temporum
dat.	patribus	abbatibus	virginibus	carminibus	temporibus
abl.	patribus	abbatibus	virginibus	carminibus	temporibus

Fourth declension

	bow	*hand*
	Singular	
nom.	arcus	manus
acc.	arcum	manum
gen.	arcus	manus
dat.	arcui	manu
abl.	arcu	manu
	Plural	
nom.	arcus	manus
acc.	arcus	manus
gen.	arcuum	manuum
dat.	arcibus	manibus
abl.	arcibus	manibus

Fifth declension

	thing
	Singular
nom.	res
acc.	rem
gen.	rei
dat.	rei
abl.	re
	Plural
nom.	res
acc.	res
gen.	rerum
dat.	rebus
abl.	rebus

Pronouns

	I/me	you (s.)	we/us	you (pl.)	himself, herself, themselves
nom.	ego	tu	nos	vos	—
acc.	me	te	nos	vos	se
gen.	mei	tui	nostri/ nostrum	vestri/ vestrum	sui
dat.	mihi	tibi	nobis	vobis	sibi
abl.	me	te	nobis	vobis	se

Singular
this, he, she, it

	masculine	feminine	neuter
nom.	hic	haec	hoc
acc.	hunc	hanc	hoc
gen.	huius	huius	huius
dat.	huic	huic	huic
abl.	hoc	hac	hoc

Plural
these, they, them

	masculine	feminine	neuter
nom.	hi	hae	haec
acc.	hos	has	haec
gen.	horum	harum	horum
dat.	his	his	his
abl.	his	his	his

Singular
that, he, she, it

	masculine	feminine	neuter
nom.	ille	illa	illud
acc.	illum	illam	illud
gen.	illius	illius	illius
dat.	illi	illi	illi
abl.	illo	illa	illo

Plural
those, they, them

	masculine	feminine	neuter
nom.	illi	illae	illa
acc.	illos	illas	illa
gen.	illorum	illarum	illorum
dat.	illis	illis	illis
abl.	illis	illis	illis

Pronouns – *continued*

	Singular			Plural		
	that, he, she, it			*those, they, them*		
nom.	is	ea	id	ei	eae	ea
acc.	eum	eam	id	eos	eas	ea
gen.	eius	eius	eius	eorum	earum	eorum
dat.	ei	ei	ei	eis	eis	eis
abl.	eo	ea	eo	eis	eis	eis

who, which

	Singular			Plural		
nom.	qui	quae	quod	qui	quae	quae
acc.	quem	quam	quod	quos	quas	quae
gen.	cuius	cuius	cuius	quorum	quarum	quorum
dat.	cui	cui	cui	quibus	quibus	quibus
abl.	quo	qua	quo	quibus	quibus	quibus

	Singular			Plural		
	he himself, she herself, itself			*they themselves*		
nom.	ipse	ipsa	ipsum	ipsi	ipsae	ipsa
acc.	ipsum	ipsam	ipsum	ipsos	ipsas	ipsa
gen.	ipsius	ipsius	ipsius	ipsorum	ipsarum	ipsorum
dat.	ipsi	ipsi	ipsi	ipsis	ipsis	ipsis
abl.	ipso	ipsa	ipso	ipsis	ipsis	ipsis

Adjectives

sanctus-a-um: blessed, saintly

Singular

	masc.	fem.	neut.
nom.	sanctus	sancta	sanctum
acc.	sanctum	sanctam	sanctum
gen.	sancti	sanctae	sancti
dat.	sancto	sanctae	sancto
abl.	sancto	sancta	sancto

Plural

	masc.	fem.	neut.
nom.	sancti	sanctae	sancta
acc.	sanctos	sanctas	sancta
gen.	sanctorum	sanctarum	sanctorum
dat.	sanctis	sanctis	sanctis
abl.	sanctis	sanctis	sanctis

omnis: all, every

Singular

	masc./fem.	neut.
nom.	omnis	omne
acc.	omnem	omne
gen.	omnis	omnis
dat.	omni	omni
abl.	omni	omni

Plural

	masc./fem.	neut.
nom.	omnes	omnia
acc.	omnes	omnia
gen.	omnium	omnium
dat.	omnibus	omnibus
abl.	omnibus	omnibus

prudens: wise

Singular

	masc./fem.	neut.
nom.	prudens	prudens
acc.	prudentem	prudens
gen.	prudentis	prudentis
dat.	prudenti	prudenti
abl.	prudenti	prudenti

Plural

	masc./fem.	neut.
nom.	prudentes	prudentia
acc.	prudentes	prudentia
gen.	prudentium	prudentium
dat.	prudentibus	prudentibus
abl.	prudentibus	prudentibus

maior: greater

Singular

	masc./fem.	neut.
nom.	maior	maius
acc.	maiorem	maius
gen.	maioris	maioris
dat.	maiori	maiori
abl.	maiore	maiore

Plural

	masc./fem.	neut.
nom.	maiores	maiora
acc.	maiores	maiora
gen.	maiorum	maiorum
dat.	maioribus	maioribus
abl.	maioribus	maioribus

Regular verbs: indicative active

amare *to love*	monere *to warn*	mittere *to send*	capere *to capture*	audire *to hear*
		Present		
amo	moneo	mitto	capio	audio
amas	mones	mittis	capis	audis
amat	monet	mittit	capit	audit
amamus	monemus	mittimus	capimus	audimus
amatis	monetis	mittitis	capitis	auditis
amant	monent	mittunt	capiunt	audiunt
		Future		
amabo	monebo	mittam	capiam	audiam
amabis	monebis	mittes	capies	audies
amabit	monebit	mittet	capiet	audiet
amabimus	monebimus	mittemus	capiemus	audiemus
amabitis	monebitis	mittetis	capietis	audietis
amabunt	monebunt	mittent	capient	audient
		Imperfect		
amabam	monebam	mittebam	capiebam	audiebam
amabas	monebas	mittebas	capiebas	audiebas
amabat	monebat	mittebat	capiebat	audiebat
amabamus	monebamus	mittebamus	capiebamus	audiebamus
amabatis	monebatis	mittebatis	capiebatis	audiebatis
amabant	monebant	mittebant	capiebant	audiebant

Regular verbs: indicative active – *continued*

amare *to love*	monere *to warn*	mittere *to send*	capere *to capture*	audire *to hear*
		Perfect		
amavi	monui	misi	cepi	audivi
amavisti	monuisti	misisti	cepisti	audivisti
amavit	monuit	misit	cepit	audivit
amavimus	monuimus	misimus	cepimus	audivimus
amavistis	monuistis	misistis	cepistis	audivistis
amaverunt	monuerunt	miserunt	ceperunt	audiverunt
		Pluperfect		
amaveram	monueram	miseram	ceperam	audiveram
amaveras	monueras	miseras	ceperas	audiveras
amaverat	monuerat	miserat	ceperat	audiverat
amaveramus	monueramus	miseramus	ceperamus	audiveramus
amaveratis	monueratis	miseratis	ceperatis	audiveratis
amaverant	monuerant	miserant	ceperant	audiverant

Regular verbs: indicative passive

Present

amor	moneor	mittor
amaris	moneris	mitteris
amatur	monetur	mittitur
amamur	monemur	mittimur
amamini	monemini	mittimini
amantur	monentur	mittuntur

audior
audiris
auditur
audimur
audimini
audiuntur

Future

amabor	monebor	mittar
amaberis	moneberis	mitteris
amabitur	monebitur	mittetur
amabimur	monebimur	mittemur
amabimini	monebimini	mittemini
amabuntur	monebuntur	mittentur

capior
caperis
capitur
capimur
capimini
capiuntur

capiar
capieris
capietur
capiemur
capiemini
capientur

audiar
audieris
audietur
audiemur
audiemini
audientur

Imperfect

amabar	monebar	mittebar
amabaris	monebaris	mittebaris
amabatur	monebatur	mittebatur
amabamur	monebamur	mittebamur
amabamini	monebamini	mittebamini
amabantur	monebantur	mittebantur

capiebar
capiebaris
capiebatur
capiebamur
capiebamini
capiebantur

audiebar
audiebaris
audiebatur
audiebamur
audiebamini
audiebantur

Regular verbs: indicative passive – *continued*

		Perfect	
amatus sum	monitus sum	missus sum	captus sum	auditus sum
amatus es	monitus es	missus es	captus es	auditus es
amatus est	monitus est	missus est	captus est	auditus est
amati sumus	moniti sumus	missi sumus	capti sumus	auditi sumus
amati estis	moniti estis	missi estis	capti estis	auditi estis
amati sunt	moniti sunt	missi sunt	capti sunt	auditi sunt

		Pluperfect		
amatus eram	monitus eram	missus eram	captus eram	auditus eram
amatus eras	monitus eras	missus eras	captus eras	auditus eras
amatus erat	monitus erat	missus erat	captus erat	auditus erat
amati eramus	moniti eramus	missi eramus	capti eramus	auditi eramus
amati eratis	moniti eratis	missi eratis	capti eratis	auditi eratis
amati erant	moniti erant	missi erant	capti erant	auditi erant

Verbs: subjunctive (active)

Present

amem	moneam	mittam	capiam	audiam	sim (esse)
ames	moneas	mittas	capias	audias	sis
amet	moneat	mittat	capiat	audiat	sit
amemus	moneamus	mittamus	capiamus	audiamus	simus
ametis	moneatis	mittatis	capiatis	audiatis	sitis
ament	moneant	mittant	capiant	audiant	sint

Imperfect

amarem	monerem	mitterem	caperem	audirem	essem
amares	moneres	mitteres	caperes	audires	esses
amaret	moneret	mitteret	caperet	audiret	esset
amaremus	moneremus	mitteremus	caperemus	audiremus	essemus
amaretis	moneretis	mitteretis	caperetis	audiretis	essetis
amarent	monerent	mitterent	caperent	audirent	essent

Pluperfect

amavissem	monuissem	misissem	cepissem	audivissem	fuissem
amavisses	monuisses	misisses	cepisses	audivisses	fuisses
amavisset	monuisset	misisset	cepisset	audivisset	fuisset
amavissemus	monuissemus	misissemus	cepissemus	audivissemus	fuissemus
amavissetis	monuissetis	misissetis	cepissetis	audivissetis	fuissetis
amavissent	monuissent	misissent	cepissent	audivissent	fuissent

Irregular verbs

esse *to be*	posse *to be able*	velle *to wish*	ferre *to carry*	ire *to go*
		Present		
sum	possum	volo	fero	eo
es	potes	vis	fers	is
est	potest	vult	fert	it
sumus	possumus	volumus	ferimus	imus
estis	potestis	vultis	fertis	itis
sunt	possunt	volunt	ferunt	eunt
		Future		
ero	potero	volam	feram	ibo
eris	poteris	voles	feres	ibis
erit	poterit	volet	feret	ibit
erimus	poterimus	volemus	feremus	ibimus
eritis	poteritis	voletis	feretis	ibitis
erunt	poterunt	volent	ferent	ibunt
		Imperfect		
eram	poteram	volebam	ferebam	ibam
eras	poteras	volebas	ferebas	ibas
erat	poterat	volebat	ferebat	ibat
eramus	poteramus	volebamus	ferebamus	ibamus
eratis	poteratis	volebatis	ferebatis	ibatis
erant	poterant	volebant	ferebant	ibant

Irregular verbs – continued

		Perfect		
esse *to be*	**posse** *to be able*	**velle** *to wish*	**ferre** *to carry*	**ire** *to go*
fui	potui	volui	tuli	ii
fuisti	potuisti	voluisti	tulisti	isti
fuit	potuit	voluit	tulit	iit
fuimus	potuimus	voluimus	tulimus	iimus
fuistis	potuistis	voluistis	tulistis	istis
fuerunt	potuerunt	voluerunt	tulerunt	ierunt

		Pluperfect		
fueram	potueram	volueram	tuleram	ieram
fueras	potueras	volueras	tuleras	ieras
fuerat	potuerat	voluerat	tulerat	ierat
fueramus	potueramus	volueramus	tuleramus	ieramus
fueratis	potueratis	volueratis	tuleratis	ieratis
fuerant	potuerant	voluerant	tulerant	ierant

Unit 1

Practice (i)
1 (a) me, her, he, us (b) silvam, mulus, sarcina, Paulum 2 (a) sarcinam; the mule carries the bag. (b) Paulus; Paul carries the mule. 3 (a) amat; the mule does not like the wood. (b) ambulat; Paul is walking in the wood. (c) spectat; the mule watches the wood (d) portat; not Paul but the mule is carrying the bag.

Practice (ii)
1
mulus	mulum	mulo
Paulus	Paulum	Paulo
sarcina	sarcinam	sarcina
silva	silvam	silva

2 (a) nominative, accusative; Benedict longs for some food. (b) accusative; the mule does not like the bag. (c) ablative; Benedict is not in the wood. (d) nominative; Paul is a monk. 3 (a) Paulus cum mulo in silva ambulat; Paul walks with the mule in the wood. (b) in mulo est sarcina; on the mule is a bag.

Revision
1 silvam, monachum, sarcina, cibo 2 (a) Benedictus in silva non ambulat. (b) Sarcina in mulo est. (c) Mulus non Paulum sed sarcinam portat. (d) Mulus silvam non amat. 3 (examples of sentences) (a) Paulus mulum non portat. (b) Cibus in sarcina est. (c) Paulus silvam spectat. (d) Paulus cum monacho ambulat.

Unit 2

Practice (i)
1 equis, equi, mulo; the mule lives in the field with the horses, but the horses do not work with the mule. 2 (a) portat; the mule carries the bag. (b) habitant; the monks live in the monastery. (c) amant; the mules do not like the horses. (d) laborat; the horse does not work in the field.

Practice (ii)

1 silvas, silvis, umbrae; the mule does not like woods because in the woods are shadows. 2 (a) sunt; the bags are on the mule. (b) amat; the mule does not like the shadows in the wood. (c) portant; the monks do not carry the bags. (d) habitant; the horses do not live in the wood.

Revision

1 (a) mulum, muli, mulis; discipulus, discipulo, discipulos; umbra, umbram, umbras; (b) equum, equo, equi, equos, equis; silvam, silva, silvae, silvis; sarcina, sarcina, sarcinae, sarcinas, sarcinis. 2 (a) Paulus saepe in agro cum monachis laborat; Paul often works in the field with the monks. (b) Sarcinae in mulo sunt; the bags are on the mule. (c) Discipuli in monasterio habitant; the students live in the monastery. (d) Mulus umbras non amat; the mule does not like shadows. 3 (a) Umbrae in silvis sunt. (b) Monachi sarcinas non portant. (c) Mulus saepe in silvis ambulat. (d) Mulus equos non amat quod cum mulis non laborat.

Unit 3

Practice (i)

1 agrum, agri, agris; unguento, unguentis, presbyterum, presbyteri, presbyteros. 2 (a) presbyteri, discipulis, laborant; the priests do not work with the students. (b) vino, oleo, unguentis, ovis; the bag is heavy with wine, oil, perfumes and eggs. 3 (a) monachi, habitant; the monks live in the monastery. (b) silvas, agros; the mule does not like the woods but the fields. (c) equi, mulis, laborant; the horses work with the mules in neither the woods nor the fields. (d) vina, unguenta; Benedict desires wines and perfumes.

Practice (ii)

1 (a) viam; the monks walk along the road. (b) agro; the mule is in the field. (c) monachis; the horse, frightened by the monks, comes out of the monastery. (d) equo, terram; the monk falls off the horse on to the ground 2 (a) in, ex, in; in the wood, the monk falls from the horse and lies on the ground. (b) e, in; the eggs fall from the bag on to the ground. (c) per, ad; the mule walks through the wood towards the monastery.

Revision

1 silva, silva, silvae, silvis; mulus, mulum, muli, mulos, mulis; puerum, pueri, pueros; vinum, vinis, libro, libri; ancillam, ancillas, ancillis. 2 (a) discipulus, ambulat; the student walks into the kitchen. (b) presbyter, desiderat; the priest often desires food and wine. (c) silvam; the mule always comes through the wood. (d) librum; the master longs for a book, the students long for wine. 3 (a) Equi neque in silva neque in agro laborant. (b) Monachus unguenta in sarcina portat. (c) Presbyter cum discipulis per silvam ad monasterium ambulat (d) Discipuli non presbyteri sunt.

Unit 4

Practice (i)

1 terram, terrae, terras, terrarum; ramum, rami, ramo, rami, ramorum, ramis; folium, folii, folio, folia, foliorum, foliis. 2 (a) monasterii; the women work in the kitchen of the monastery. (b) feminae; the eggs fall on to the woman's tunic. (c) Benedicti; the students drink Benedict's wine. 3 (a) nominative, genitive; the students desire the maids' wine. (b) nominative, genitive; Stephen is the master of the school. (c) genitive, nominative; Paul is Stephen's student. (d) genitive; the mule is fearful of woods. 4 (a) rami, ramorum; (b) agri, agrorum (c) ovi, ovorum (d) umbrae, umbrarum (e) ancillae, ancillarum

Practice (ii)

1 (a) Sum Paulus. (b) Sumus Stephani discipuli. (c) Est episcopus. (d) Es in silva. 2 (examples) (a) Ubi est mulus? (b) Cur Paulus in bibliotheca laborat? (c) Femina-ne mortua est? (d) Quis est Stephanus? (Quis est magister?)

Revision

1 (examples) (a) Femina est in silva. (b) Equus umbras non amat. (c) Magister in bibliotheca laborat. (d) Mulus unguenta oleum vinum ovaque portat. 2 (a) Sumus-ne in silva? (b) Equus feminae audire ventum potest. (c) Mulus sarcinas monachi portat. (d) Num discipuli vinum Benedicti desiderant? 3 ventus, ventum, venti, ventos, ventorum, ventis; tunicam, tunicae, tunicae, tunicarum, tunicis; ovum, ovum, ovi, ovo, ova, ovorum.

Unit 5

Practice (i)

1 umbrae, ovi, pueri, magister, episcopi, Egberta, libri. 2 (a) umbra-ae, sarcina-ae, Lucia-ae, domina-ae, filia-ae, via-ae, etc. (b) episcopus-i, Paulus-i, equus-i, etc. (c) ovum-i, castellum-i, unguentum-i, oppidum-i, monasterium-i, etc.

Practice (ii)

1 (a) Bestiae furiosae Christianos sanctos fugant. (b) Christianus furiosus bestias sanctas fugat. (c) Christianum furiosum bestiae sanctae fugant. 2 (a) Bestiae furiosae sanctum monachum spectant; the furious beasts watch the saintly monk. (b) Libri magni in bibliotheca sunt; there are great books in the library. (c) Discipuli ignavi mulos furiosos in agris vident; the lazy students see the furious mules in the fields. (d) Monachi somnulenti in bibliotheca non laborant; the sleepy monks do not work in the library.

Revision

1 lucid; wall; mural; animal; bestial; leaf; foliage; dubious; loquacious; virile; irate 2 (a) Monachi-ne ignavi in agris laborant? Do lazy monks work in the fields? (b) Num discipuli cognati Luciae sunt? Surely the students are not kinsmen of Lucia? (c) Paulus magistri libros in

bibliotheca spectat; Paul is looking at the teacher's books in the library.
(d) Num Benedictus ancillarum avunculus est! Surely Benedict is not the
maids' uncle!

3

		Singular				Plural	
	masc.	*fem.*	*neut.*		*masc.*	*fem.*	*neut.*
nom.	sanctus	sancta	sanctum	*nom.*	sancti	sanctae	sancta
acc.	sanctum	sanctam	sanctum	*acc.*	sanctos	sanctas	sancta
gen.	sancti	sanctae	sancti	*gen.*	sanctorum	sanctarum	sanctorum
abl.	sancto	sancta	sancto	*abl.*	sanctis	sanctis	sanctis

5 nocturnal, canine, culinary, decimal, domestic, ecclesiastical, filial,
fraternal, maternal, solar, bovine. **6** (a) Num episcopus gulosus est? (b)
Discipuli fessi in agro saepe sedent. (c) Domina-ne (femina-ne) furiosa
est, Stephane? (d) Muli-ne obscura in silva laborant?

Unit 6

Practice (i)
(a) possunt; the monks cannot see the abbess (b) debet; vult; the abbess
ought to be working in the kitchen, but wants to watch the monks in the
church.

Practice (ii)
1 ager, agro, agro, agri, agros, agrorum, agris; coquus, coquum, coqui,
coquo, coqui, coquos, coquorum, coquis; culina, culinam, culinae,
culina, culinae, culinas, culinis, culinis; oleum, olei, oleo, olea, olea,
oleis, oleis   **2**   (a) ancilla, discipulis; the maid brings food for the
students. (b) episcopo, abbatissae; the student gives perfume not to the
bishop but to the abbess.   **3**   (a) Episcopus historiam monasterii
presbytero monachoque narrat; the bishop narrates the story of the
monastery to the priest and the monk. (b) Discipulus ignavus Luciam
spectat; the idle student watches Lucia. (c) Miser mulus sarcinam
onerosam semper portat; the poor mule is always carrying a heavy bag.
(d) Cur ancilla cum monacho laborare debet? why should the maid
work with the monk?

Revision
1 (a) ab initio; (b) anno Domini; (c) curriculum vitae; (d) et cetera;
(e) ad nauseam; (f) ad infinitum.   **2**   (a) Bestiae-ne Christianos in
amphitheatro devorant? Are the beasts devouring the Christians in the
amphitheatre? (b) Monachi boni ludos saevos non amant; Good monks
do not like the cruel games. (c) Paulus-ne coquis cibum vinumque
semper portat? Does Paul always bring food and wine for the cooks? (d)
Cur discipulo libros magister dat? Why does the master give books to
the student? **3** paganus, paganum, pagani, pagano, pagani, paganos,
paganis, paganis; oppidum, oppidum, oppido, oppido, oppida,
oppidorum, oppidis, oppidis; bestia, bestiam, bestiae, bestia, bestiae,

bestiarum, bestiis, bestiis   4   (a) Paulus multum cibum coquo dat.
(b) Discipulus ambulare non cum ancillis sed cum monachis debet.
(c) Monachi ludos spectare volunt sed in monasterio laborare debent.
(d) Lucia-ne in culina laborare potest?

Revision I

1 (a) Abbatissa bestiam sanctam timet. (b) Ova in episcopum ignavum
cadunt. (c) Liber Augustini non discipulis furiosis sed ancillae gratus est.
(d) Benedictus gulosus unguenta abbatissae odorae desiderat.   2   (a)
Monachi muros monasterii videre possunt; the monks can see the walls
of the monastery. (b) Miserae ancillae in culinis semper laborant; the
wretched maids are always working in the kitchens. (c) Pueri mulis
cibum dant; the boys give food to the mules. (d) Cur sunt abbatissae in
bibliotheca? why are the abbesses in the library? (e) ludos monachus
non spectat; the monk does not watch the games. (f) Episcopus-ne in
monasterio habitat? does the bishop live in the monastery? (g) Monachi
feminis aquam dant; the monks give water to the women.   4   (a)
Discipuli-ne fessi sunt? (b) Malus monachus in monasterio habitare non
potest. (c) Magister furiosus libros discipulis miseris dat. (d) Filia
dominae laborare in culina non potest. Num ambulare cum discipulis
debet? (e) Equi-ne mulum in silva audire possunt? Cibum equorum ad
monasterium portat.
5

	Singular				Plural		
	masc.	*fem.*	*neut.*		*masc.*	*fem.*	*neut.*
nom.	magnus	magna	magnum	nom.	magni	magnae	magna
acc.	magnum	magnam	magnum	acc.	magnos	magnas	magna
gen.	magni	magnae	magni	gen.	magnorum	magnarum	magnorum
dat.	magno	magnae	magno	dat.	magnis	magnis	magnis
abl.	magno	magna	magno	abl.	magnis	magnis	magnis

7 (a) a wasp

Unit 7

Practice (i)
1 (a) abbatibus; (b) arboribus; (c) virginis; (d) patri; (e) abbate; (f)
arborum (g) patre; (h) virginibus; (i) patris; (j) abbatem   3   (a) Reges in
monasterio non habitant; kings do not live in the monastery. (b)
Monachus boves in silva potest videre; the monk can see oxen in the
wood. (c) Virtutem matrum laudant; they praise the courage of the
mothers. (d) Amici-ne abbatum grati sunt militibus? are the friends of
the abbots pleasing to the soldiers?

Practice (ii)
2 (a) nomina abbatum; (b) munera matris; (c) multa opera (multi
labores); (d) corpora bestiarum; (e) carmina abbatis; (f) gratis carminibus

Revision
1 corpus, corporis, corpore, corpora, corporum, corporibus, corporibus; homo, hominis, homini, homine, homines, homines, hominibus, hominibus; potio, potionem, potioni, potione, potiones, potionum, potionibus, potionibus 2 (a) Munera discipuli dominae grata sunt. (b) Num magister in superstitiones credit? (c) Augustinus carmina virginibus recitat. (d) Monachi pacem, milites bellum desiderant. 3 (a) Quis est dea amoris? Est-ne Diana? (b) Abbatissa in silvam cum Patre Benedicto ambulat. (c) Carmina-ne virginis grata abbati sunt? (d) Cur Benedictus carnem panem crustaque semper desiderat?

Unit 8

Practice (i)
2 (a) exspectant; (b) laudamus; (c) vacat; (d) laboratis; (e) recito; (f) susurrant; (g) equitat; (h) parant; (i) salutat; (j) volitant; (k) praedicat; (l) curat; (m) castigas

Practice (ii)
2 (a) sedemus; (b) timent; (c) monet; (d) ridetis; (e) manemus; (f) respondent; (g) doces; (h) dolent

Practice (iii)
1 (a) iacet; (b) cantat/cantabit 2 (a) monebit; (b) amabunt; (c) laudabimus; (d) sedebitis; (e) cantabis; (f) iubebimus; (g) praedicabit; (h) videbis; (i) manebimus

Revision
1 (a) Equi in caelo volitabunt; horses will fly in the sky. (b) In ecclesia sedebo; I shall sit in the church. (c) Discipulos somnulentos castigabunt; they will punish sleepy students. (d) Lucia mihi in ecclesia susurrabit; Lucia will whisper to me in the church. 2 (a) O Domina, cur doles? mistress, why do you weep? (b) Philosophiam te doceo, o Paule; I am teaching you philosophy, Paul. (c) Labores in agris non toleramus; we do not endure the toils in the fields. (d) Nonne, o virgo, Augustinum amas? surely, maiden, you love Augustinus? 3 munus, munus, muneris, muneri, munera, munerum, muneribus, muneribus; laborem, labori, labore, labores, labores, laboribus, laboribus; allegoriam, allegoriae, allegoria, allegorias, allegoriarum, allegoriis, allegoriis; dei, deo, deo, deos, deorum, deis, deis 4 (a) Abbatissa magnam cenam parabit. (b) Discipuli-ne in bibliotheca adhuc laborant? (c) Quid, o Lucia, susurras? (d) In ecclesia dolebunt.

Unit 9

Practice (i)
2 (a) omnibus discipulis; (b) breve carmen; (c) difficilia opera; (d) humilium monachorum; (e) turpis superstitio; (f) mollis tunica; (g) fortibus militibus; (h) dulcis amica (domina)

Practice (ii)
1 a song not to be heard; an abbess to be revered; tasks to be done; a monk to be praised; gifts to be distributed; words to be added; an abbot to be revered; a maid to be admired 2 (a) audiendus; the abbot has to be heard. (b) amandi; the soldiers are not to be loved. (c) perficiendum; the work is to be finished.

Revision
1 (a) Magnae cenae in culina parandae sunt; large dinners have to be prepared in the kitchen. (b) Dulcis domina semper audienda est; a sweet mistress must always be heard. (c) Turpes discipuli excitandi sunt; the disgraceful students ought to be woken. (d) Humilis servus etiam laudandus est; a humble serf should also be praised. (e) Cur abbas reverendus est? why must an abbot be revered? 2 (a) Carmen fortibus militibus ancillaeque humili dedicabimus. (b) Doleo quod Lucia me amore inflammabit sed non amabit. (c) Nunc puella carmen dulce cantabit et pueri historiam monasterii narrabunt 3 dulcis: see omnis, sanctus in Tables.

Unit 10

Practice (i)
1 (a) mittit; (b) capimus; (c) audiunt; (d) capio; (e) mittunt; (f) auditis; (g) mittimus; (h) audis 3 (a) lego; (b) currunt; (c) scribit; (d) incipimus; (e) sepeliunt; (f) fugiunt; (g) bibitis; (h) venit; (i) audiunt

Practice (ii)
(a) mittet; (b) capiemus; (c) audient; (d) sedet; (e) audietis; (f) videre poterunt; (g) venire vis; (h) aderimus

Practice (iii)
(a) fourth; (b) first; (c) mixed; (d) third; (e) first; (f) second; (g) third; (h) fourth; (i) mixed; (j) second; (k) first; (l) third

Revision
1 (a) ducet; the monk will lead the mule into the wood. (b) perficient; today the students will finish the tasks. (c) relinquemus; shall we leave the monastery? (d) potero; I shall not be able to hear Augustine. 2 (a) credo; I do not believe in superstitions. (b) inflammat; (my) girlfriend inflames me with love. (c) audis; do you hear Augustine's poems? (d) legunt; the students read from the Vulgate. 3 (a) Ancillae carmina Augustini semper audire volunt! (b) Lucia iam legere et cantare et in agris laborare potest. (c) Animas humilium servorum et regum magnorum curabimus. (d) Cur monachi e silva (ef)fugiunt? 4 See Tables of nouns: opus: third declension; nox: third; fabula: first; sepulcrum: second; annus: second

Unit 11

Practice (i)
1 (a) amabat; (b) audiebant; (c) mittebamus; (d) eras; (e) poteram; (f) monebat; (g) erant 2 (a) pluebat; it was raining. (b) iacebat; the pitiable

body lay on (in) the ground. (c) legebamus; we were reading the poems of Catullus. (d) sepeliebant; they were burying the monk near the church. (e) flebat; the maiden was weeping.

Practice (ii)
1 (a) praedicantem; (b) dormientes 2 (a) ovum... cadens; Egberta sees the egg falling from the bag. (b) monachum... cantantem; Lucia was listening to the monk singing in the church. (c) discipulis stertentibus; Paul was sitting with the snoring students. (d) monacho dormienti; the abbess will not give food to the sleeping monk. (e) ancillas... susurrantes; Benedict was listening to the maids whispering in the kitchen. (f) feminae... poterant; the women could see Theodorus running in the wood.

Revision
1 (examples) (a) Coquum cibum devorantem in culina videre poteram. (b) Monachos in silva ululantes audiebamus. (c) Abbatissa discipulum vinum bibentem spectat. (d) Nunc abbas audiendus est. 2 (a) Augustinus duodecim horas dormiebat. (b) Sapientes/prudentes magistri cum discipulis semper bibebant. (c) Mulum-ne, o Lucia, in agro bibentem audire poteras? (d) Discipuli abbatem ex ecclesia pompam ducentem spectabant. 3 laboratis, mittere, mittam, come, venire, scribere, scribunt, scribebant, capere, capiet, capiebat, fear, times, timebas, dare, dabit, dabat, aperire, aperiam, aperiebam, see, videre, videbunt, videbant, praise, laudare, laudabimus, laudabamus, facit, faciet, docere, docebitis, docebatis

Unit 12

Practice (i)
1 (a) ambulavit; (b) viderunt; (c) venimus; (d) cepi; (e) monuisti; (f) audivit; (g) misimus; (h) monuit 2 (a) dixit; the monk (has) spoke(n) to the serf. (b) laudavimus; we (have) praised the maids in the kitchen. (c) ceperunt; have the Danes captured all the monasteries? (d) scripsisti; have you written a letter to the bishop?

Practice (ii)
(a) nos, vestram; (b) meum, vobis; (c) mea, tibi; (d) tibi

Revision
1 ambulabit, ambulabat, veniemus, veniebamus, praise, laudare, laudatis, laudabatis, docere, docebo, docebam, say, dicere, dicebas, dixisti, write, scribere, scribunt, scribent, scripserunt, capere, capimus, capiebamus, cepimus, see, vident, videbant, viderunt, esse, est, erat 2 (a) dulcia carmina tua; Augustine, will you read to me your sweet poems? (b) discipulis; poor Stephen was always working with the students in the library. (c) peregrinum; did Lucia hear the stranger/pilgrim in the wood? (d) ancillae... monuerunt; the maids have warned us. 3 (a) Theodorus-ne vobiscum in silva ambulabat, o discipuli? (b) Abbatem-ne praedicantem audivisti, o Augustine? (c) Abbatissam coquo susurrantem vidi. (d) Epistulam-ne Luciae scripsisti, o Paule?

Revision II

1 (a) cantabit; (b) dormiunt, devoraverunt; (c) vidi; (d) scribit
2 (a) recitabit, recitabat, recitavit (b) ridebunt, ridebant, riserunt
(c) audietis, audiebatis, audivistis (d) scribam, scribebam, scripsi
3 (a) docendi; (b) sepeliendum; (c) laudandi; (d) scribenda **4** (a) fugiens;
(b) ducentem; (c) sedentes; (d) cantantes **5** See Table of nouns: annus-
i: second declension; vita-ae: first; oppidum-i: second; potio-nis: third;
clamor-is: third; tempus-oris: third. **6** (a) Virginis-ne carmen audivisti,
o Pater Stephane? (b) Episcopus omnibus monachis praedicabat.
(c) Mox corpus miserabile monachi sepeliemus. (d) Coquus vinum cum
tristi discipulo per totam noctem bibebat.

7 hospes, hospitis   host, hospital, hostel, hotel, hospice
    caput, capitis   capital, cattle, chattel, chapter
    discus-i   dish, discus, disk, disco
    dignitas, dignitatis   dainty, dignity
    phantasia-ae   fancy, fantasy
    praedico-are   predicate, preach
    blasphemo-are   blame, blaspheme
    securus-a-um   sure, secure
    computo-are   count, computer

8 (c) an ancient inn or take-away

Unit 13

Practice (i)
aestimavi, station, salutatum, recitare, vacatum, damnation, mansion,
ridere, sessum, tentum, vision, monere, monitum, dictum, ducere,
ductum, relinquere, scriptum, ascensum, actum, auditum, ventum,
perfectum, receptum

Practice (ii)
(a) sepultus; Theodorus was buried in a field. (b) visi; the pilgrims were
seen in the wood. (c) territus; the mule was terrified by the shadows.
(d) laudata; the maiden was praised by her father.

Practice (iii)
(a) Mulus in silvam ductus umbras timet; the mule having been led into
the wood fears the shadows. (b) Discipuli a Stephano docti
obdormiverunt; the students having been taught by Stephen fell asleep.
(c) Cenam ab ancillis paratam Benedictus devoravit; Benedict devoured
the meal which had been prepared by the maids.

Practice (iv)
(a) legente; while Augustine was reading the poems of Tibullus, Paul was
copying out the rule of the monastery. (b) susurrantes; Theodorus saw
strangers whispering in the wood. (c) devorato; after much food had
been devoured (after devouring much food) Benedict fell asleep.

Practice (v)
(a) abimus (b) redibunt; (c) adibamus; (d) abierunt; (e) exit; (f) exeunt

Revision
1 (a) Theodorus, peregrinos timens, e silva exiit. (b) Coquus ancillas in horto laborantes diu spectabat. (c) Pater Stephanus dolens in ecclesia sedebat. (d) Paulo in stagno natante, peregrini silvam adibant. **2** (a) Lucia, Danis auditis, ad monasterium rediit. (b) Cena ab ancillis parata, a monachis devorata est. (c) Epistula a monacho scripta, comiti tradita est. (d) Discipulus, equo arbori ligato, in stagno natavit (natabat). **3** delinquent; ridere; ducere; scribe, scribble; recipient **4** Past participle of desidero-are, neuter plural: the desired things.

Unit 14

Practice (i)
2 (a) vultu tristi; (b) casu; (c) grati versus; (d) manu; (e) spiritus sancti; (f) gemitu; (g) exercitus comitis; (h) virginis arcus sagittaeque

Practice (iii)

Prefix	Simple verb		Compound	
ad	ire	*go*	adire	*go to, approach*
ex	ire	*go*	exire	*go out*
ab	esse	*be*	abesse	*be absent*
ad	esse	*be*	adesse	*be present*
ab	mittere	*send*	amittere	*send away, lose*
ad	capere	*take*	accipere	*receive, welcome*
circum	venire	*come*	circumvenire	*surround, come around*
cum	vocare	*call*	convocare	*call together*
de	mittere	*send*	demittere	*send down, lower*
ad	facere	*make*	afficere	*treat, afflict*
cum	putare	*think*	computare	*sum up, reckon*
e	rapere	*take, snatch*	eripere	*snatch out*
in	ruere	*rush*	irruere	*rush in*
in	venire	*come*	invenire	*come upon, find*
per	facere	*make*	perficere	*make thorough, finish*

Revision
1 See Tables: (a) gradus: fourth declension; corpus: third; monachus: second (b) dies: fifth; miles: third; sagitta: first **2** (a) Virgo numquam in stagno nataverat. (b) Peregrini, cibo multo devorato, monasterium reliquerunt. (c) Neque cibum neque aquam inveneramus sed numquam spem amisimus. (d) Discipuli, in gradibus ecclesiae sedentes, versus Augustini audiebant. (e) Monachi omnes libros manu scripserant.

Unit 15

Practice (i)
1 (a) Luciae; Lucia's face was sad. (b) ancillarum; the maids' food was devoured by Benedict. (c) Monachi; the monks live in the monastery. d) vinum; wine was desired by the abbot. **2** (a) illius; his daughter lives in the castle. (b) hac; the abbess was praying in the church with her. (c) ei; Paul always gave food to him/it. (*Note: even an inanimate 'it' may*

be masculine or feminine, depending on the gender of the noun which the pronoun represents). (d) illi, his; those men were seen in the wood with these men.

Practice (ii)
1 (a) haec silva; (b) haec unguenta; (c) horum discipulorum 2 (a) illa domina; (b) illa carmina; (c) illum mulum video 3 (a) ea epistula; (b) cum eis monachis; (c) id est

Practice (iii)
(a) se; (b) ipsa

Practice (iv)
amabitur, videbunt, audiebat, *s/he was being heard, s/he will capture,* capiet

Practice (v)
1 duxerunt, *they were led,* audivit, auditus est, cepit, capta est, monuit, monitus est
2 (a) Discipuli in schola a Patre Ricardo castigantur; the students are punished in the school by Father Richard. (b) Omnes sarcinae ex oppido a mulo portabantur; all the bags were being carried out of the town by the mule. (c) Carmen Catulli ab Augustino amicis recitatum est; the poem of Catullus was read by Augustine to his friends. (d) Virgo matri dicens a Paulo visa est; the maiden, while speaking to her mother, was seen by Paul. 3 (a) Benedictus cibum devoravit; Benedict devoured the food. (b) Paulus virginem in silva vidit; Paul saw the maiden in the wood. (c) Monachi historiam monasterii narrabunt; the monks will relate the history of the monastery. (d) Dani corpus in horto sepeliverunt; the Danes buried the body in the garden.

Revision
1 (a) scriptae; many letters were written by Augustine to Lucia. (b) relictum; the monastery was left (abandoned) by the pilgrims. (c) sepultum; the body of the monk was buried. (d) positi; the books were placed in the library. 2 (a) Mox discipuli se liberabunt. (b) Monachi-ne ipsi docent? docere-ne docentur? (c) Paulus Luciaque e silva ambulantes visi sunt. (d) Paulus, peregrinis adeuntibus, in stagno se celavit. (e) Multae bestiae a virgine ipsa captae sunt. (f) Boves a Danorum exercitu custodiebantur.

Unit 16

Practice (i)

Present indicative		Present subjunctive	
we live	**vivimus**	**vivamus**	*may we live*
s/he (it) stands	**stat**	**stet**	*may s/he (it) stand*
we love	**amamus**	**amemus**	*may we love*
you forgive	**ignoscis**	**ignoscas**	*may you forgive*
s/he is careful	**cavet**	**caveat**	*may s/he be careful*
we rejoice	**gaudemus**	**gaudeamus**	*may we rejoice*
we praise	**laudamus**	**laudemus**	*may we praise*
s/he drinks	**bibit**	**bibat**	*may s/he drink*
you are quiet	**taces**	**taceas**	*may you be quiet*

Practice (ii)
(a) festinate; (b) festinetis; (c) tacete; (d) taceas

Practice (iii)
May you be quiet! Taceas! If only you'd be quiet! Ut taceas! If only he'd believe us! Ut nobis credat! Do not be afraid of the wood. Ne silvam timeas. Careful lest they hear. Cave ne audiant. I believe so that I may understand. Credo ut intellegam.

Practice (iv)
(a) intellegam; I drink so that I may understand. (b) celaret; Lucia plunged herself into the pond in order to hide herself. (c) dicit, intellegant; Students, as Stephen says, are taught theology that they may understand the work of God. (d) audiremus; Augustine advised us to listen to his songs/poems.

Revision
1 (a) Mulus, sarcinis omnibus visis, gemuit. (b) Paulus, Ricardo audito, in monasterium festinavit. (c) Stephanus, corpore amici sepulto, in ecclesiam abiit. (d) Coquus, cibo devorato, in silvam ambulavit. 2 (a) Danos omnes capiant! (b) Ne abbas librum carminum tuum videat, o Augustine! (c) Vinum bibite, o amici! omnes vinum bibant! (d) Abbas eum monuit ut monasterium relinqueret 3 See Tables. (a) gaudeo-ere: second conjugation; scribo-ere: third; laudo-are: first

Unit 17

Practice (i)
(a) laudor; What good fortune! I am praised by my mistress. (b) audimur; we are being heard by the maiden sitting in the rafters. (c) castigaberis; o wicked boy, you will be punished by the master.

Practice (ii)
(a) secuta est; Lucia followed Richard into the monastery. (b) mirabuntur; all men will admire my songs/poems.

Practice (iii)
1 (a) The maid is more furious than the monk. (b) The students are lazier than the maid. (c) The abbess is holier than the soldiers. (d) The horse is faster than the mule. 2 (b) Discipuli ignaviores ancilla sunt. (c) Abbatissa sanctior militibus est. (d) Equus celerior mulo est.

Practice (iv)
1 (a) sanctissimus; is the abbot the holiest of all the monks? (b) suavissima; Benedict's perfumes are the most delightful. (c) bellissima; Charles' daughter is the most beautiful in the land.
2

Meaning	Adjective	Comparative	Superlative	Derivative
good	**bonus**	**melior**	**optimus-a-um**	*optimist*
bad	**malus**	**peior**	**pessimus-a-um**	*pessimist*
great, large	**magnus**	**maior**	**maximus-a-um**	*maximum*
small	**parvus**	**minor**	**minimus-a-um**	*minimum*

Revision

1 (a) secuti sunt; the students followed the Danes into the wood. (b) progressa est; Lucia went forward into the church. (c) locuti/ae sumus; we spoke in the wood. (d) miratus est; Augustine admired the daughter of the count. 2 (a) sequitur; Lucia follows the pilgrims into the monastery. (b) loquor; I speak about most serious matters. (c) videntur; the pilgrims are seen conspiring in the wood. (d) miraris; do you admire the song/poem of Augustine? 3 (a) Equi-ne ignaviores quam muli/mulis sunt? (b) Augustinus-ne optimus discipulus est? (c) Abbatissam-ne sanctiorem umquam vidisti, o Paule? (d) Ricardus quam Dani ipsi / Danis ipsis saevior erat.

Unit 18

Practice (i)

(a) If the mule were wealthy, he would not be pulling carts. (b) If he tries to escape, kill him! (c) If the master had remained in the school, he would be alive now. (d) If you were beautiful, I would love you.

Practice (ii)

1 (a) Stephanus pius est. (b) Abbas scelestus est. (c) O discipuli, in monasterium festinate! (d) Ubi sunt peregrini? 2 (a) Abbas dixit puerum scelestum poenas dare debere. (b) Paulus abbati dicit corpus magistri in sarcina esse. (c) Augustinus rogat ubi versus Catulli sint.

Revision

1 (a) Si illi discipuli Danos non timerent, stulti essent; if those students were not afraid of the Danes, they would be foolish. (b) Stephanus nobis dixit cucullum monachum non facere; Stephen told us that a hood does not make a monk. (c) Qui ab amicis amatur est felix; he who is loved by his friends is fortunate. (d) Monachi, si avaritia non moventur, laudandi sunt; if the monks are not moved by greed, they should be praised. 2 (a) Credo Augustinum Paulo amicum bonum esse. (b) Si Ricardum invenies, o Stephane, eum roga ut in claustrum veniat. (c) Discipuli Luciam ex omnibus virginibus/omnium virginum esse bellissimam dicunt. (d) Num comitis filiam discipulum humilem amare credimus.

Latin–English vocabulary

a(b) *by, from*
abbas-atis [m] *abbot*
abbatissa-ae [f] *abbess*
abeo-ire-ii-itum *go away*
absum-esse *be away, absent*
accipio-ere-cepi-ceptum *receive*
ad *to, towards*
addo-ere-idi-itum *add*
adduco-ere-xi-ductum *bring*
adeo *so much*
adeo-ire-ii-itum *go to,*
  approach
adhaereo-ere-si *stick*
adhuc *still*
adiuvo-are *help*
adsum-esse *be here, present*
adultero-are *be adulterous*
advena-ae [f] *newcomer*
aedifico-are-avi-atum *build*
aequor-is [n] *water, surface*
aestas-tatis [f] *summer*
aestimo-are-avi-atum *value*
aestuosus-a-um *hot*
ager, agri [m] *field*
agnosco-ere-ovi-otum *recognize*
ago-ere, egi, actum *do, drive,*
  perform
agricola-ae [m] *farmer*
alienus-i [m] *stranger*
aliquando *sometimes*
aliquis *someone*
alius-a-um *some, other*
allegoria-ae [f] *allegory*
alter-a-um *another*

ambo *both*
ambulo-are-avi-atum *walk*
amicus-i [m], amica-ae [f]
  friend
amitto-ere *lose*
amo-are-avi-atum *like, love*
amor-is [m] *love*
amphitheatrum-i [n]
  amphitheatre
amphora-ae [f] *jug*
an *or*
anas-atis [f] *duck*
ancilla-ae [f] *maid*
angelus-i [m] *angel*
anima-ae [f] *soul*
animal-is [n] *animal*
animus-i [m] *mind*
annus-i [m] *year*
anser-is [m] *goose*
ante(a) *before(hand)*
antrum-i [n] *cave*
anxius-a-um *concerned*
aperio-ire-ui-itum *open*
appareo-ere-ui *appear*
apud *at, in the presence of*
aqua-ae [f] *water*
ara-ae [f] *altar*
arbor-is [f] *tree*
arcus-us [m] *bow*
argentum-i [n] *silver*
ars-tis [f] *art, skill*
ascendo-ere-endi-ensum *climb*
aspicio-ere *look at*
at *but, yet*

atque *and*
attonitus-a-um *astonished*
audio-ire-ivi-itum *hear*
aura-ae *air*
aurora-ae [f] *dawn*
aurum-i [n] *gold*
austerus-a-um *severe, gloomy*
aut *or*
autem *however*
auxilium-i [n] *help*
avunculus-i [m] *uncle*

balbus-a-um *stammering*
basio-are-avi *kiss*
basium-i [n] *kiss*
bellum-i [n] *war*
bellus-a-um *beautiful*
bene *fine*
benignus-a-um *kind*
bestia-ae [f] *beast*
bibliotheca-ae [f] *library*
bibo-ere-bibi *drink*
blasphemo-are *blaspheme, swear*
bonus-a-um *good*
bos-vis [m/f] *ox*
brevis-e *short*

caballus-i [m] *horse*
cado-ere, cecidi, casum *fall*
caedo-ere, cecidi, caesum *kill, cut*
caelum-i [n] *heaven, sky*
calamus-i [m] *reed*
calidus-a-um *warm*
campana-ae [f] *bell*
candela-ae [f] *candle*
canto-are-avi-atum *sing*
capio-ere, cepi, captum *take, capture*
captivus-i [m] *prisoner*
caput, capitis [n] *head, capital*
carmen-inis [n] *song, poem*
caro, carnis [f] *flesh, meat*
carus-a-um *dear, special*
castellum-i [n] *castle*
castigo-are-avi-atum *punish*
castitas-tatis [f] *chastity*
casus-us [m] *chance*
Catullus-i *Catullus*

caveo-ere *be careful*
celebro-are-avi-atum *celebrate*
celeriter *quickly*
cella-ae [f] *cell, room*
cellerarius-i [m] *procurator*
celo-are-avi-atum *hide*
cena-ae [f] *dinner*
centum *hundred*
certe *certainly, yes, at least*
certus-a-um *sure, unerring*
ceterus-a-um *other*
chorus-i [m] *choir*
Christianus-i [m] *Christian*
Christus-i *Christ*
cibus-i [m] *food*
circum *around*
circumspicio-ere-exi-ectum *look around*
cito-are-avi-atum *stir up, rouse*
clamo-are-avi *shout*
clamor-is [m] *shout, cry*
clarus-a-um *bright*
claudo-ere *lock*
claustrum-i [n] *cloister*
cogito-are *think*
cognatus-i [m] *kinsman*
cognosco-ere-ovi *discover, learn*
colligo-ere-egi-ectum *recover*
combustus-a-um *incinerated*
comes-itis [m] *count*
comitor-ari *accompany*
commemoror-ari *remember, relate*
computo-are *sum up*
confirmatus-a-um *confirmed*
conicio-ere *throw*
coniunx-gis [m/f] *husband/wife*
conor-ari, conatus *try, attempt*
consilium-i [n] *plan*
consisto-ere-stiti *stop*
consocius-i [m] *associate*
consolatio-nis [f] *consolation*
conspicio-ere-spexi-spectum *catch sight of*
conspiro-are *conspire*
constituo-ere-ui-utum *decide*
contentio-nis [f] *dispute, competition*
contineo-ere *contain, hold*

contradico-ere   *contradict*
convalesco-ere   *recover*
convocatio-nis [f]   *conference*
convoco-are-avi-atum   *call together, assemble*
coquus-i [m]   *cook*
cor-dis [n]   *heart*
Corinthi-orum [m]   *Corinthians*
corpus-oris [n]   *body*
cras   *tomorrow*
creator-is [m]   *creator*
credo-ere [+dat.]   *believe, trust*
crepito-are   *rustle*
cresco-ere   *grow*
crimen-inis [n]   *charge, crime*
crudelis-e   *cruel*
crustum-i [n]   *pastry, cake*
cucullus-i [m]   *hood*
cui, cuius   *to whom, whose*
culina-ae [f]   *kitchen*
cum [1]   *with, in the company of*
cum [2]   *when, since*
Cupido-inis [m]   *Cupid*
cur   *why*
cura-ae [f]   *anxiety, stress*
curo-are [+acc.]   *care for*
curro-ere   *run*
custodio-ire   *guard, watch over*
custos-dis [m/f]   *guardian*

damno-are   *condemn*
Danus-i [m]   *Dane, Viking*
de [+abl.]   *from, about*
dea-ae [f]   *goddess*
debeo-ere-ui-itum   *owe, have to*
declino-are   *swerve*
dedico-are   *dedicate*
defessus-a-um   *exhausted*
deinde   *then, next*
deleo-ere-evi-etum   *destroy*
deliro-are-avi   *be silly, insane*
demitto-ere   *lower*
densus-a-um   *thick*
depono-ere-sui-situm   *put down*
desidero-are-avi-atum   *long for, desire*
desilio-ire-ui   *leap out*
desino-ere, desii   *stop, abandon*
desisto-ere   *stop*

despicio-ere   *look down*
deus-i [m]   *god*
devoro-are-avi-atum   *devour, eat*
diabolus-i [m]   *devil*
dialectica-ae [f]   *discussion, argument*
dico-ere-ixi-ictum   *tell, say*
dies-iei [m]   *day*
difficilis-e   *difficult*
dignitas, dignitatis [f]   *distinction*
digredior-i, digressus   *depart*
diligentia-ae [f]   *attentiveness*
diligo-ere   *love*
discedo-ere-essi   *depart*
discipulus-i [m]   *student*
discus-i [m]   *disc*
diu   *for a long time*
divido-ere   *divide*
divitiae-arum [pl.]   *riches*
divus-i [m]   *god*
do-are, dedi, datum   *give*
doceo-ere-ui, doctum   *teach*
doctus-i [m]   *learned man*
doleo-ere   *grieve*
dolus-i [m]   *deceit*
domina-ae [f]   *lady, mistress*
dominus-i [m]   *lord, sir*
domum   *homewards*
donum-i [n]   *gift*
dormio-ire-ivi-itum   *sleep*
duco-ere-uxi-uctum   *lead*
dulcis-e   *sweet*
dum   *while, as long as*
dumus-i [m]   *thicket*
duo   *two*

e(x)   *from, out of*
ecce   *look*
ecclesia-ae [f]   *church*
effugio-ere, effugi   *flee away*
Egberta-ae [f]   *Egberta*
eho   *eh*
elephantus-i [m]   *elephant*
emo-ere   *buy*
enim   *for, you see*
eo, ire, ii, itum   *go*
episcopus-i [m]   *bishop*
epistula-ae [f]   *letter*

equidem   *indeed, to be sure*
equito-are-avi   *ride*
equus-i [m]   *horse*
ergo   *so, therefore*
eripio-ere-ripui-reptum   *take out, snatch*
erro-are-avi   *make a mistake*
eruditio-nis [f]   *learning*
et   *and*
et... et   *both... and*
etiam   *also*
evanesco-ere, evanui   *disappear*
exanimatus-a-um   *breathless*
excito-are   *wake, arouse*
exemplar-is [n]   *copy*
exemplum-i [n]   *example, precedent*
exerceo-ere-ui-itum   *occupy, practise, train*
exercitus-us [m]   *army*
exhalo-are-avi-atum   *breathe out*
exhaurio-ire-ivi, exhaustum   *drain, empty*
exhilaro-are-avi-atum   *cheer*
exiguus-a-um   *slender, scant*
existimo-are   *think*
explico-are-avi-atum   *explain, undo*
exscribo-ere-ipsi-iptum   *write out*
exsequiae-arum [f]   *funeral*
exspecto-are-avi-atum   *wait for*

fabula-ae [f]   *story*
facies-iei [f]   *face, appearance*
facilis-e   *easy*
facio-ere, feci, factum   *do, make*
faenum-i [n]   *hay*
falsus-a-um   *false*
fama-ae [f]   *story, report*
familia-ae [f]   *family*
famulus-i [m]   *attendant*
fas   *not blasphemous*
fatum-i [n]   *fate*
faveo-ere [+dat.]   *favour*
felix   *fortunate, happy*
femina-ae [f]   *woman*
fenestra-ae [f]   *window*
fervidus-a-um   *burning, impetuous*

fessus-a-um   *tired*
festino-are-avi   *hurry*
fibula-ae [f]   *brooch*
fictilia-ium [n]   *earthenware*
fidelis-e   *loyal*
fides-ei [f]   *faith, loyalty*
figura-ae [f]   *shape*
filia-ae [f]   *daughter*
flecto-ere   *bend*
fleo-ere   *weep*
folium-i [n]   *leaf*
fortasse   *perhaps*
fortis-e   *brave*
fortuitus-a-um   *accidental*
fortunatus-a-um   *happy, lucky*
fragrantia-ae [f]   *odour*
frater-tris [m]   *brother*
frigidus-a-um   *cool, cold*
frigus-oris [n]   *chill, cold*
frondesco-ere   *put forth leaves*
frustra   *in vain, to no avail*
frux-gis [f]   *fruit*
fugio-ere, fugi   *flee*
fugo-are   *chase*
fundo-ere   *pour*
furiosus-a-um   *furious*
furtim   *secretly*
furtum-i [n]   *theft*

garrulus-a-um   *talkative*
gaudeo-ere   *rejoice*
gelidus-a-um   *cold*
gemitus-us [m]   *groan, sigh*
gemo-ere-ui   *groan*
genae-arum [f]   *cheeks*
gero-ere   *conduct, manage*
gestus-us [m]   *gesture*
gladius-i [m]   *sword*
gracilis-e   *elegant, slender*
gradatim   *gradually*
gradus-us [m]   *step*
Graecus-i [m]   *Greek*
gratia-ae [f]   *favour, grace*
gratias tibi   *thank you*
gratus-a-um   *pleasing*
gravis-e   *serious*
gulosus-a-um   *greedy*

habena-ae [f]   *rein*
habeo-ere-ui   *have*

habito-are-avi *live*
herba-ae [f] *grass*
heus *hey!*
hic *here, this*
hiems, hiemis [f] *winter*
historia-ae [f] *story*
hodie *today*
homo-inis [m] *man*
honestus-a-um *decent, honourable*
honoro-are *honour*
hora-ae [f] *hour*
horrendus-a-um *fearful, to be feared*
hortus-i [m] *garden*
hospes-itis [m] *host, guest*
humilis-e *humble, meek*

iaceo-ere-ui *lie*
iam *now, already*
ibi *there*
ictus-us [m] *blow*
igitur *and so*
ignavus-a-um *lazy*
ignis-is [m] *fire*
ignosco-ere [+dat.] *forgive*
ille [m], illa [f] *he/she, that*
illic *over there*
immergo-ere-si-sum *plunge*
immo *no, on the contrary*
immotus-a-um *stationary*
impero-are [+dat.] *order, instruct*
impetus-us [m] *attack*
improbus-a-um *troublesome*
in *in, on*
incensum-i [n] *incense*
incipio-ere-cepi-ceptum *begin*
inde *after that, next*
induo-ere *put on*
ineptus-a-um *foolish*
infirmus-a-um *sick*
inflammo-are-avi *inflame*
infra *below*
ingredior-i, ingressus *enter*
inicio-ere, inieci, iniectum *throw in*
inimicus-i [m] *enemy*
iniuria-ae [f] *harm*

inno-are-avi *swim, float*
inquit *(s/he) says, said*
insolitus-a-um *unusual, unfamiliar*
intellego-ere *understand*
intendo-ere *aim*
inter *among*
interea *meanwhile*
interficio-ere *kill*
intro-are-avi *enter*
invado-ere *go, come into*
invenio-ire-veni-ventum *find*
invidia-ae [f] *grudge, jealousy*
io! *heyup!*
iocosus-a-um *full of jokes, humorous*
ipse *s/he her/himself*
iratus-a-um *angry*
irruo-ere-ui *rush in*
ita *thus, so*
itaque *and so, therefore*
iter-ineris [n] *way, route*
iterum *again*
iubeo-ere, iussi *order, tell*
iudicium-i [n] *trial, judgment*
iudico-are *try, adjudicate*
Iuppiter, Iovis [m] *Jupiter*
iuvenis-is [m] *youth, young man*
iuvo-are *help, please*
iuxta *next to*

Karolus-i [m] *Charles*

labor-is [m] *work*
laboro-are-avi *work*
lacertus-i [m] *arm*
lacrima-ae [f] *tear*
laetus-a-um *happy, cheerful*
lapis-idis [m] *stone*
lascive *wantonly*
lascivus-a-um *wanton*
latebra-ae [f] *hiding-place*
laudo-are-avi-atum *praise*
lego-ere, legi, lectum *read*
lente *slowly*
lentus-a-um *slow*
levis-e *light*
libellus-i [m] *(little) book*
libens *glad*
libenter *gladly*

liber-bri [m]   *book*
liber-a-um   *free*
Liber-i [m]   *Liber, god of wine*
libero-are-avi-atum   *free, deliver*
licet   *it is permitted*
ligo-are-avi-atum   *tie, bind*
lilium-i [n]   *lily*
linteum-i [n]   *linen cloth*
locus-i [m]   *place*
longe   *far, distant*
loquax   *noisy*
loquor, loqui, locutus   *speak*
Lucia-ae [f]   *Lucia*
ludus-i [m]   *game, show*
lux-cis [f]   *light, life*

madidus-a-um   *soaked*
magister-tri [m]   *master, teacher*
magnus-a-um   *great, large*
maiores-um   *betters, ancestors*
maledico-ere   *slander*
malus-a-um   *troublesome, bad*
maneo-ere-nsi-nsum   *remain, stay*
manus-us [f]   *hand*
mare-is [n]   *sea*
Martialis-is [m]   *Martial*
mater-tris [f]   *mother*
medicus-i [m]   *doctor*
medius-a-um   *mid-, middle of*
mehercule   *well I be Hercules*
mens, tis [f]   *mind*
mensis-is [m]   *month*
mercator-is [m]   *trader*
meridies [m]   *midday*
meto-ere   *gather, reap, mow*
metus-us [m]   *fear*
meus-a-um   *my*
miles-itis [m]   *soldier*
mille   *thousand*
minime   *no, certainly not*
minus   *less*
mirabilis-e   *wonderful,
   marvellous*
miror-ari-atus   *wonder at*
miserabilis-e   *pitiable*
miser-a-um   *wretched*
misericordia-ae [f]   *pity*
missa-ae [f]   *mass*
mitto-ere-isi-issum   *send*

modicus-a-um   *modest, small*
modo ... modo   *one minute ...
   the next*
molestus-a-um   *troublesome*
mollio-ire   *soften, calm*
mollis-e   *soft*
monachus-i [m]   *monk*
monasterium-i [n]   *monastery*
moror-ari-atus   *delay, wait*
mors, mortis [f]   *death*
mortuus-a-um   *dead*
mox   *soon, presently*
multus-a-um   *much, many*
mulus-i [m]   *mule*
munimentum-i [n]   *protection*
munus-eris [n]   *gift, show*
murmuro-are   *murmur*
murus-i [m]   *wall*
musca-ae [f]   *fly*
mutilo-are-avi   *mutilate*

nam   *for*
narro-are-avi-atum   *relate, tell*
natalis dies [m]   *birthday*
nato-are-avi   *swim*
nec   *and ... not*
nec multo post   *not long
   afterwards*
neque ... neque   *neither ... nor*
nescio-ire   *do not know*
nil (nihil)   *nothing*
nisi   *except*
nobilis-e   *noble*
nomen-inis [n]   *name*
non   *not*
non ita   *no, not so*
non numquam   *sometimes*
non solum ... sed etiam   *not only
   ... but also*
nos   *we, us*
nox, noctis [f]   *night*
nugae-arum [f]   *trifles, nonsense*
nullus-a-um   *not any, no one*
num   *surely ... not*
numquam   *never*
nunc   *now*
nuntii-orum [m]   *news*
nuper   *recently*
nusquam   *nowhere*

obdormio-ire *fall asleep*
oboedientia-ae [f] *duty*
obscurus-a-um *dark*
obsecro-are *implore*
observo-are-avi-atum *observe*
obstupefactus-a-um *stupefied*
occido-ere-cidi *fall*
occido-ere-cidi-cisum *kill*
oculus-i [m] *eye*
odorus-a-um *scented, sweet-
  smelling*
ohe *whoa*
oleum-i [n] *oil*
olim *once (upon a time)*
omnis-e *all, every*
onerosus-a-um *heavy*
oppidum-i [n] *town*
opprimo-ere *attack*
opto-are *choose*
opulentia-ae [f] *wealth*
opulentus-a-um *wealthy*
opus-eris [n] *task, work*
origo-inis [f] *origin*
oro-are *pray, beg*
os, oris [n] *mouth*
ostento-are *show (off)*
otiosus-a-um *lazy*
ovis-is [f] *sheep*
ovum-i [n] *egg*

paganus-i [m] *pagan*
pagina-ae [f] *page*
palma-ae [f] *palm*
panis-is [m] *bread*
par *equal*
pareo-ere [+dat.] *obey*
paro-are-avi-atum *prepare*
pascor-i *graze, eat*
paucus-a-um *few*
paulisper *a little while*
Paulus-i [m] *Paul*
pauper-is [m] *pauper*
pavidus-a-um *fearful*
pax, pacis [f] *peace*
peccator-is [m] *sinner*
pecunia-ae [f] *money*
pecus-oris [n] *herd, flock*
per *through, across, along*
percutio-ere *strike, beat*

peregrinus-i [m] *foreigner,
  pilgrim*
perficio-ere-feci-fectum *finish*
periculum-i [n] *danger*
perpetuus-a-um *unending*
perterritus-a-um *thoroughly
  scared*
perturbo-are-avi-atum *confuse,
  disturb*
pervigilo-are *lie awake all night*
peto-ere *seek*
phantasia-ae [f] *fancy, notion*
pharetra-ae [f] *quiver*
philosophia-ae [f] *philosophy*
philosophus-i [m] *philosopher*
pius-a-um *pious, dutiful*
placeo-ere [+dat.] *please*
placet *it pleases*
placidus-a-um *calm*
plaustrum-i [n] *cart, wagon*
plenus-a-um [+abl.] *filled (with)*
pluit *it is raining*
plurimi *most people*
pluvia-ae [f] *rain*
poena-ae [f] *penalty*
poeta-ae [m] *poet*
pompa-ae [f] *procession*
pomum-i [n] *fruit*
pono-ere-sui-situm *place, put*
populus-i [m] *people*
porta-ae [f] *gate*
porto-are-avi-atum *carry*
possideo-ere *occupy*
possum, posse *be able*
post *after*
postea *afterwards*
potio-nis [f] *drink*
praebeo-ere *give, offer*
praeda-ae [f] *loot*
praedico-are-avi *preach*
praedium-i [n] *store, barn*
praemium-i [n] *reward*
praepono-ere *prefer*
praeter *except, besides*
praeterea *besides*
pravus-a-um *wicked*
presbyter-teri [m] *priest*
primus-a-um *first*
pro *on behalf of*

pro certo   *for certain*
procedo-ere   *go forward*
proditor-is [m]   *traitor*
profero-ferre   *put forward*
proficiscor-i, profectus   *set out*
progredior-i, progressus
  advance, go forward
prope   *near*
Propertius-i [m]   *Propertius*
propter   *because of*
protego-ere   *cover*
proximus-a-um   *nearest,*
  previous
prudens   *wise*
pudor-is [m]   *shame*
puer-i [m]   *boy*
pueritia-ae [f]   *childhood*
purpureus-a-um   *purple*
puto-are-avi   *think*

quaero-ere   *seek*
quam   *than, which*
quam celerrime   *as quickly as*
  possible
quando   *when*
quatio-ere   *shake*
qui, quae, quod   *who, which*
quia   *that, because*
quidam   *somebody, a certain*
quidem   *in fact, indeed*
quintus-a-um   *fifth*
quis, quid   *who, what?*
quo   *where (to)*
quod   *because*
quomodo   *how*
quoniam   *since*
quoque   *also*

raeda-ae [f]   *carriage*
ramus-i [m]   *branch*
recipio-ere-cepi-ceptum
  welcome, take back
recito-are   *recite, read aloud*
recupero-are   *recover*
redeo-ire   *return*
refero, referre   *report*
regio-nis [f]   *region*
regnum-i [n]   *kingdom*
rego-ere, rexi, rectum   *rule*
regula-ae [f]   *rule*

reicio-ere-eci-ectum   *reject,*
  refuse
relinquo-ere-liqui-lictum   *leave,*
  abandon
remaneo-ere-si-sum   *remain*
requiesco-ere   *rest*
res, rei [f]   *thing, possession*
resono-are   *resound*
respondeo-ere, respondi   *reply*
resurgo-ere   *reappear*
reus-i [m]   *defendant*
revelo-are-avi-atum   *reveal*
revenio-ire   *return*
revereor-eri   *hold in awe*
revoco-are   *recall*
rex, regis [m]   *king*
rideo-ere, risi   *laugh, smile*
ripa-ae [f]   *bank*
rivalis-is [m]   *rival, competitor*
rogo-are-avi   *ask*
Romanus-i [m]   *a Roman*
rosa-ae [f]   *rose*
rudo-ere   *bray*
rumor-is [m]   *rumour, gossip*
rursum (rursus)   *again*

saepe   *often*
saevio-ire   *rage*
saevitia-ae [f]   *cruelty*
saevus-a-um   *cruel, mean*
sagitta-ae [f]   *arrow*
sagittaria-ae [f]   *archeress*
saltem   *at least*
salutem dicere   *greet*
saluto-are   *greet*
salve   *hello*
salvus-a-um   *safe*
sanctus-a-um   *holy, blessed*
sane   *certainly*
sanguis-inis [m]   *blood*
sapiens   *wise*
sapientia-ae [f]   *wisdom*
sarcina-ae [f]   *bag*
satio-are   *fill, satisfy*
satis   *enough*
saucius-a-um   *wounded, smitten*
scelestus-a-um   *wicked*
schola-ae [f]   *school*
scientia-ae [f]   *knowledge*

scilicet! *my foot!*
scio-ire *know*
scissus-a-um *torn*
scribo-ere-ipsi-iptum *write*
scutum-i [n] *shield*
se *her(him/them)self*
secundus-a-um *second*
securitas-tatis [f] *peace of mind*
securus-a-um *sure, secure*
sed *but*
sedeo-ere *sit*
semel *once*
semper *always*
sentio-ire *notice, feel*
sepelio-ire-ivi, sepultum *bury*
septem *seven*
sepulcrum-i [n] *grave*
sequor-i *follow*
servo-are *save*
servus-i [m] *serf, slave*
severus-a-um *severe*
si *if*
sic *thus*
sicut *just as, as if*
silentium-i [n] *silence*
silva-ae [f] *wood*
simul *at the same time*
sincerus-a-um *sound, genuine*
sine *without*
sino-ere *allow*
sisto-ere *stop*
sitiens *thirsty*
socius-i [m] *colleague, associate*
sol-is [m] *sun, day*
solium-i [n] *seat*
solus-a-um *only, alone*
somnium-i [n] *dream, fantasy*
somnulentus-a-um *sleepy*
somnus-i [m] *sleep*
sonitus-us [m] *sound, noise*
specto-are-avi-atum *watch*
spelunca-ae [f] *cave*
spes-ei [f] *hope*
spiritus [m] *spirit*
splendeo-ere *be bright, resplendent*
st! *ssh!*
stabulum-i [n] *stable*
stagnum-i [n] *pond, lake*

statim *immediately*
stella-ae [f] *star*
sterto-ere *snore*
stimulus-i [m] *sting*
sto-are, steti, statum *stand*
strenuus-a-um *energetic*
strideo-ere *hum, whistle*
stringo-ere-inxi-ictum *draw (sword)*
studiosus-a-um *hard-working*
studium-i [n] *study*
stultus-a-um *foolish*
stupor-is [m] *senselessness*
sub *beneath*
subito *suddenly*
subsellium-i [n] *pew, bench*
subvenio-ire [+dat.] *help*
suffragium-i [n] *vote*
superbus-a-um *proud*
supero-are *surpass*
superstitio-nis [f] *superstition*
surgo-ere *rise*
suspiro-are-avi *sigh*
susurro-are-avi *whisper*
suus-a-um *his/her/their own*

taberna-ae [f] *inn*
taceo-ere-ui *be quiet*
tacitus-a-um *silent, quiet*
tam cito *so quickly*
tamen *however*
tandem *at last*
tectum-i [n] *ceiling*
telum-i [n] *missile*
temperantia-ae [f] *restraint*
tempus-oris [n] *time*
tendo-ere *stretch*
teneo-ere-ui, tentum *hold*
tener-era-erum *tender*
tentatio-nis [f] *temptation*
tergo-ere *wipe*
terra-ae [f] *ground*
terreo-ere-ui-itum *frighten*
terribilis-e *terrible*
territus-a-um *scared*
tertius-a-um *third*
testimonium-i [n] *evidence, proof*
theologia-ae [f] *theology*

theologus-i [m]   *theologian*
thesaurus-i [m]   *store*
timeo-ere   *fear*
timidus   *fearful*
timor-is [m]   *fear*
tolero-are   *endure, support*
tollo-ere   *lift, raise*
tot   *so many*
totus-a-um   *whole*
trabs-bis [f]   *beam*
trado-ere-didi-ditum   *hand over*
traho-ere   *pull, drag*
trans   *across*
transeo-ire   *pass, go by*
trepidus-a-um   *nervous*
tres, tria   *three*
tristis-e   *sad*
trucido-are-avi-atum   *slaughter*
tumultus-us [m]   *din*
tunica-ae [f]   *tunic, dress*
turbulentus-a-um   *disturbed, confused*
turpis-e   *disgraceful*
turpitudo-inis [f]   *disgraceful behaviour*
tutus-a-um   *safe*
tuus-a-um   *your*

ubi   *when, where*
ulterior   *farther*
ululo-are   *howl*
umbra-ae [f]   *shadow*
umbrosus-a-um   *full of shadows*
umquam   *ever*
unde   *from where*
unguentum-i [n]   *scent, perfume*
unus-a-um   *one*
usque   *and on to*
ut   *as, so that, that*
ut, utinam   *if only*
utilis-e   *useful*

vaco-are-avi-atum   *be idle, empty*
vacuus-a-um   *empty*
vado-ere   *go*
vae   *alas, woe*

valde   *very much*
vale dicere   *say goodbye*
valeo-ere   *be well*
vanus-a-um   *empty, false*
vel   *or*
venatio-nis [f]   *hunt*
venatrix-icis [f]   *huntress*
venatus-us [m]   *hunt*
venio-ire-i, ventum   *come*
ventus-i [m]   *wind*
verbero-are   *beat*
verbum-i [n]   *word*
ver-is [n]   *spring*
veritas-tatis [f]   *truth*
vero   *indeed*
versus-us [m]   *verse*
vester-tra-trum   *your*
vestio-ire   *clothe*
vestis-is [f]   *clothing*
veto-are   *forbid*
via-ae [f]   *road*
viator-is [m]   *traveller*
vicesimus-a-um   *twentieth*
victima-ae [f]   *victim*
victoria-ae [f]   *victory*
video-ere, vidi, visum   *see*
vigilo-are   *be awake, watchful*
viginti   *twenty*
vinclum-i [n]   *chain*
vinolentus-a-um   *fond of booze*
vinum-i [n]   *wine*
virga-ae [f]   *rod*
virgo-inis [f]   *maiden*
vir-i [m]   *man*
virtus-tutis [f]   *courage, virtue*
vita-ae [f]   *life*
vitium-i [n]   *vice*
vivo-ere   *live*
volito-are   *fly*
volo, velle   *want*
voluto-are   *ponder, turn*
vos   *you*
vox, vocis [f]   *voice*
Vulgatum-i [n]   *the Vulgate*
vulnero-are-avi-atum   *wound*
vultus-us [m]   *face, expression*

abbess   abbatissa-ae [f]
abbot   abbas-atis [m]
about   de [+ abl.]
advise   moneo-ere-ui-itum
all, every   omnis-e
already   iam
always   semper
also   etiam, quoque
amphitheatre   amphitheatrum-i
   [n]
and   et, atque
angry   iratus-a-um
animal   bestia-ae [f], animal-is
   [n]
approach   adeo-ire-ii-itum
army   exercitus-us [m]
arrow   sagitta-ae [f]
ask   rogo-are-avi
astonished   attonitus-a-um

bad   malus-a-um
bag   sarcina-ae [f]
be able   possum, posse
be away, absent   absum-esse
be here, present   adsum-esse
be quiet   taceo-ere
beast   bestia-ae [f]
beautiful   bellus-a-um
because   quod
believe, trust   credo-ere [+dat.]
bishop   episcopus-i [m]
book   liber-bri [m]
both   ambo
both ... and   et ... et
bow   arcus-us [m]

boy   puer-i [m]
branch   ramus-i [m]
brave   fortis-e
bray   rudo-ere
bread   panis-is [m]
brother   frater-tris [m]
build   aedifico-are-avi-atum
bury   sepelio-ire-ivi, sepultum
but   sed
buy   emo-ere
by   a(b)

cake   crustum-i [n]
capture   capio-ere, cepi, captum
care for   curo-are [+acc.]
carriage   raeda-ae [f]
carry   porto-are-avi-atum
cart   plaustrum-i [n]
castle   castellum-i [n]
chase   fugo-are
cheerful   laetus-a-um
church   ecclesia-ae [f]
cloister   claustrum-i [n]
clothing   vestis-is [f]
come   venio-ire-i, ventum
condemn   damno-are
conspire   conspiro-are
cook   coquus-i [m]
copy   exscribo-ere-ipsi-iptum
count   comes-itis [m]
cruel   saevus-a-um, crudelis-e

Dane   Danus-i [m]
danger   periculum-i [n]
dark   obscurus-a-um

daughter filia-ae [f]
day dies-iei [m]
dead mortuus-a-um
death mors, mortis [f]
devour devoro-are-avi-atum
difficult difficilis-e
dinner cena-ae [f]
disgraceful turpis-e
do facio-ere, feci, factum
dress tunica-ae [f]
drink bibo-ere-bibi
drink potio-nis [f]
duty oboedientia-ae [f]

easy facilis-e
eat devoro-are-avi-atum
egg ovum-i [n]
elegant gracilis-e
elephant elephantus-i [m]
endure tolero-are
enough satis
enter intro-are-avi
ever umquam
eye oculus-i [m]

face vultus-us [m]
fall cado-ere, cecidi, casum
fall asleep obdormio-ire
farmer agricola-ae [m]
fear timeo-ere
fear timor-is [m], metus-us [m]
few paucus-a-um
field ager, agri [m]
filled (with) plenus-a-um [+abl.]
find invenio-ire-veni-ventum
finish perficio-ere-feci-fectum
fire ignis-is [m]
first primus-a-um
flee fugio-ere, fugi
food cibus-i [m]
foolish stultus-a-um
foreigner peregrinus-i [m]
forgive ignosco-ere [+dat.]
free liber-a-um
free libero-are-avi-atum
friend amicus-i [m], amica-ae [f]
frighten terreo-ere-ui-itum
furious furiosus-a-um

garden hortus-i [m]

gift donum-i [n], munus-eris [n]
give do-are, dedi, datum
go eo, ire, ii
go away abeo-ire-ii-itum
god deus-i [m]
goddess dea-ae [f]
gold aurum-i [n]
good bonus-a-um
great magnus-a-um
greedy gulosus-a-um
grieve doleo-ere
groan gemo-ere-ui
groan gemitus-us [m]
ground terra-ae-us [f]

hand manus-us [f]
hand over trado-ere-didi-ditum
happy laetus-a-um
have habeo-ere
hear audio-ire-ivi-itum
heavy onerosus-a-um
here hic
hide celo-are-avi-atum
history historia-ae [f]
hold teneo-ere-ui, tentum
holy sanctus-a-um
hope spes-ei [f]
horse equus-i [m], caballus-i [m]
hour hora-ae [f]
however tamen, autem
humble humilis-e
hundred centum
hurry festino-are-avi

if si
if only ut, utinam
immediately statim
inflame inflammo-are-avi

kill interficio-ere
kitchen culina-ae [f]
know scio-ire

lady domina-ae [f]
large magnus-a-um
laugh rideo-ere, risi
lazy ignavus-a-um
lead duco-ere-uxi-uctum
leaf folium-i [n]
leave relinquo-ere-liqui-lictum
letter epistula-ae [f]

library bibliotheca-ae [f]
lie iaceo-ere
life vita-ae [f]
listen to audio-ire-ivi-itum
live habito-are-avi, vivo-ere
long for desidero-are-avi-atum
lose amitto-ere
love amo-are-avi-atum
love amor-is [m]

maid ancilla-ae [f]
maiden virgo-inis [f]
make facio-ere, feci, factum
man vir-i [m], homo-inis [m]
meat caro, carnis [f]
mind animus-i [m]
monk monachus-i [m]
monastery monasterium-i [n]
money pecunia-ae [f]
mother mater-tris [f]
much, many multus-a-um
mule mulus-i [m]
my meus-a-um

name nomen-inis [n]
near prope [+acc.]
neither … nor neque … neque
never numquam
night nox, noctis [f]
noble nobilis-e
not non
nothing nil (nihil)
now nunc, iam

obey pareo-ere [+dat.]
often saepe
one unus-a-um
order impero-are [+dat.]
order, tell iubeo-ere, iussi
other ceterus-a-um
owe, ought debeo-ere-ui-itum
ox bos-vis [m/f]

peace pax, pacis [f]
people populus-i [m]
perfume unguentum-i [n]
philosophy philosophia-ae [f]
pilgrim peregrinus-i [m]
pitiable miserabilis-e
plan consilium-i [n]
pleasing gratus-a-um

poem carmen-inis [n]
poet poeta-ae [m]
pond stagnum-i [n]
praise laudo-are-avi-atum
pray oro-are
preach praedico-are-avi
prepare paro-are-avi-atum
priest presbyter-teri [m]
prisoner captivus-i [m]
procession pompa-ae [f]
punish castigo-are-avi-atum

read lego-ere, legi, lectum
recite, read aloud recito-are
rejoice gaudeo-ere
relate narro-are-avi-atum
remain remaneo-ere-si-sum
return redeo-ire, revenio-ire
ride equito-are-avi
road via-ae [f]
rule regula-ae [f]
run curro-ere

sad tristis-e
say dico-ere-ixi-ictum
scared territus-a-um
school schola-ae [f]
see video-ere, vidi, visum
seek peto-ere, quaero-ere
send mitto-ere-isi-issum
serf servus-i [m]
serious gravis-e
shadow umbra-ae [f]
shout clamo-are-avi-atum
shout, cry clamor-is [m]
sing canto-are-avi-atum
sit sedeo-ere
slaughter trucido-are-avi-atum
slave servus-i [m]
sleep dormio-ire-ivi-itum
slow lentus-a-um
slowly lente
snore sterto-ere
soldier miles-itis [m]
song carmen-inis [n]
soul anima-ae [f]
spirit spiritus-us [m]
spring ver-is [n]
stay maneo-ere-nsi-nsum
step gradus-us [m]

still adhuc
story fabula-ae [f]
student discipulus-i [m]
surely ... (not) nonne ... (num)
sweet dulcis-e
sweet-smelling odorus-a-um
swim nato-are-avi

teach doceo-ere-ui, doctum
teacher magister-tri [m]
than quam
there ibi
thick densus-a-um
thing res, rei [f]
think puto-are-avi
thousand mille
three tres, tria
through per [+acc.]
tie ligo-are-avi-atum
time tempus-oris [n]
tired fessus-a-um
town oppidum-i [n]
trust credo-ere [+dat.]
twenty viginti
two duo

understand intellego-ere

value aestimo-are-avi-atum
verse versus-us [m]
voice vox, vocis [f]

walk ambulo-are-avi-atum
wall murus-i [m]
want volo, velle
wanton lascivus-a-um
war bellum-i [n]
watch specto-are-avi-atum
watch over custodio-ire
water aqua-ae [f]
way, route iter-ineris [n]
weep fleo-ere
whisper susurro-are-avi
who? what? quis? quid?
why cur
wicked scelestus-a-um
wind ventus-i [m]
window fenestra-ae [f]
wine vinum-i [n]
wise prudens, sapiens
with cum [+abl.]
without sine [+abl.]
woman femina-ae [f]
wood silva-ae [f]
word verbum-i [n]
work opus-eris [n], labor-is [m]
work laboro-are-avi
wound vulnero-are-avi-atum
wretched miser-a-um
write scribo-ere-ipsi-iptum

year annus-i [m]